THE WISDOM OF IMPERFECTION

The Wisdom of Imperfection

The Challenge of Individuation in Buddhist Life

Rob Preece

SNOW LION PUBLICATIONS
ITHACA, NEW YORK • BOULDER, COLORADO

Snow Lion Publications
P. O. Box 6483
Ithaca, NY 14851 USA
(607) 273-8519
www.snowlionpub.com

Printed in USA on acid-free recycled paper.

ISBN-10 1-55939-252-5
ISBN-13 978-1-55939-252-5

Library of Congress Cataloging-in-Publication Data
Preece, Rob.
 The wisdom of imperfection : the challenge of individuation in Buddhist
life / Rob Preece.
    p. cm.
 Includes bibliographical references.
 ISBN-13: 978-1-55939-252-5 (alk. paper)
 ISBN-10: 1-55939-252-5 (alk. paper)
 1. Religious life—Buddhism. 2. Buddhism—Psychology. 3. Psychother-
apy—Religious aspects—Buddhism. 4. Buddhism—China—Tibet. I. Title.

BQ7775.P74 2006
294.3'422—dc22   2006005963

Designed and typeset by Gopa & Ted2, Inc.

Contents

List of Illustrations

Drawings by Rob Preece

Acknowledgments

T HIS BOOK IS DEDICATED to Lama Thubten Yeshe, Thubten Zopa Rinpoche, and Gen Jhampa Wangdu, who have given their lives for the benefit of sentient beings. I would like to offer my gratitude to my wife Anna, who has constantly supported me in the process of writing. I wish to remember the help and support of Ian Gordon Brown and Barbara Somers, who provided invaluable aid to my becoming a psychotherapist when I returned to the West from India. I would like to offer my thanks to all those who have shared their experiences and struggles of integrating Buddhism into their lives. They have been a rich source of insight and understanding. Finally, I would like to dedicate this book, with love, to my sons Alex and Toran, who may also embark upon this journey at some point in their lives.

Introduction

✦ ✦ ───

O NE OF MY GREATEST CHALLENGES as a practicing Tibetan Buddhist of some thirty years has been to reconcile two worldviews—namely, those of Buddhism and Jung. By some coincidence, I
first encountered both of these at the same time, while at university.
Finding that both approaches offered something very important in
understanding my life, I have never felt the desire to abandon one for
the sake of the other. As a consequence, I needed to find some way of
bringing these views together. As my exploration of these approaches
of self-actualization has unfolded, I have become increasingly aware of
distinctions among what might be described as a journey, a path, and
a process.

My early encounters with Jung gave me the invaluable recognition
that life could be seen as a journey with phases and rites of passage that
are crucial to our unfolding maturation. When I encountered the
Tibetan Buddhist tradition, I found that it offered a path that could be
followed—a clear and systematic method of self-transformation. When
I later trained as a psychotherapist, I became increasingly aware that we
are constantly passing through a psychological process, something that
Jung also recognized in his explorations of alchemy.

Each of these subtle distinctions sheds a different light on our self-
actualization. In Jung's view, the journey symbolized since time imme-
morial in myths and legends expresses an archetypal unfolding of the
individual through life: the journey of individuation. This stands in
contrast to the philosophical precision and systematic method with
which Buddhist practice approaches a path to the attainment of

enlightenment. It is assumed that an individual following this path has already reached a certain level of development in his or her life. Again, both approaches stand in contrast to the psychotherapeutic emphasis on a process of transformation, an alchemical process that occurs in the context of therapy.

The classical Buddhist teachings, particularly in the Tibetan tradition, define a path on which experiences and insights evolve as we engage in specific practices. What is so extraordinary about the Tibetan tradition in particular is its wealth of methods, coupled with teachings that explain the nature of mind and of the reality we experience. In this respect, the Buddhist tradition offers what many of us look for: a clear and concise way to cultivate the mind and free our lives from needless confusion and suffering.

While Buddhist teachings offer a means of resolving our life issues, they have less to say about the subjective experience of that path and what its psychological effects might be. The insights or experiences we might gain emerge through a psychological process that is different for each of us. For example, in the Tibetan tradition there are instructions on how to evoke a particular tantric deity, or gain an experience of emptiness (*shunyata*), but seldom is there an explanation of how the individual experiences the effects of practice. This insight may be found only if one spends time with experienced meditators who are willing to speak about their own experience. Unfortunately, most Tibetans I have encountered are reluctant to speak of their own inner process. This is in part because they do not use a psychological language, but also because they seldom allow such intimate questioning.

What this dilemma brings to light is the important difference between a path and a process. We could say that a spiritual path is more structured and doctrine-centered, while its underlying psychological process is more organic and person-centered. While these two are radically different, they are intrinsically interwoven. This has led me to wonder how we might map the underlying psychological process, or indeed the journey, of someone who is practicing the Buddhist path. What kinds of problems might we encounter? And are there any common elements of that journey from which we can learn as Westerners trying to bring Buddhism into our lives?

As a psychotherapist as well as a Buddhist practitioner, I am inevitably affected greatly by these questions. Over the years, many of my clients have been Buddhists attempting to look at the integration of Buddhist principles into their lives. Part of my intention in writing this book, therefore, has been to bring together these two worlds: the Western understanding of psychological processes and Buddhist practice. One dimension of this will be to see how Buddhist insights and practice influence and enable our psychological journey. The other will be to explore how the process of psychological individuation, as described by thinkers such as C. G. Jung, is reflected in the Buddhist path.

Individuation, in Jungian terms, is essentially the process of becoming a psychological "individual" who is a separate, indivisible unity or whole. To individuate is to bring into being our innate nature and to manifest this in our life as an individual. Individuation implies becoming ever more conscious of, and fully open to, all that we are, be it good or bad, so as to become increasingly whole. This is a path that values our individual qualities and potential, along with all of our human frailty and fallibility.

Individuation as a process of self-actualization is at the heart of the path of the bodhisattva, one who dedicates his or her life to attaining buddhahood for the welfare of all sentient beings. Although not couched in terms of individuation, Buddhist understanding offers a path of practice that profoundly supports this process. If we consider the Buddha's life, it was a demonstration of exactly this. His teachings describe a path of gradual self-transformation and self-realization: the awakening of his innate true nature. Placing the bodhisattva's path alongside the Western psychological understanding of individuation enables us to make valuable connections that inform both approaches.

Buddhism, because of its non-theistic approach to self-realization, has more in common with the psychotherapeutic world than most other spiritual traditions do. We can see this reflected in the way Buddhist principles are increasingly becoming incorporated into a more contemplative style of psychotherapy.

The spiritual–psychological journey is, however, no simple path to travel. All too often we fail to recognize our capacity for self-deception. Having been a Buddhist for many years, I am continually amazed at my own capacity, and that of some of my peers, to distort our understanding of Buddhism to suit personal inclinations. This is often done in order to maintain and justify habits and beliefs that secure a familiar sense of identity in the world. Freud said that neurosis is a kind of personal religion. We could equally well say that we collectively and individually shape our religious beliefs to affirm our neuroses. Nowhere is this tendency more evident than in religious dogmatism and fundamentalism.

In his seminal book *Cutting Through Spiritual Materialism,* Chögyam Trungpa began to open the eyes of Westerners to their tendency to adopt Eastern, and particularly Buddhist, practices and beliefs in a way that turned them into exotic trinkets to be collected and played with. My own teacher, Lama Thubten Yeshe, often spoke of the Western "supermarket mentality" that wants quick and easy solutions to our problems. The Western disposition to try a little of this and a little of that could create what he called "spiritual soup," all mixed up together.

For Westerners, translating the doctrine and practices of Eastern spiritual traditions into experience is not straightforward. In my time as a member of Buddhist communities, I have seen how easily we distort and confuse the essential meaning of practice and misinterpret basic principles of doctrine. It has also become evident how easily we place a veneer of spiritual practice and spiritual correctness over deeply unresolved personal problems. We create a kind of spiritual pathology.

Over my past eighteen years working as a psychotherapist, many Buddhist practitioners have come to see me. Most have been genuinely attempting to reconcile Western life with the Buddhist tradition. More is at issue, however, than the contradictions between Buddhist ideals and Western life-style. It is increasingly noticeable that the Western psyche, with its particular cultural inheritance and emotional wounding, does not always fit comfortably within an Eastern approach to spiritual practice. This is not to conclude that an Eastern tradition does not suit us, or that Western people are spiritually inept. It is true, however, that our Western upbringing does make our emotional life and sense of identity very different from what one finds in the East.

Whether we recognize it or not, in the West we live with deeply entrenched Judeo-Christian values. These permeate our culture in ways that are often very subtle. They influence our worldview, our values, and our experience of the body, sexuality, and gender. They form deeply ingrained attitudes towards good and evil, spirit and matter, and sexuality and spirituality, as well as color our view of reality.

Eastern teachers from different Buddhist traditions are often surprised by the depth of emotional wounding they encounter in Westerners. It is hard for them to conceive of the pressures and stresses that impinge upon our psyches from early infancy. As a consequence, they can sometimes seem surprisingly simplistic in their responses to Westerners' questions about their problems. Buddhism has no developmental model that addresses the unfolding of the personality and ego-identity through childhood. Consequently, it is not easy to explain in Buddhist terms the nature of the development of self-identity and how it can be damaged. Furthermore, the influence of this damage in the adult is hard to clarify and often more complex than any model to be found in the traditional teachings.

Western psychotherapy has charted the kinds of psychological damage we suffer, but we cannot assume that Eastern teachers will address these problems. It takes time for Eastern teachers even to begin to understand the kind of life we lead in the West and the nature of the pressures, insecurities, and stresses that affect us. Fortunately, some Eastern teachers take time to learn about our experience so that they can tailor their guidance to Western needs rather than simply following doctrine.

Many Westerners explore spiritual traditions because they seek a solution to their psychological malaise. However, it is evident from my work as a psychotherapist that these "spiritual" solutions do not always address the root cause. Many people on the "spiritual" path have more of a problem with their basic identity in the world than they do with their relationship to the divine. Likewise, spiritual organizations often attract distressed people seeking spiritual solutions that do not necessarily address their core suffering. It can take a sophisticated insight to understand the nature of our emotional wounding and the patterns and defenses that crystallize around it. Perhaps, therefore, it is unwise to assume that a spiritual practice will automatically resolve these deep psychological issues.

In my search for a resolution to these dilemmas, I have learned a great deal from my own process and that of my psychotherapy clients. Moreover, certain themes have emerged that I feel must be looked at more deeply. When we examine our personal pathology more closely, we may discover a way to become liberated from it. If we fail to do so, these unaddressed issues may color our spirituality and distort our understanding. Ultimately, nothing is gained by blindness and unconscious self-deception, but we often fail to see these weaknesses in ourselves.

The Shadow—to use the name that Jung gave to our blind spots— is notoriously elusive. It feeds on our denial and lack of awareness. In this book, I wish to explore some of these blind spots—not to provide solutions, but to help us to see the potential pitfalls in our path. Much of what I am introducing is from my own, often painful, experiences. My own spiritual path has seldom been filled with glorious realizations, visions, or magical insights. Perhaps one could see the recognition of my blindness and mistakes as a kind of insight. I hope that is so, but it never feels as exotic as the profound realizations described in the teachings.

We need a deep-rooted compassion for ourselves in order to allow for our fallibility and vulnerability on the path. There is little point in trying to base our lives on unreal ideals that only cripple us. My experience has led me to conclude that a fundamental aspect of the journey is the uncovering of our personal spiritual pathology and its gradual resolution. At each stage on the path, new aspects of pathology may emerge, and their resolution will enable us to move forward. Our willingness to learn and grow from this process is perhaps one of the most extraordinary qualities of our human nature. Considerable wisdom comes from our state of imperfection.

In what follows, I have tried to draw on the insights of both Buddhist and Western psychology to explore what can be seen as the process of individuation of Buddhist practitioners in the West. In particular, I am grateful for the insights of my teachers Lama Thubten Yeshe and Thubten Zopa Rinpoche, and for the ideas of C.G. Jung. Most of all, however, I owe a debt to the invaluable experience of the many people I have seen over the years in therapy and to those with whom I have worked in workshops and retreats.

PART I
The Call to Awaken

Shakyamuni Buddha

Life's Challenge 1

LIFE IS A RICH but fragile mystery. As depicted in Tibetan paintings of the Wheel of Life, from the moment of conception we are held in the jaws of Yama, the Lord of Death. Perhaps the greatest miracle is that some of us actually survive and are able to engage in life. In the womb, the likelihood of a fetus living through the duration of pregnancy is not great. The instinctual cries of an infant after birth are a powerful reflex for survival. By the time we have been in this life for a decade, this challenge to survive has become a normality to which we are largely oblivious. By adulthood, we have developed sophisticated psychological strategies and patterns to deal with the uncertainties and unpredictability of life. These strategies shape the person we become and, unfortunately, can do so in increasingly limiting and rigid ways.

As our personality and ego-identity become stronger, they can also become less flexible, so that our capacity for adaptation and change also slows and freezes. What were once natural mechanisms for adaptation, growth, and survival can begin to be limitations that actually accentuate our suffering. Life then presents us with a further challenge. Are we ready and willing to wake up, to let go and open to our intrinsically fleeting, illusory nature and allow ourselves to change? If we do not do so willingly, then it is inevitable that life circumstances will eventually demand that we face ourselves and shed the skin of our limiting self-conceptions to discover our true nature. Some may take up this challenge, this call, while others choose to do otherwise.

It may be difficult to imagine the internal struggle taking place in a young man trapped in stultifying luxury, desperate to break free and search for truth. Siddhartha, the son of a rich Nepalese raja, had been cosseted in circumstances that were primarily intended to prevent him from seeing the world at large. His father dreaded the path that his son might follow, should the inclination arise. At the time of Siddhartha's birth, a prediction had been made that he would either become a great king or else renounce the kingdom, follow the path of a mendicant, and become a fully enlightened Buddha. In an attempt to prevent the latter from happening, the King contrived circumstances that would enclose Siddhartha in a world that was effectively a prison. In time, these conditions became intolerable. Siddhartha began surreptitiously venturing out of his enclosure in an attempt to discover more of the world outside. This only exacerbated his frustration and disillusionment with the false world he inhabited.

One can only speculate upon the torment Siddhartha must have gone through to respond to the call that was growing within. To leave a father, wife, and child would, I imagine, be extremely difficult, but this is what he was driven to do. Knowing that he would never gain his father's approval, Siddhartha Gautama, the future Shakyamuni Buddha, had to leave in the dark of night knowing that he would probably never return.

Seldom is someone destined to become the king of a rich kingdom, but it is not uncommon to discover ourselves at odds with the circumstances in which we find ourselves. As a psychotherapist, I often encounter people who are tormented and depressed by the sense that their lives lack direction and meaning. These are often very capable and successful people who have materially accomplished a great deal in their lives. They have, however, gradually come to feel stuck in a world they have created for themselves, working hard but going nowhere.

The growing urge to break out should not be seen as running away. It may be tempting to suggest, cynically, that Siddhartha, like a lot of young men, could not bear the responsibilities of parenthood and simply ran away. Indeed, I have seen many clients whose disposition was to try to escape in this way. The inner call to change, however, often arises in those who have worked hard. They may, it is true, have focused their attention narrowly—perhaps on sustaining a relationship, bringing up children, or developing a career. Conversely, there are those who suddenly wake up to the fact that they have drifted through their lives and gone nowhere.

The call to wake up and change comes in many guises, and it may come at virtually any age. Possibly the most noticeable ingredient of any call, however, is a profound sense of malaise—a growing recognition of what the Buddha would have called the truth of suffering. The Buddha's understanding of suffering was not a simplistic notion of pain or discomfort. Suffering, or *dukkha* in Sanskrit, relates particularly to a recognition of the fundamental unsatisfactoriness or pointlessness of what we experience. We may put effort and time into things that at first seem to offer a sense of meaning, only to find, at some point, that they begin to feel hollow and unsatisfactory. We may suddenly stop and ask ourselves why we are bothering. Money, status, self-esteem, reputation, security, material success, self-image, self-validation, approval, duty—the list of possible reasons is endless. Life may be insisting that we begin to face ourselves and honestly admit to our self-imposed restrictions and limitations.

When I was around nineteen or twenty, I experienced an initial call that gradually changed my life. Having left school at sixteen, I had been engaged in an electronics apprenticeship for several years in a "new town" called Crawley in Sussex, UK. I found myself becoming deeply disaffected and disillusioned by the factory environment I was working in. I began to see the routine of hundreds of people clocking-in in the early morning to work on production lines as numbingly meaningless. Being a late teenager, I expressed my inner angst in the form of poetic monologues. Some of these, in retrospect, were embarrassingly naïve, while others were surprisingly insightful. It was, however, a dawning of the realization that the factory worker life was not for me. I found it increasingly depressing and repellent.

My training officer at the time was surprisingly astute and had a significant influence on the call that was awakening in me. He could see my inner struggle with the world I was in, and he gradually shifted my perspective towards potentials that I had never considered. The narrow view of life I had grown to accept, even at such a young age, was beginning to break apart and open up to new possibilities. I realized I had to get out and eventually finished my apprenticeship, after four years. I went to university, something unusual in my family, and there found a response to my inner searching in the form of Jungian psychology and Buddhism.

While my call occurred at a relatively early age, for many it happens later in life, after many years of following a particular path. Typical of this phenomenon was the experience of a client who worked as an accountant and who was, on the surface, a safely settled family man with a wife and two children. When he discovered his wife had been having an affair for several years, he was thrown into a devastating crash, partly precipitated by his wife saying she wanted to be with a "real man." This caused him to begin to look deeply at the situation he had set up for himself, which consisted of a secure yet undemanding job in a career he had entered by default, having followed his parents' wishes. His relationship was with a strongly career-minded woman who had become the primary earner while he looked after the children.

Following the discovery of his wife's affair, he began to wake up to the life he had created for himself, which was cut off from his feelings, safe, and without any real sense of his own identity as a man. He became acutely aware of his lack of fulfillment and a lack of real engagement in what he was doing. He felt impotent and as though he had never really stepped into his life. This painful wake-up call opened him to his emotional life and also to the recognition that he needed to embark upon a period of self-exploration if his life and relationship were going to have any real sense of meaning. He began to recognize how much he had become stuck in an unconscious need for a safe maternal cocoon and thus had run away from actively and passionately living his life.

Another example is the story of a client who had remained in a stultifying and potentially destructive relationship because she was afraid to move on. The combination of a chronic lack of self-esteem, a deep sense of duty, and a fear of breaking free held her in paralysis. Gradually she become ill, which made her aware of how much she was imprisoning her potential to be true to herself. Eventually the conflict between how she knew she could be and what she had forced herself to be became so painful she began to make the changes she needed. She then had the courage to leave the relationship.

The call so often comes because we have unwittingly dug a hole for ourselves that has limited and constricted our innate potential in increasingly unhealthy ways. At some point, an inner impulse to change becomes inevitable. It is our deeper instinct for health and wholeness.

This inner call awakens us to the need for change. Sometimes it is initiated by outer circumstances, such as an illness or losing a job or a partner, but it may also arise from something less specific: life may simply have become stagnant and apparently meaningless. There may also be a profound sense of incongruity between our outer life circumstances and our inner needs.

When people speak of the need for change, one often feels that an irresistible impulse is at work. It is as if they are being moved by a force in their lives that is greater than themselves. Jung spoke of the power of the Self as the inner archetype of wholeness, one that can unfold our life for us. However, its effect may not always be comfortable. The inner impulse towards wholeness can create an almost intolerable pressure to break through to a new way of being. This often precipitates the experience of a breakdown.

What eventually called me to the path I was to follow was an intense period of suffering which was accompanied by a growing recognition that I had to go on a journey. I needed to leave my familiar surroundings and take the risk of stepping out into the world on my own. Following university I left on my travels, which took me gradually around the world until I eventually arrived in Nepal. There, several months later, I found myself sitting at the feet of a Tibetan Lama receiving instructions on Buddhist meditation practice. I had a profound sense that I had come home.

In *Man and His Symbols,* Jung speaks of the journey as a central theme of the process of individuation.[1] The journey that emerges as a result of the call does not require that we travel in a physical sense: the traveling must be done inwardly. However, what it does require is that we begin to question the underlying assumptions upon which we have based our lives. Leaving home to go to foreign lands is one way of shaking up our preconceptions. The cultural shifts we encounter can help to detach us from the social and cultural conditioning by which we have become trapped. In the absence of physical travel, this detachment can equally well be achieved through a process of self-exploration such as therapy. What seems crucial, however, is that we allow ourselves to become dislodged from what was familiar and step into a place of liminality, of uncertainty, where we do not have to retain the sense of ourselves we once had. We may do this voluntarily and consciously, or this may be thrust upon us by circumstances, such as an illness or bereavement.

If we are to change and grow, we must allow ourselves to become fluid, not static and ossified. Then we can change shape as necessary. We also need others to allow us to change. In teachings on the bodhisattva's way of life, it is sometimes mentioned that we may need to change our place of dwelling if staying in one place causes others to become fixed in their view of us.[2] When this happens, the demands, expectations, or opinions of others can make it very difficult to change. I often hear clients in therapy saying that they are beginning to change and their friends or family don't like it.

The call to travel, either inwardly or outwardly, is in part the call to break free of the constraints of a psychological environment that locks us into all manner of preconceptions and expectations. The sense of imprisonment that can ensue calls forth something from deep within that demands that we break up, break down, or shatter our solid reality so that growth can occur. This force from within is a natural expression of our own potential for health. I am reminded of the city of Rangoon, which I visited on my travels in 1973. There were the remains of many-storied Victorian buildings, left by the British. But, extraordinarily, trees, vines, and creepers were now growing through the pavements, walls, and ceilings, pushing their way through the layers of brick and plaster. The irresistible force of nature was reclaiming the city for itself.

If we listen to the call that is coming from deep within, we can begin to trust in a process that will lead us towards health and wholeness, towards individuation. If we do not—and some will not do so—the consequence may be dire. There are times in our lives when the call comes. If we fail to follow it, resisting change, plastering up the cracks, and attempting to carry on with the status quo, the call may return later. When it does so it will often be more forceful, more dramatic, and more devastating. At such times the consequences may be less easily resolved. Nature may reassert its need for our attention through chronic physical illness. The heart attack in middle age is a typical manifestation.

The call need not come through suffering alone, but it often does. In folk tales, there is usually dis-ease in the home. The King is old and sick, the land is barren, and there is trouble in the kingdom. The youngest son, the one taken least seriously, is usually the one called to heal the malaise. The possibility of healing is usually summoned by the realization that only by finding the sacred pearl, the healing elixir, or the sacred firebird will the kingdom be restored. The symbolism of this is charted in Jungian writings time and again.

The King symbolizes the ego within its increasingly unhealthy world. It is the ego that must evolve, gradually emerging from its origins in primitive, instinctual needs, and grow to inhabit a more conscious and healthy relationship to life. This is a hazardous journey—a journey of awakening and the emergence of consciousness. The call makes us begin to face the wounding that has inevitably occurred in the process of incarnating again in this material existence. We may have brought our susceptibilities with us from previous lives, and the early moments of this life will have reconstellated some of them. To quote Barbara Somers, with whom I trained to become a psychotherapist, many of us are like plants that have grown in rough, stony, poor soils and become damaged, contorted, and unhealthy, yet still manage to flower. Like these plants, by the time we reach relative adulthood, we may have been damaged in ways that we ourselves can barely see. The journey begins as we start to acknowledge our wounding and slowly take steps to heal ourselves.

One of the most common responses to the call to heal our sense of self is the search for what we call spirituality. This seems to be a kind of instinct that we possess as an aspect of our human condition. For Jung, the Self was indeed a core of being that, even though unconscious, stirs us with a deeply felt yearning for wholeness. The Buddha's truth of cessation[3] can be seen as an archetypal, primordial knowledge of our Buddha nature, which we each have buried in us "like a precious jewel buried beneath the house."[4] This archaic memory may have been carried through countless lives and generations. When we are called, something in us begins to stir, and this memory and a yearning for its restoration awaken. We are instinctively drawn to those experiences that offer solutions to our life malaise. Many of us embark upon what we have come to call a "spiritual path." It remains to be seen whether this will ultimately cure our malaise.

O UR SENSE OF DIS-EASE may lead many of us to seek solutions in the world's spiritual traditions. This was exactly why I found myself, in my twenties, sitting in a Tibetan Buddhist monastery in Nepal listening to the velvety voice of a maroon-robed Lama. I was like a sponge soaking in his wisdom and the sheer beauty of his quality of being. I was an emotionally damaged Westerner whose need for a resolution to my struggles, and deeply felt spiritual yearning, made me ripe for this wonderfully rich and inspirational experience.

I was not alone. Many people who had experienced emotional fragility and a lack of ego strength as a result of wounding from childhood were seeking a spiritual solution to their malaise. Eventually this led me, along with some of my peers, to establish a spiritual community that would offer us a sanctuary in which to live and practice the teachings we had been given.

There are today many spiritual organizations that contain people searching for spiritual sanctuary, in part as a place to heal, but also—and this can be even more significant—as a safe haven to shield them from the alienation and hostility of the world around. It can be a great relief to be able to relinquish some of this struggle and live under the guidance of a teacher in a safe community. While there are times in everyone's life when finding an oasis of sanctuary is vital, nevertheless a fundamental question is whether this environment addresses the real issue. Is this spiritual process actually healing our psychological difficulties?

In my work as a psychotherapist it has become increasingly appar-

ent that for some engaged in a spiritual path the difficulty relates not
only to the need for spirituality but also to how they incarnate within
a normal identity. This leads to a further question concerning how we
bring our spirituality to earth. When we have a relatively poor sense of
identity, we tend to relate poorly to the concrete, material world and,
particularly, to the body. Spirituality can then become seriously
ungrounded. If our sense of ego-identity is weak, it is relatively easy for
our so-called spiritual search to potentially take us further away from
our normal day-to-day conventional reality. For some, this may manifest in a kind of idealistic, mystical hysteria where everything is wonderfully positive, magical, and beautiful but has little relationship to
the normal world and fails totally to include the dark, painful side of
life. For others, it can lead to a fanaticism that drives them into strict
and intense practice in order to attain spiritual realizations. I was certainly not immune to the latter and can see that such tendencies to desperately seek spiritual salvation will often cover deep-seated problems
that are not resolved.

An example of this came to me some years back when a client began
working with me in therapy. She was a middle-aged, middle-class
woman who found herself suffering increasingly from depression. This
depression, however, she would mask in a veneer of positive spiritual
niceness that turned whatever suffering she might encounter into an
attempt to be more spiritual, which meant more positive. She would
smile a lot, even when touching on something potentially painful, and
talk about love and light and how she could see that all the things she
experienced were clearly sent to test her spirituality. When we got closer
to any of her inner struggle, she would rapidly dissociate from it and
seek a spiritual rationalization. Her spiritual search was for light and
transcendence because she could not bear to directly confront her distress. While her emphasis on light and transcendence gave, on the surface, a sense of her being highly spiritual, it covered a deep-rooted
wounding that had much to do with her inability to accept her Shadow,
or her darker side. She would resist looking at her darker side because
it did not accord with her ideal, spiritual self-image. She wanted me to

affirm her somewhat grandiose positive spiritual identity so that she might feel validated in the illusion she was creating of being OK. Even so, her depressions would haunt her like a demon.

Only as she began to see that her divine ideals and her veneer of positivity and light were really an avoidance did she begin to allow the therapeutic process to unfold. She needed someone to help her see that she was acceptable with her Shadow and that it was normal to have uncomfortable emotions. If she could heal her split between spiritual goodness and an unacceptable Shadow, then she would be more grounded as someone who had both positive qualities and faults and who could accept this. Part of this split was also a struggle in relation to her body and its more base needs. Her spiritual search was based on a desire to transcend her troubles without really addressing them, combined with a kind of addiction to the positive and the light.

This confusion brings into serious question what we mean by "spiritual." This word, which has no Buddhist equivalent, can be deeply misleading. Western concepts of spirituality contribute greatly to the split that often occurs between daily life and so-called spiritual life. So often, people speak of a difficulty integrating their spirituality or spiritual practice into their life. Fortunately, in relation to Buddhist practice, there is no notion of spirituality as distinct from "normal" life. The focus is not on some sort of transcendental, paranormal, or psychic opening to a higher state. For a Buddhist there is no external divine being that is going to save us. Rather, Buddhism focuses upon an ever-deepening awareness into the nature of reality, experienced in each moment. In this respect, the meaning of spirituality has its roots in the capacity to be truly present in daily life.

It would seem that our Western concept of spirituality actually shapes our view of what we expect to experience. Our conception of spirituality as a peaceful, light, and transcendent quality profoundly influences our focus, along with notions such as piety, purity, and holiness. Historically, this has separated spirituality from the body, sexuality, and earthly or worldly life. Notions of salvation and the presence of a higher omnipotent authority in monotheistic belief systems can also contribute to a lack of personal responsibility for emotional and psychological self-transformation. Spirituality can then become something that is both un-grounding in its move to transcend worldly life and, to some extent, infantilizing, giving over responsibility to a higher power.

Most people engage in some form of spiritual life because they wish for solutions to their life problems and to gain a deeper sense of meaning or purpose. Monotheistic religions differ from non-theistic religions such as Buddhism in what may be seen as the route towards, and source of, salvation. In Buddhism there is a notion of liberation from suffering, but not in the sense of an escape from normal life. Nirvana as a state of being free of suffering is not, as some consider it to be, a dimension of heaven that is other than normal life. Liberation comes through an insight into the nature of life, not through avoiding its reality. It is a fundamental change in how we see life, not an escape from it. In this respect, there is little room for avoidance of what is present in our physical and emotional experience.

When I encountered Buddhist psychology, I naturally assumed that its practices and teachings would help to heal my life problems. This assumption, however, is valid only if we have not misjudged what really are the roots of our problems. It is natural to enter a spiritual path because we seek meaning and a deeper understanding of the fundamental questions in life. This need is like an instinct that must be satisfied. Searching for some sense of the transpersonal or the divine can give us a feeling of trust, optimism, and security as the foundation of our lives. This may enable us to be more stable in our sense of who we are, but not always. In my own experience, the Buddhist teachings were addressing a deep-rooted spiritual yearning in my life and yet did not always resolve the real struggle, which had less to do with my spirituality than with my basic ego wounding. I began to see that seeking a so-called spiritual solution to the problems I experienced was not the only answer; it was also necessary for me to address my normal functioning identity in the world. I needed to look at psychological problems that affected my relationships to women in particular.

If we do not uncover these problems—and I saw this in myself—
we risk placing a veneer of spirituality over deeply buried emotional
wounds from childhood that do not simply go away. Spirituality can
then lead us to actually split off from our emotional problems, repress
them, and even deepen them, by what Welwood calls "spiritual bypassing."[5] If we have buried a part of ourselves we felt was unacceptable
and bad because of its emotional nature, our spirituality may exacerbate feelings of worthlessness or "sinfulness" and actually re-wound
us. Rather than healing deep-rooted wounds, our spiritual beliefs may
cause them to become repressed and strengthened. In my own early
years as a Buddhist I made great attempts to follow a collective expectation of how I should behave in order to be a wholesome, acceptable
practitioner. I became a good, peaceful, soft-spoken, repressed, puritanical Buddhist. Unfortunately, this created a veneer of peacefulness
that buried much of my inner emotional turmoil because I believed it
needed to be tamed.

When this happens there is greater potential for our spirituality to
become simply another expression of our personal pathology. We can
falsify the qualities valued in the path without realizing it. Renunciation
can become another level of denial and avoidance; compassion can
become a sickly sentimentality that has no substance to it. Our desire
to help others can come from "compulsive caring," or a compulsion to
sacrifice ourselves because we feel worthless. The Buddhist idea of
emptiness can likewise be falsified by the desire to disappear psychologically and merge or lose ego boundaries. Lack of identity, formless
vagueness, and absence of boundaries do not exemplify the Buddhist
idea of emptiness. My own version of this misconception was to try
to live an ideal of the pure and pious only to find it was a form of
repression I could not ultimately sustain.

At the heart of Buddhist practice is the search for a solution to our
fundamental wounds. Healing the emotional damage we often carry
within is truly the object of this practice. If we wish to resolve these
problems, we need to be open and honest about their reality within us.
Only when we do will any spiritual practice address what we need. The

aim of Buddhist practice is not a spiritual transcendence that dissociates from our suffering. Nor is it the search for salvation in some form
of external divine being that we hope will save us in our distress. As
one of my teachers, Lama Thubten Yeshe, once said, "Buddhism is
very practical; you just have to recognize that your mind is the cause of
suffering. If you change your mind, you can find liberation." This message is very simple but by no means easy to follow. In order to do so,
however, we must begin to recognize where we are psychologically
wounded.

The Wound 3

♦ ♦ ───

THE ROOT OF SUFFERING

A T TWO AND A HALF, my younger son's capacity to scream relentlessly when he did not get what he wanted seemed quite extraordinary. His anger and distress had a determination behind it that was
hard to know how to respond to. When in full voice, he had the capacity to go on for long periods of time, and nothing would abate the
flow, even if he got what he wanted. His suffering was raw, immediate,
uncontrived, and unmasked by adult constraints. He was expressing
the most basic experience of not having what he wanted, with little or
no capacity to rise to a more conscious level of understanding. This
suffering will be very familiar to any parent. We may as adults consider
that this is not something we would allow ourselves to express; we are
above such infantile responses, or are we? How often do we react to
not getting what we want and find someone to blame, rapidly distract
ourselves, rationalize our feelings away, or find some substitute indulgence? I recall seeing a smartly dressed woman in her thirties on the
steps of the Royal Academy in London shouting at her husband that
it was raining and she would get wet. She was like a little child, blam-
ing him for her discomfort or even for the rain itself.

Our suffering arises because our minds react to our experiences in
ways that are often uncontrollable. We cannot always change the world
and make the rain stop, but we can change our internal response to
what is happening. As we grow up we gradually learn to let go of
immediate gratification of our needs. Our suffering may then become
less raw and immediate, but the more sophisticated our mind becomes,

the more subtle our suffering becomes. I may not have tantrums when I do not get what I want, but I may feel disappointment, dissatisfaction, frustration, anxiety, and a host of other feelings. They may be brief or I may ignore them, but they are often there.

In Buddhist psychology the primary cause of suffering originates in the mind from a basic disposition of clinging and grasping. While these are the traditional terms used to describe a particular habit in the mind, I have often found it more useful to see this as a kind of contraction. We contract around a sense of self-identity, and if we are aware of ourselves, we can feel this as a kind of physical or energetic contraction. This may have originated in the mind, but it manifests subtly on a physical level. This disposition, in turn, responds to the environment in a tight, obsessive way that leads to an endless cycle of pain and reaction. Without realizing it, we lock and fix our reality in a way that does not allow its natural ebb and flow. One could say that the degree to which we actually suffer is then directly related to the degree to which we are contracting or locking. Our life may become tight and fearful as we struggle to protect ourselves from what we believe to be "reality." The more we contract, the more we fill our world with stress and tension, the more we feel insecure and fear change. There is less and less room to move; less time; less actual freedom; less real personal space. The environment may contribute the outer conditions to this distress, but the primary cause originates in the mind.

In our contracted state we lose relationship to the innate space that is present in reality. If we could open to it, our reality is in fact spacious, fluid, and essentially free. Because of our deep-rooted insecurity, however, spaciousness is intolerable to our fragile hold on self-identity. It becomes a source of profound anxiety. In our ignorance we are blind to this spacious nature and live in a contracted state called in Sanskrit *dukkha* (literally "contracted space"), in contrast to an open spaciousness known as *sukkha*. The term *dukkha* is, however, usually translated as "suffering" or "unsatisfactoriness," while *sukkha* is a quality of bliss.

I see this reaction in myself when I can turn something that is relatively simple into a drama as I contract and tighten. I recall an occasion when I was working on our house, gradually tiling the kitchen. I had planned to do it in a particular way and felt all was going as I had hoped. We did not have enough tiles to complete the job at that time, and so it was suggested we should do it a different way. I began to feel myself contracting. This would require taking half the tiles off in a particular area to finish another part. I could feel myself gradually closing in to a narrow, defended place that was totally locked and unmovable. I was beginning to feel pressured to do something that felt utterly unacceptable to me. There was no space to move, and I was ready to explode. In a matter of minutes I had turned the open spaciousness with which I was working into a contracted hell of my own making.

While there is a kind of simplicity in this Buddhist view of the root of suffering, Western psychotherapy offers us a variety of notions of the roots of suffering that in many ways complement this Buddhist principle, but which are more complex. The most familiar psychotherapeutic view is that much of our suffering originates with emotional wounding, particularly in childhood. Western psychology has explored in depth the developmental processes of the individual and generally orients towards the idea that our emerging self grows from conception and encounters various environmental factors that gradually both shape and distort its growth. This emphasizes the view that the combination of stresses in the environment and our innate disposition together make us grow and can also leave us wounded psychologically. Where Buddhism and Western psychology meet is in the idea that the wounding we experience arises through an interaction between inner propensities and outer conditions.

Although Western psychology tends not to look for a specific root cause of suffering, a generalized principle could be to see the root of suffering as our relative capacity or incapacity to respond healthily to the trials of life. Our ability to adapt to and maintain relative health in distressing or traumatizing circumstances is a remarkable homeostatic capacity within our nature. The degree to which we experience suffering is relative to our capacity to respond to life's demands in a healthy way. The responses we make as we grow shape who we become in both healthy and unhealthy ways. Often, however, we adopt ways of coping with trauma that, while appropriate at the time, later in life become a source of habitual patterns of reaction that limit and frustrate us. An example of this is the way in which a child will close off and bury the effects of sexual abuse to survive. This can be seen as the most natural and healthy mechanism in the circumstances. It is only later in life that this response to trauma proves to be an obstacle to further healthy development and must be healed. A historical process of wounding will then echo through much of our life as painful, habitual emotional patterns.

A man I once saw in therapy brought this experience clearly to mind when he began to touch on the possibility that he had been sexually abused as a child by his father. Gradually he began to uncover an experience that he had long ago locked in the unconscious so that he could survive. Burying the trauma of the abuse served to protect him at a time when he did not have the psychological resources to integrate its depth of distress. In adulthood, however, the presence of this trauma, albeit within the unconscious, was becoming increasingly disturbing. During the therapeutic process, as different aspects of this abuse became more conscious, it was important to allow him to find his own pace so that he could live with the pain he was releasing. In time, he was able to bring much of the experience to the surface and could slowly allow the significant changes this was bringing in his sense of self, his relationships, and his capacity to meet the world. Prior to this he was always caught in habitual, often fearful, responses to situations and people he encountered, never really able to understand why. Once he had uncovered this wounding, he began to change his relationship to the world around him and for the first time felt he was responding from a sense of inner health rather than pain, fear, and confusion.

While we can see that there are many situations in life where people clearly are the victims of circumstances, our individual susceptibility and the way we respond to circumstances will alter the degree to which they traumatize us. One could say that both Western psychology and Buddhism point to the idea that our response to the world, not necessarily the world itself, is the basis of our problems. The world itself will always manifest the conditions that potentially cause suffering; we have only a limited capacity to alter this. Our inner response to those conditions can, however, be cultivated. In his *Guide to the Bodhisattva's Way of Life*, Shantideva says we can try to cover the surface of the world with leather, but it would be much simpler just to cover our feet.[6] Shantideva's observation counteracts the ordinary view that needs to find someone or something to blame for all the ills we suffer. Indeed, if we consider the suffering of the child who has been abused, it would be inappropriate to say that his or her suffering is just a consequence of mental attitude. Both Buddhist and Western psychology assert, however, that we must begin to take responsibility for our responses to our experiences rather than endlessly blame something or someone out there. When we do so, we move out of the infantile position into an adult place.

Buddhist psychology particularly emphasizes the cultivation of a quality of awareness that directly recognizes our mind's response to each moment of experience as it unfolds. Western psychology particularly illuminates the nature of emotional patterning and wounding that shape our responses. Together, these two approaches provide insight into the cause of suffering, especially in relation to the nature and wounding of the ego. While Buddhist practice pays little attention to the historical evolution of individual pathology, its approach to healing relies on direct insight into the nature of experience as it arises. Western psychology pays great attention to the evolution of and wounding to our sense of self. There is much psychotherapy can learn from the Buddhist emphasis on cultivating awareness of the immediacy of the present experience, just as Buddhist psychology can benefit from a more detailed and personal understanding of the psychological development of the ego and its wounding.

THE WOUNDING OF THE EGO

In Buddhism there is no developmental model of the complexity understood by the Western therapeutic world. The practice and theory

of Buddhist psychology is based on a view of the person as an established, relatively conscious individual. This view assumes that we have
reached a certain level of psychological development and have a com-
paratively stable and cohesive sense of self. This does not imply, however, that we have developed a great depth of self-awareness.

Western psychology has clearly charted the development of the ego
as it evolves from conception and is shaped by our experiences of
infancy in relation to our individual susceptibility. There is what might
be called an innate instinct to constellate a sense of self; to function and
survive in the world. For some, this constellation of an ego does not
form well, and the sense of self remains fragile and unclear. For others, its formation is affected by circumstances that cause varying degrees
of wounding. Even without this wounding, a sense of self, albeit a
healthier one, must grow for our normal functioning in the world.

As we grow, our felt or emotional experience of "me" may become
increasingly wounded by the surrounding environment; in particular,
by the presence of dysfunctionality in the family. This emotional
wounding is often very painful and causes a kind of contraction
around an identity that slowly becomes fixed and solid. For example,
a child with a parent who constantly disapproves of or is angry with
her, and who thus surrounds her with a persistently negative emotional atmosphere, can develop painful self-beliefs that she is not good
enough, is unlovable, not wanted, and so forth. We contract into this
wounding, limiting and narrowing our sense of self into something
that is solid and intractable. This wounded self underlies the way we
feel about ourselves in the world and then permeates our life, shaping
our emotional responses to situations and experiences.

We will become most clearly aware of our wounded self when our
"buttons are pushed" and we feel a vividly appearing, emotionally
charged sense of *me*. This "vividly appearing I," as the Tibetans call it,
is associated with what in Buddhist psychology is known as "ego-
grasping." This is the experience of an ego, or "I," that is instinctually
contracted around a solid *me* and has a strong emotional flavor. Ego-
grasping holds on to a sense of *me* that is self-existent and independ-

ent of any process of creation. Possibly the most obvious time we recognize this vivid sense of "I" is when someone threatens or insults us. Strong emotions such as fear, grief, shame, desire, jealousy, guilt, and so on bring into clear relief our cherished and protected sense of *me*.

From a Buddhist point of view this solid sense *of me* is the aspect of ego-grasping at the root of all of our suffering. It is grasped at and *felt* to be true, permanent, and solid and yet is merely a constructed sense of ego. It does not actually exist as a solid entity anywhere in our continuum. I emphasize the word *felt* because this is not an intellectual construct, it is a *felt* experience, irrespective of one's philosophical notions.

To recognize this contracted sense of self is vital if we are to understand what is meant by "the emptiness of self" in Buddhism. This is particularly so because even among Buddhists, there can be a misunderstanding as to what is being negated by the notion of emptiness of self, or no-self.

When I experience someone threatening or insulting me I experience a kind of contraction in myself that grasps at a sense of *me*. This is a tangible, almost physical contraction that causes a strong emotional tightening in my chest. From this place, before I have a chance to do anything about it, I can react defensively with anger or aggression to protect myself. Alternatively, I may feel hurt or insulted and withdraw into myself for comfort and safety. In all of these reactions I can feel a vivid expression of my grasping at a solid sense of *me*. At first, this sense of *me* and its defensive reactions feel as though they relate to something that is a definite central part of me, something solid that must be defended. Only by looking more deeply will I begin to recognize that these reactions hold on to something that is not actually substantial, and they paint a picture of the world that is not real. Even though I may have feelings that I am hurt, frightened, or rejected, if I look deeply at this reactive *me,* I can see that it is not fixed, permanent, or true. There is no solid base for its existence. It is not to be found in my body, feelings, mind, perceptions, and so on as something existent.

The emotional process is real enough, but the "I" that I am grasping at as a fixed sense of self doesn't exist. It is like an emotionally charged bubble that pops when looked at more closely. As this bubble pops, the sense of contracted surface tension that held it together begins to open. A quality of inner space begins to be restored that is not tight and contracted.

The recognition of the lack of solid self and the subsequent release of the contraction around it don't mean we have no ego at all. It is important to distinguish between the normal, functional ego that acts as a focus of our relationship to the world and this emotionally charged, solid sense of ego.

Clearly differentiating these two is vital if we are truly to understand the notion of emptiness of self that is spoken of in Buddhism. Failing to differentiate can lead us to perceive emptiness as a kind of nihilism where we negate too much or the wrong thing. I recall that in the early seventies when I first encountered books on Zen, some of my friends and I got into a way of thinking that said, "Well, there is no ego, so nothing matters; just do what you like because there is no one doing it anyway." Our notion of no-self led to a kind of formlessness that had no sense of personal responsibility. It is not, however, the ego that needs to go but the ego-grasping that holds on to a self as solid and ultimately existent.

Having a stable center of self-awareness is crucial to relative daily experience. Although it creates a duality of subject and object, of self and other, this is necessary on the level of our everyday reality. This stable center forms the basis of our capacity to live in the relative world and function. It provides a focus to our life and a sense of continuity and self-awareness. In Buddhism this is called the "relative I," which is merely a label placed upon the basis of the person as a whole. From a Buddhist perspective, this capacity of focused awareness is a necessary facet of existence which is consistent with the understanding that arises from Western psychology. We need an ego as a focus of consciousness, for without it we would be extremely vulnerable to psychosis. We need a stable identity to give us a sense of form and shape in the world.

The relative "I" that enables us to function in the world does, however, become mixed up and confused with our emotional ego-grasping
so that we cannot see the difference. To realize emptiness of self we
must differentiate the two and understand clearly what ego-grasping
holds on to. The vivid emotional "I" that becomes so deeply entrenched in our sense of self has a number of significant ingredients:

1. We experience an emotional wounding to the sense of self that
   manifests when our "buttons are pushed."
2. This wound colors our entire experience of the world, projecting
   a view that is largely a distortion of reality.
3. We contract around and cling to this sense of self as if it were a
   solid, absolute, true self.
4. This ego needs to relate to things, either pleasurable or painful,
   to reinforce its sense of existence.
5. Underlying the grasping at self is a fundamental anxiety that
   makes us keep "doing" because the space of "being" is unbearable.

As Stephen Batchelor says in his little-known book *Flight*,[7] the underlying disposition of ego-grasping is a flight reaction from the essential,
spacious nature of our being. Anxiety, he says, is the fundamental emotional tone of the existential uncertainty intrinsic to this grasping at
identity. This existential anxiety is bound up with our struggle to cope
with the essentially empty nature of the ego. It leads us to grasp at anything that will reinforce a sense of self. We will grasp at pleasurable
things that will substantiate our existence and will fight defensively
anything that threatens us. Alternatively, we may try to deny and anesthetize ourselves from the pain. These are the three fundamental dispositions of attachment, aversion, and ignorance. Inevitably, however,
the transitory nature of our materiality, our mortality, will always haunt
us and may eventually lead us to face our basic anxiety.

Western psychotherapy has well charted the nature of our wounding and goes some way towards its healing. Conventional psychotherapy may enable a healthier sense of self to emerge, but even though

most of our emotional wounding is addressed, so long as there is still the root tendency to hold an "I" as self-existent, fundamental anxiety will remain. This deep-rooted tendency to cling to a sense of identity may be addressed only in a more contemplative style of therapy. As I have found personally and in my work as a therapist, the essential anxiety of ego-grasping is extremely difficult to overcome. It is only when we begin to place our minds into a quieter, less conceptual awareness that we will see through the subtle illusion of a self. For this, the practice of meditation is fundamental.

Healing the Wound

The development of an ego-identity is not an option that we can avoid or bypass; it is a factor of the human condition. Without it, we will experience serious psychological problems. As I have said at some length in *The Psychology of Buddhist Tantra,*[8] the need for a stable identity is vital in deepening the Buddhist path. For those whose sense of self is weak or seriously wounded, this wounding must be addressed before the journey can go forward. If our spiritual practice does not address it, then a psychotherapeutic path may be a necessary preliminary.

Whatever the nature of our wounded identity, it will always be felt as an absolute, irresolvable, inescapable truth. In psychotherapy clients I have often sensed a kind of stubborn determination that this is so. This emotional identity is often highly charged, overwhelming, and deeply painful. What gives it so much power is the disposition to grasp at it as true. We believe what we feel, and seldom does a more positive view of ourselves come close to changing it.

We may try to replace wounded concepts about ourselves with healthier, more loving and self-accepting ones. Much psychotherapy is aimed at gradually restoring a healthier sense of identity to free the ego from its wounding. When this happens in therapy it can radically alter how a person then relates to the world. This process requires much time and loving support. In time, the therapist can enable a kind of re-parenting that helps to establish a more healthy state of being.

This does not always work, however, when the strength of ego-grasping stubbornly holds onto a destructive self-belief that does not shift. We may attempt to place a veneer of positive thinking on top of this negative self-belief but still not actually touch the root wound. Positive veneers may serve for a while, but at some point the actual sense of self will come to the surface again and need to be addressed.

In the practice of meditation we can infuse our experience with a quality of ease and acceptance that allows us to just be without judgment. This helps to replace the harsh inner landscape that is so often connected to our wounding. I have found this in my own practice and while teaching meditation of quiet present awareness. By gently introducing a sense of acceptance, meditation can be pervaded by an atmosphere of compassion that helps soften the contraction around negative beliefs. This practice of compassion towards ourselves can be like the cultivation of an inner parent who is unconditional and accepting. This can enable a softening and letting go of negative self-beliefs so that we inhabit a more caring inner landscape.

Through this healing process, a more healthy flexible, fluid, and permeable sense of self may begin to emerge. Even this positive state of self-identity, however, will have a subtle ego-grasping tendency. We can just as easily grasp at being valuable, loveable, and precious as at feeling worthless. A particularly clear example of this arose during a retreat I was leading. A woman came to speak to me about a painful experience that kept arising during meditation. She had had a number of particularly damaging relationships with men, which began as a child with her father, and, later, in her marriage, and even in relation to a psychotherapist. Her experiences had left her with a deep-rooted sense of not being good enough that would manifest in a ferocious, extremely distressing rage. She had worked hard in psychotherapy looking at the emotional roots in childhood of this damaged sense of self. Replacing the negative belief with a positive one seemed reasonable but did not seem to actually work. She was confronted time and again by this solid, fixed sense of herself being not good enough.

During our discussion I was reminded of the Tibetan practice of

Chöd (literally "to cut off"), during which a meditator would go to a particularly frightening place, like a cremation ground, and deliberately generate a state of fear so that the vivid sense of "I" would arise. Once this vivid feeling of "I" was generated, the meditator would look it directly in the face, so to speak, and recognize its completely fabricated nature. Recognizing that this "I" had no true existence would directly cut through ego-grasping (hence the name *Chöd*), releasing the mind from the emotional distress of the fear.

In effect, this woman had the perfect Chöd context. She was constantly confronted by this vivid sense of her ego-grasping and could, if she faced it, recognize its empty nature. As we spoke, it was clear that she had previously thought she needed to replace the negative sense of self-identity with a positive one. The danger with this approach was that she would cling to this new identity just as solidly. It would then be cracked by some experience and she would again be back to the wound. I suggested that clinging to a fixed identity, whether positive or negative, was just another form of ego-grasping that needed to be cut through. Returning to her meditation, she had a clear sense of the object of ego-grasping and, for the first time, could begin to loosen the ego's grip.

So long as we still hold on to a sense of self, even a positive one, we are caught in the roots of anxiety and suffering. Only once we can go beyond this disposition can we experience liberation. However, the journey must begin with recognizing the wounding that lies at the heart of our sense of self. This recognition of suffering is part of the call that brings us to the path of awakening. When I reflect upon the elements of my own life that caused me to embark upon the spiritual path, I am aware that anxiety was central. The absence of any satisfactory solution to my deep existential anxiety gave me little choice but to embark upon a journey to find an inner peace. In my journey it became apparent that the only thing that truly gave a sense of relief was meditation and the cultivation of a particular quality of awareness that enables a gradual opening of the ego's contraction.

In meditation we can gradually release the surface tension that holds together our ego-identity like a bubble of water. As this tension releases, our sense of self becomes more permeable and more flexible. As the contraction opens, it gives a profound sense of spaciousness and restores the natural fluidity of our responses. We will live with a more natural capacity to be in harmony with the events and experiences of our lives, whether positive or negative. In our happiness there will be less need to grasp and hold on to our experiences. In our distress we will no longer cling to and identify with a sense of disaster that is permanent and unchanging. When we let go of the contraction around our identity we open to our inner space, to a freedom that is no longer wounded. Life can then unfold freely. This may sound simple, but the habit of contraction is ingrained in every cell of our being and takes time to unravel. The journey, however, must begin with the knowledge of what is at the root of our suffering and that we *can* reach a place of wholeness and liberation.

A Vision of Wholeness 4

THE BUDDHA'S TEACHING of the four noble truths is a wonderfully insightful paradigm for healing and transformation. Its simplicity belies its profundity. We may recognize the challenge present in the first noble truth, the truth of suffering, as the underlying malaise we experience in life becomes apparent. The second truth, the truth of the cause of suffering, leads us to honestly face the underlying issue of the wounding we have experienced that is echoed time and again through life. The third noble truth leads us to recognize that there is another possibility. The truth of cessation gives us a vision of what is possible. It strikes an optimistic note and shows us that there is a place of wholeness if we choose to travel the path. This realization can be a welcome relief when we are in the midst of some period of intense distress or crisis in our life. If we were sick, it would possibly be the most challenging encounter of our lives to be informed that there is no cure. The truth of cessation gives us the insight and confidence to see that we have the potential to be whole.

There is another important consideration reflected in the truth of cessation, which is the recognition of our fundamental human value. From a therapeutic perspective one of the most insidious aspects of distress that emerges within psychotherapy is a deep-rooted lack of self-value. Growing up in a Judeo-Christian culture that tends to emphasize man's fallen and sinful nature exacerbates this lack of intrinsic value. It engenders a somewhat bleak and depressive attitude towards human nature as fundamentally flawed. We can be redeemed only by a determined struggle against our darker side and if we cast out our badness. To then consider that salvation is possible only through the selfless sacrifice of a savior does not exactly engender a sense of empowerment or appreciation of our human value. Growing up in a culture that has these values deeply entrenched in its spiritual roots can have a profoundly damaging effect on the sense of self. Fundamental to our potential for change must therefore be a restoration of our intrinsic value.

Within Tibetan Buddhism, one of the primary aspects of understanding our fundamental human value is reflection on the preciousness of human life, or what is often called the "precious human rebirth." Traditionally, this preciousness is understood in terms of both its value and its potential freedom. Its value is bound up in the knowledge that our innate potential is extraordinary. Unfortunately for many of us, the stressful life we live, the materialistic preoccupations we have, and the education we receive seldom give us the freedom to understand our intrinsic nature. Our ignorance of the innate quality of the mind is such that it often requires the presence of someone who has a deeper wisdom to point out our potential. This is why the presence of the Buddha and his teachings in our time is so important. It is through the existence of rare beings of his depth of insight that we can actually be shown the potential that lies hidden within our normal distressed, neurotic, and busy minds.

When we begin to explore the nature of the mind we will inevitably encounter the wild and uncontrollable aspects of our normal, somewhat overcrowded, habitual mind. Only with guidance and skillful practice will we begin to recognize that the mind has an undercurrent of clarity and luminosity that is of a very different order. To open or awaken this innate clarity is to expand our ground of being into a state free of much of the emotional psychological distress that comes from our contracted, dysfunctional self-identity. This state of "Buddha nature," or awakened potential, is possibly the single most important recognition at the beginning of our journey. Within each of us, our nature is primordially pure, even though the vessel may be flawed.

In the *Uttaratantra* by Maitreya, a treatise on the Buddha nature, a number of metaphors for the presence of Buddha nature are given. It is like a golden statue wrapped in filthy rags; a jewel buried beneath the house of a pauper; honey surrounded by a swarm of bees; a seed contained within rotting fruit; gold buried in mud.[9]

These metaphors are a way of conveying the notion of an intrinsic primordial purity that is temporarily obscured from view. When I first encountered these metaphors I found they had a surprisingly profound effect upon my mind. Until that time I don't think I had ever been given the message that my innermost being was healthy. Rather, I had somehow learned to fear that if I revealed my deepest nature, it would be found unacceptable and even dangerous or evil. To then begin to trust that something positive could be revealed dramatically changed my self-perception. I could begin to let go of my tight self-control and trust that within my chaos and confusion was an innate potential for something positive and healthy. So long as I failed to recognize this, it was like living in poverty and not realizing there is a valuable treasure hidden beneath the floor. My sense of self-value was indeed like a golden statue hidden within filthy rags, and I was completely identified with the rags.

The freedom this life can offer us is the capacity to understand this intrinsic value. Once it is recognized, we can make a choice to awaken. Perhaps our most remarkable gift that distinguishes us from, for example, animals is the capacity of consciousness and reason. While, according to Buddhist philosophy, all sentient beings possess Buddha nature, the human condition is of particular importance in enabling this to manifest.

We have emerged into consciousness over many thousands of years, and while this may have separated us from our animal ancestors, it also has given us a freedom to awaken still further. Our minds have a remarkable gift of language that enables us to understand and communicate. In principle, we have the physical and mental freedom to develop our awareness if we are willing and ready to use it skillfully.

Regrettably, much of our time is caught up in a preoccupation with life struggles and emotional insecurities that distract us from what might be possible. Even in the West, where we are much more materially fortunate than many parts of the world, we are still dogged by psychological habits that block our potential. Far from using this human potential meaningfully, we use it to indulge our insecurities and exploit the natural environment around us. Blindly, we create more suffering and harm in the world rather than truly recognizing our potential. As Shantideva points out, we all wish to have happiness but constantly create the causes for suffering.[10] While this is so, only when something wakes us up do we start to take responsibility for this remarkable gift of life.

This call to awaken may in part come from an experience of suffering; it may also come through the experience of what we might call a vision of our innate wholeness. This vision may be utterly mysterious and incomprehensible, but its effect is almost always dramatic. While I use the term *vision,* this is not to imply it is always through a symbolic appearance. We may be made aware of our intrinsic nature during a time of what Maslow called a peak experience, when we open to a quality of our nature that is spacious, lucid, and free of conceptual clutter. There is no set time in life when this may happen, and it cannot be contrived; the question is whether we can consciously respond to the insight it brings concerning our potential.

When I was about eleven, I had an experience which I could only in retrospect comprehend, even though at the time its impact was dramatic. It was an experience I have never forgotten. I was a Boy Scout going on a weekend hike in the country with a close friend. We had walked through farmland for most of the first day and were due to find a location to camp for the night. It had been arranged that we would stay in a farmer's field.

In mid-afternoon my friend and I stopped in a field beside a wood for a rest. I decided I wanted to explore the woods behind us, leaving my friend in the field. I climbed the fence and began to enter the wood. At first, the undergrowth was quite dense, but as I went further this opened out and I eventually found a path that was winding before me. I followed the path and found it led to an extensive bed of reeds which, from my perspective at the age of eleven, seemed to reach over my head. I went on and soon came to a wooden walkway with water beneath, winding its way through the reeds. I was getting more and more excited because I anticipated that this might be leading me to a pond. Suddenly the reeds parted and the sight before me froze me to the spot like a rabbit blinded by headlights. I was looking across a lake and in its center was a small island upon which stood a magnificent stone pagoda.

I did not know what I was looking at except that I had a feeling it was oriental and utterly magical. It brought to the surface feelings that I can still recall to this day. I was in a state of complete wonder. I knew deep down that this was a special moment.

As part of my weekend hike I was supposed to make notes and record what had happened. Consequently, I spent about half an hour making drawings of that lake with its temple in the middle. When I returned to my friend it was hard to convey what had happened, and it was only many years later that I recognized the importance of this vision of wholeness. It did not matter that it had come at a time in my life when I could not really understand what I had experienced. It had penetrated deep into my psyche and would come to life when the right time came, which it certainly did some twelve years later when I arrived in Bali on my travels and encountered similar temples on lakes.

In the stories of both Parzival, the central figure of the Grail legend, and the Buddha, their entry into the journey was initiated by an important vision of possibility. For the Buddha this vision was evoked by the tranquil simplicity of a wandering mendicant seen on the fourth occasion that he ventured out of his enclosure. He encountered someone who, without any of the comfortable luxury he had, could appear self-contained, content, and at one with himself and life. For Parzival, who in the Grail legend had also been enclosed in a protected, secluded environment, it was the sight of a radiant knight he at first thought was a manifestation of God.[11] Responding to this vision became irresistible. It was an opening to another reality previously concealed from view. However, both Parzival and the Buddha had to defy the established order to venture into the world.

In folk tales the hero is often given a lure to set the journey in motion. A wise person or messenger may appear who imparts the knowledge of the existence of a symbolic object that promises to heal the state of dis-ease. It may be an inexhaustible treasure, an elixir of life, a sacred pearl, a golden fleece, a firebird, the well at the world's end, the lost city, or some such thing. To find this object, however, will usually entail traveling into hazardous, unknown territory. The messenger initiates an insight or vision that is numinous, enthralling, and irresistible. This vision creates the aspiration and motivation to go on, with the knowledge that there is a truly meaningful and worthwhile goal.

An absence of this kind of vision can be a terrible experience in people's lives. It can leave some feeling desperate and hopeless and that life lacks all meaning. At such times, the pull towards anesthetics to deaden the feeling of emptiness may be very tempting, but this only prolongs the agony. If we give ourselves time and allow ourselves to wait and remain open to the process we are going through, a change can occur. The germ of a renewal of vision and a sense of purpose grows gradually from within; it cannot be implanted from outside. Forcing this process by fabricating something that is not genuinely emerging from within seldom works for long. This "dark night of the soul" is not resolved by someone trying to make us feel positive and give us hope. As T. S. Eliot writes in his "Four Quartets," "I said to my soul, be still, and wait without hope / For hope would be hope for the wrong thing."

The Buddha taught the truth of cessation before the truth of the path because without some insight into the possibility of liberation or totality, there would be little incentive to travel the path. A vision of the goal is therefore an important part of the Buddhist journey. Longchenpa, a Tibetan master, used a phrase translated as "goal-sustained refuge"[12] to convey the way in which a taste or vision of the goal generates the faith and inspiration to go forward. Once we experience this refuge, our life direction changes radically, turning increasingly from unsatisfactory worldly refuges. Strength of purpose becomes reinforced by the experience of renewed reminders of that vision. In the Tantras in particular, this constant re-visioning of the goal is brought into the present by repeatedly visualizing oneself as the deity, the essence of our innate Buddha potential. This process establishes our commitment to embark on what will inevitably be a difficult journey. Without the inspiration, faith, and understanding a sense of vision brings, it can prove extremely difficult to overcome the challenges we will meet.

Within the Buddhist Mahayana tradition, great emphasis is placed upon the cultivation of a quality of intention or motivation known as *bodhichitta*, or the awakening mind. Bodhichitta is seen as the principal seed that creates the fruit of buddhahood. It is the growing strength of the aspiration to accomplish a state of wholeness or full awakening for the welfare of others.

Bodhichitta has three components that are equally significant. The first of these is a deep and expansive quality of compassion that recognizes the suffering of others and the need to take responsibility for its alleviation. This great compassion feels the unbearable nature of our collective suffering and cannot simply remain passive. The second component is the vision of wholeness. This is the recognition that we each have the potential to benefit others in ways that are inconceivable in our limited ordinary state. It is this vision of buddhahood that also enables us to cope with the potentially overwhelming depth of distress and suffering present in the world. This vision reminds us that we can achieve a state of being that can hold the immensity of this awareness. The third factor of bodhichitta is a quality of will that is able to take on the task.

The vision of our innate potential at the heart of bodhichitta is conveyed in the metaphors that are used to describe its nature. In his *Guide to the Bodhisattva's Way of Life,* Shantideva calls it the supreme ambrosia that overcomes death, the inexhaustible treasure, the supreme medicine, the tree that shelters all, the universal bridge, the dawning moon, and the great sun.[13] All of these images have, at one time or another, appeared as symbols of what Jung called the "treasure hard to attain"[14] that recur in many myths and fairy tales. This treasure can be understood as the healing vitality that is released from the depth of the psyche when we are in touch with our sense of wholeness, the Self.

Within our Western culture there are constant reminders of symbols of wholeness if we are open to them and can recognize their meaning. In architecture in particular we often see mandala images, radiant suns, flower motifs, pergolas, domes, spires, triumphant archways, and countless others. In ornate stucco relief work on ceilings, we are reminded time and again of the symbols of wholeness. The recurrence of cupolas, fountains, and pools placed in the center of classical symmetrical garden designs all reflect the same symbolism. The alchemists of the Middle Ages saw the *fons mercurialis,* the mercurial fountain, as a profound symbol of the goal of the alchemical art.[15]

Today, unfortunately, we have all but lost the capacity to recognize the meaning behind these symbols, even though they often remain numinous for us. These archaic metaphors continue to emerge in our creative lives in strange circumstances. I was amused by wedding cakes I saw displayed in the window of a cake shop close to where I once lived. These symmetrical structures with bride and groom standing on the top layer were very elaborate optimistic symbols of wholeness. One of them even had on the lower layers a little plastic fountain. I don't imagine that the cake designer was aware of the alchemical significance of this symbolism; even so, there was clearly an unconscious resonance. When we are receptive, as I was when I encountered the pagoda in the lake as a child, this symbolism will penetrate the veil and touch our inner nature.

A vision of the goal helps to generate the inspiration and strength of motivation to venture out on the journey of awakening. This journey asks us to gradually surrender to and serve the Self, our Buddha nature. Such service is an act of loving-kindness and compassion for the welfare of others, which is like the moisture of nourishment that makes the journey worthwhile. Without this love and compassion, the journey would become arid and dry. Bodhichitta is an expression of the heart of the path that combines a deep sense of service towards those around us with the vision of the goal and a willingness to engage in the path.

However we choose to engage in the journey, a vision of the goal will be a guiding light that provides hope when we are struggling. If we lose this vision, we may find ourselves snuffling around in the dirt with no idea of why we are there. We can become so ground down by the demands and responsibilities of life that our world comes to lack vision and inspiration. Inspiration is a vital part of the path, particularly at the beginning. While the call may come from painful circumstances that need to change, we may also need to listen to our inner visions and respond to their inspiration.

Our vision may not be as grand as the idea of enlightenment. It may, however, be an instinctual sense that there can be something different. The seed or germ of our capacity to change is often found in the darkest moment. When the Buddha taught the third noble truth, the truth of cessation, his intention was to wake us up to our potential. This may be like the recognition that we are living like a poor man under whose shack lies a buried treasure. We may be surrounding ourselves by protective rubbish and fail to see our innate potential, like a golden statue wrapped in filthy rags. These metaphors for Buddha nature show us our inner potential, encouraging us not to be bound by our limited, low-quality perceptions of ourselves, as Lama Thubten Yeshe used to say. The goal of the vision is not something outside of ourselves that is unreachable; it is our own true nature, the nature we can easily lose sight of in our complicated, high pressure, and often destructive materialistic culture.

Chenrezig

The Noble Imperfection   5

COMPASSION DOES NOT ARISE from ideals of perfection but from a recognition of and concern for our own fallibility. At the heart of our potential for health and wholeness is the need for a fundamental quality of acceptance, an unconditional compassionate presence. Without this capacity either for ourselves or for others, even our spirituality can become harsh and uncompromising.

While we may begin to understand our intrinsic potential, our human fallibility is nevertheless glaringly evident in so many aspects of life. We may try to overlook it or strive towards some ideal or vision of perfection, but even then, our humanity is just below the surface. The spiritual search and the quest for personal growth is often an attempt to transcend this fallibility. We may have a vision of wholeness, but if we relate to this vision unskillfully, it may not lead us beyond suffering but instead perpetuate its causes.

For many of my early years as a Buddhist I was driven by a desire to live up to an ideal of the bodhisattva, whose exemplary life and attitude were models of virtue. This desire provoked a kind of obsession with trying to be virtuous, peaceful, and well-behaved. The group of peers with whom I lived was equally caught up in presenting a veneer of goodness and piety. Furthermore, this ideal acted as a stick with which to beat myself. I berated myself for not being good enough, for falling short of the ideal. I would sometimes feel unworthy of my teacher's attention and would fear that he must be able to see how gross and deluded I was.

When I think of how uncomfortable this experience was, I am shocked at the depth of my self-negation and self-judgment. I was caught in a state of mind that had no love and acceptance of myself for who I was. There was no compassion in my self-view and I had internalized the view that self-improvement was the goal. I had to set my sight on becoming a better, more wholesome, less selfish, good person; then I would be acceptable. I am not alone in becoming involved in a Buddhist culture that neurotically sees striving for self-betterment as the goal. If our wounded lack of self-value is at the root of our striving to attain a state of perfect enlightenment, then we are in serious danger not just of deluding ourselves but of actually aggravating our emotional wounding.

Today as never before there is a vast industry based upon self-improvement, which has at its heart the sense that we are not acceptable as we are. We must be better, faster, slimmer, more attractive, more dynamic, etc. This is our twenty-first-century version of original sin. Our sin is that we are not good enough and there are countless icons, presented particularly in the media, of what we must live up to. Perhaps the most obvious examples of this are in the cult of the celebrity and the culture of fashion and body shape. But there are many ways in which we constantly measure and judge ourselves.

Unfortunately for many of us, the spiritual side of our lives is not immune to this same disposition. If the ideals by which we measure ourselves are spiritual, then the desire to be seen as spiritually evolved can be just as pressuring and demanding. We must become more conscious, more caring, more open, more pure, more enlightened, and so on. In many ways, idealism can be seen as being at the very heart of a spiritual path. The idea of self-development or spiritual development usually has an ideal as its central premise, couched in terms such as "living to one's full potential" or "becoming enlightened."

While self-improvement may sound reasonable as an aspect of Buddhist practice, this view needs to carry something of a health warning. The intention of self-betterment carries a potentially unhealthy Shadow which is, often, a fundamental lack of self-worth and self-acceptance. The need to be different and live up to an ideal can lack an essential compassion that allows us to be who we are.

In the therapeutic setting, I encounter Buddhist practitioners whose view of the path seems driven by an intense striving to be a better person. This striving is based on a fundamental lack of self-acceptance. Their spiritual urgency is often born out of a desire to be good, caring, sensitive, and wise, as this will lead to a sense of self-affirmation. Scratch the surface of this spiritual correctness and we discover deep insecurities, lack of self-worth, and lack of self-acceptance. The resulting need for love and acceptance is what the psychotherapy world calls narcissistic wounding and can make spirituality self-preoccupied. We may attempt to cover this wounding with a veneer of spiritual goodness, but this does not heal the root. It will often feel inauthentic.

I recall a young Western Tibetan Buddhist nun living within a community I was part of. She tried hard to live the pure, selfless existence she saw exemplified in the teachings. She seldom if ever considered her own needs. She would sleep very little and constantly worked to take care of others. Many of us would say, "Look at her, she is such a bodhisattva." Sadly, it was evident that beneath this utter dedication to serve her teachers and work tirelessly for others was a desperately sad and unhappy person. She would seldom acknowledge this because to do so would be to think of herself. Suppressing her own inner need or pain was crucial to her.

In time, however, she became sick and her inner struggle started to break through the veneer of her idealized bodhisattva persona. Fortunately, she was taken in hand by a very kind visiting old lady who could see straight through her mask. Letting go of the imperative to negate herself in order to feel acceptable would not be easy. She did eventually do so and let go of something of the fanatical ideal she had set herself to live by. Her example stood out for me of how the ideal of a bodhisattva's total selflessness must be born out of a healthy sense of self-worth and self-love if it is not simply to become part of our pathology.

It was Freud who first introduced the notion of a superego as the internalized image of the ideal we *should* live up to, the internal ideal against which we judge ourselves. Whether one can say that in all cultures a superego is developed to the same degree is not certain. In Western culture there are high expectations and pressures placed upon the individual, beginning in childhood, to live up to ideals of material success, physical excellence, intelligence, perfection, and goodness. Whether these ideals are defined in the family by parental expectations or in broader society, their power can be immense. To internalize a process of self-judgment against an ideal can lead to a constant feeling that we are fundamentally not acceptable as we are. We must do better, improve, grow, and develop.

The desire to improve and be a better person has, it would seem, a double edge to it. Yes, why not try to clean up our lives and be a more kind, caring, and considerate person? Why not aspire to be more ethically wholesome, more tolerant, and to stop harming others? But the desire to live up to some ideal has a number of hazardous consequences. What is unacceptable will become suppressed into what Jung called a Shadow. When we learn to hide and eventually deny our failings, it can lead to an unconscious spiritual grandiosity. Cultivated goodness and piety can eventually cause an individual to see him- or herself as special and spiritually gifted. If this way of being gains outer acclaim and approbation, the grandiose self-deception can grow, making it increasingly hard to acknowledge failings. Once again, scratch the surface and we find a lack of compassion, a failure to accept who we are, with our positive qualities and our failings.

In my early years as a Buddhist I readily confused the difference between a path that was about becoming perfect and one that led to the understanding that all things, as they are, are intrinsically perfect. Despite the underpinning view of nonduality, in Buddhist philosophy the search for perfection is glaringly dualistic and yet so central to many people's thinking. The Buddhist understanding of emptiness and nonduality is that all relative phenomena are contingent, lacking an inherent, independent nature. Attempting to perfect a relative state of being is to attempt to make relative truth into an absolute. This fails to recognize the essential Buddhist understanding that only by going beyond such distinctions of good and bad, perfect and imperfect, can we discover the ultimate truth beyond duality. As the Buddha taught in the *Heart Sutra*, phenomena are neither impure nor are they free of impurity.

The idealism that leads to a desire for or addiction to perfection on the spiritual path can be, psychologically, very damaging. The Buddhist path recognizes that it is folly to search for perfection in life. All this searching does is lead to endless suffering and dissatisfaction. As Chögyam Trungpa pointed out, we go around and around, trying to improve ourselves through struggle, until we realize that the ambition to improve ourselves is itself the problem.[16] The only road to perfection is for the ego to finally give up this search and allow what is, recognizing that our innate Buddha nature is beyond the relative qualities of good and bad. To become enlightened is not about perfecting our relative state of being but is about recognizing our true nature.

At the heart of our striving is our fundamental wound, our wounded ego-identity. If we can address this problem we can alter the whole basis of our life. When we begin to see our wound it is tempting to think we must change, we must make it different so that we can live our lives the way we might wish. I am reminded of a discussion with a client who recognized his deep-rooted fear, vulnerability, and lack of self-acceptance. He saw these as the ingredients that always made him profoundly fearful and uncomfortable with others, and he desperately wanted to get rid of them. His inclination was to embark upon endless workshops and therapy techniques to find the solution. He felt unacceptable as he was and would brutally berate himself for not being able to be with people without severe anxiety.

As we spoke, it was clear that the only way to resolve this struggle was to begin to give up the pressure to be something he was not. Rather than forcing himself to be different, he needed to fundamentally accept his distressed sense of self and begin to create an atmosphere that cared for and allowed it to be as it was. If he could establish a depth of acceptance that did not judge and criticize this wound, there would be a greater ease within himself about his distress. It was as though he needed to set up an internal environment that was like a loving, compassionate parent who simply held his painful self-identity without judgment. With this inner environment he could be more at ease with himself. In time he indeed began to struggle less within, not by trying to change but just by cultivating a growing sense of compassion and acceptance of who he was as a whole, with strengths and weaknesses. As this has happened, his capacity to cope with previously paralyzing social settings has also radically changed.

There is humility, honesty, and compassion in the capacity to allow our fallibility and frailty as human, sentient beings. To try to be otherwise can be seen as embracing a kind of false self that is in denial of our fallibility. This compassion allows us to be who we are without destructive judgment and self-criticism. This does not mean we do not address our faults or our Shadow, but that we see them with far greater acceptance, lightness, and humor. If we can live openly and honestly, we can relax and be more present. For me, the experience of accepting myself more made it possible to be present with my teachers in a more comfortable way. I was not pretending or trying to be something I was not.

With greater self-acceptance and love also comes a diminution of the intensity of striving, and a greater capacity to be present and authentic to where we are. When I was in India living close to Tibetan monks and lamas, I was often surprised at the apparently easy-going, laid-back way in which many of them seemed to live their practice. They often responded to my intensity and fervor with the expression *kale kale pe ro nang* (literally "please go slowly"). Essentially, what they were saying was take it easy, go slowly, and you get there. They seemed highly amused by the attitude I had towards my practice, as though they could not understand why I was so driven. They did not have the underlying emotional disposition in their psyches that said they were not good enough. This does not mean they did not practice and work hard. It meant that they let things be and did not have the neurotic intensity of striving many of us suffer from in the West.

This more compassionate attitude of deeper self-acceptance enables us to practice with a much lighter touch. It enables a deeper sense of ease with ourselves that influences our capacity to sit in meditation. When there is less intensity, the mind becomes more relaxed and thereby able to quieten and open to its innate spaciousness and clarity.

As we deepen our sense of ease with ourselves, the fundamental wounding to our self-identity will soften. This softening leads to a greater inner space that can more naturally respond to others. While we are caught in our wounded self-preoccupations, we have no space for others. An inner atmosphere of compassion and acceptance slowly softens the rigidity of our wounding. As we become less self-preoccupied we begin to find a capacity to respond to others, and we may discover that we are able to be present, compassionate, and caring without judging. Our compassion grows as we allow others to be who they are with their faults and struggles, their unique qualities and gifts.

If we can bring together a vision of our innate potential with the compassion that recognizes and accepts where we are as human beings, our path can be caring and honest while being rich in creative potential. Our path must begin from where we are, not from some false distortion of ourselves in an attempt to be spiritual and special. Grandiosity comes when we get hooked on our visions and fail to live honestly and compassionately with our fallibility. There is nobility in our humanity and when we truly accept and surrender, we open naturally to our clear, brilliant nature because it is always there in the present in each moment. As we do so we must learn to live with a central paradox, which is that while we may endeavor to change and grow, change actually comes when we accept fully what is.

♦ ♦ ———————————————————————————————

THERE OFTEN COMES A POINT in our lives when we are unable to go forward without help. We may feel the need for some form of spiritual guidance and yet not know where to look. Even when we find such guidance, we may be reluctant to trust it or afraid to relinquish our pride in self-reliance. In mythology a significant aspect of the heroic quest is the appearance of some form of guide, what Joseph Campbell called a "supernatural aid." He writes, "The hero to whom such a helper appears is typically one who has responded to the call."[17] This figure may have a number of functions, one of which is to initiate a vision of the goal. The guide may indicate that if the hero or heroine seeks a certain object or accomplishes a particular task, salvation will occur. While the mythical guide may symbolize some aspect of our own deeper nature, what Jung called "the Self," this inner figure is often projected onto an external person. There is, in this respect, a strong disposition, almost an instinct, to find a guide or teacher, or what in the East is known as a *guru*.

I recall, in my late teens and early twenties, a growing desire to find someone with genuine wisdom who could lead me out of the painful confusion I experienced. In my childhood background there was no one who really understood my search for meaning. I found some answers through reading, but this remained somewhat arid.

Following university, my travels to the USA, Australia, the Far East, and finally India and Nepal were marked by a growing sense that I was searching for a teacher. Although this is something of a cliché, it nevertheless became clearer as I continued. I was not alone; in the early sev-

enties, there were many others on this "hippie" trail, searching for Eastern wisdom. I kept meeting individuals who were a little further along
on the journey than myself and who seemed to be pointing me in the
right direction. It was not until I reached Nepal that I attended a meditation course and met the Tibetan lamas who were to be so important
to my path. Ironically, just before doing so, I met a Sikh in Calcutta
who spent some time advising me that I should not go in search of
gurus but should follow my own truth. His advice was very powerful
and almost caused me to not attend the meditation course. At that
moment I was torn between thinking I could undertake the journey
on my own and feeling it required help and guidance. In the end I realized I needed help and that I had to trust the guidance of these lamas.

When we are unable to access our own "inner knowledge wisdom,"
clearly we will need an outer relationship to help us. This is not a failing or weakness; it is a simple reality of the path. It may be a great
challenge to our potentially arrogant Western belief that we can do it
all ourselves. The question is, Can we find someone who is authentic
and trustworthy to place in this position? When I met the lamas, I
spent considerable time with this question in mind. In time I began to
recognize that they had a quality of insight and integrity that I felt I
could trust. As this trust developed I also had the intense feeling that
I had come home; that I had truly re-connected to the underlying
thread of my life journey. I had no doubt. I also knew that I could not
do this on my own.

During that first period of study with these teachers, I learned that
many circumstances in our lives could be seen as the guru. We constantly encounter situations and people that challenge us or open our
eyes to insights that we need to become aware of. It may be an illness
that wakes us up to the fact that we are not living in a healthy way. It
may be a person who confronts us with our limitations so that we have
to grow through them. It may be our children who endlessly push us
to our limits of patience. It may be the person who irritates us so much
that we must face our inner prejudices and Shadow. From one perspective, these experiences are the guru waking us up to know our-

selves better. The question will always be whether we are willing to face these things and change.

It is often said that the sun is always waiting to shine; the question is whether the clouds part and we are able to receive it. So it is with our experience of the guru. The guru is like an innate wisdom that is ready to illuminate an understanding of the way when we are open to receiving it. Life is always presenting us with messages that can show us the way, if we are willing to hear them.

It is commonly said in spiritual circles that when a student is ready, the teacher will appear. This may well be true, but I have also known those who do not find someone they feel they can trust. The guide, teacher, or mentor, however we name him or her, may well come as a person who can just nudge us along at an important moment. Such a person may point the way, teach us the skills we need, or open our eyes to the hazardous places on the road. Sometimes we run across someone who utterly inspires us. The danger may be in looking for the exotic and missing the simple and ordinary. Naropa, a famous Indian yogi, nearly missed finding his teacher, Tilopa, because Tilopa appeared in the form of a scruffy beggar eating fish entrails beside a river.[18] The Indian scholar Asanga's teacher appeared as a sick dog at the side of the road. When, out of compassion, Asanga began to clean the dog's wounds, suddenly the Buddha Maitreya manifested before him.[19]

This latter example points to the sudden, sometimes magical transformation that occurs when we recognize the nature of the guru in a situation. It can transform the ordinary into something extraordinary and awesome. In these moments we touch another level of meaning in our reality we had not been previously aware of.

From a Buddhist perspective, the guru is a manifestation of Buddha nature, or what is called *dharmakaya*. This could be described as the wisdom attained by all Buddhas, which consists of insight into the underlying, empty nature of reality. This clear, luminous ground of being manifests in the forms and appearances that make up our normal reality. When we are open, we may discover the guide manifesting in the most unlikely places or people.

When I was traveling in the early seventies, I had a curious confidence that I was led in certain directions because there was someone or something I needed to meet. It is perhaps the experience of traveling, more than any other circumstance, that brings this kind of awareness. Our lives are usually so ordered by the demands of work, family, and so on that we do not have the degree of freedom to flow where life takes us, as one does when traveling. As a consequence I found myself able to respond to the synchronicity of situations that were presented to me.

In the summer of 1973, while hitchhiking across Canada, I was dropped at the side of the road near a place called Barry, Ontario. This was not where I wanted to stay, but being unable to get a lift further, I had little choice but to walk down to the hostel set up in the local school for summer travelers. I was sitting playing a guitar someone had brought when a scruffy, rather sick looking man in his thirties came through the door. He was unshaven and was sweating profusely. After a few minutes he sat at an upright piano in the school hall and began to tentatively touch the keys. I stopped what I was doing and listened. He began to play some extraordinary Gershwin jazz. I could hardly believe my ears as I listened to this bedraggled traveler playing beautiful music. It seemed so incongruous. After a while he stopped playing and I went over to speak with him. His story shocked me. He said he was once a pianist with the Toronto Philharmonic and had left to join the jazz circuit. The pressure of playing had led him to become a cocaine addict and he had not long before come out of a hospital where he had been trying to kick the habit.

We sat and talked for a long time and I learned a huge amount about his philosophy of music and its spiritual significance to him. He was totally enthralling as he spoke of how he had begun to see the subtle ways in which different musical keys affected the psychological state of a person. I think this man was probably the one who first introduced me to a love and appreciation of jazz that has grown over the years. He showed me how jazz could be a road to a profound sense of spiritual ecstasy and yet, equally, reflect a depth of pain. In a situation that seemed so unlikely I learned something from this man that touched me deeply. It was a moment of connection that was very special. He was not the only person to touch me this way as I traveled during those years. Similar connections occurred many times as I slowly made my way around the world, eventually arriving in Nepal.

We may resist the idea that we need guidance. Sometimes our ego defenses will not let us be open to another's influence, particularly when we are young. We may be resistant to accepting another's help. But if we need it and do not respond to this potential opening, we may endlessly wander around in the dark. There are times when it is very important to be self-sufficient and work it out for ourselves. We can, however, fool ourselves, and there are certain times in our life when we cannot find our way. These are moments when it is wise to surrender to the guidance of someone who has gone further than we have.

When I was in my twenties I knew that the answers I needed would never come from my own attempts to understand. They would never come from books. My search for answers in the psychology department at university proved to be unsatisfactory and disappointing. I had to find guidance elsewhere. I feel supremely fortunate that I was able to find teachers who had genuinely gone farther than I could ever imagine. I could not tell whether my Tibetan guides were Buddhas; this is beyond my comprehension. They were nevertheless profoundly insightful and genuinely willing to respond to my search for understanding. Without them, I do not believe I could have embarked on the path with any clarity about where I was going. I would have stumbled around trying a bit of this and a bit of that.

Many of us in the West try to travel a spiritual path by exploring all kinds of approaches. One of the dangers of having no guide to focus that process for us is that we can have a great breadth of knowledge but no depth of insight or experience. This can lead to a grandiosity that assumes that we have great spiritual understanding when in fact it is rather limited. One of the hazards of our Western individualism is that we are often reluctant to take advice from others. When we can, however, with skillful support, our journey does become easier as we are guided in the dark. We may feel held in a way that enables us to open to our true nature. We will also discover that there is no contradiction between finding a guide on our journey and the continuing need to individuate. There is no inherent contradiction unless the guides we choose have a tendency to hold us back and disempower rather than liberate us. Regrettably, this can sometimes be the case, but if we grow to trust our inner wisdom, even this need not be an obstacle.

WHEN EASTERN TEACHERS first encounter Western students, one aspect of our character must become immediately prominent: we are determinedly individualistic. In the West we pride ourselves on our individuality. From the moment we begin to engage in the world, there are expectations and pressures on us to be able to express our own particular personal character and capacities. During our education this tendency is deepened as we are compared to others, measured, and encouraged. Self-expression and creativity are generally rewarded and applauded.

As children we rapidly grow to understand that as we move from the family out into the world around, we are expected to become increasingly self-reliant. Ultimately there will be little help in the fiercely competitive environment of work and relationships. As Erich Fromm so clearly expressed in his book *Fear of Freedom,* we may be free to do with our lives pretty much as we wish, but the cost to our emotional security is very great.[20]

To grow up in the West we must become psychologically robust enough to cope with the alienation that accompanies our independence. We must be able to cope with the demands of a relatively hostile, competitive, and insecure world. Individuality is a way of living, and it is also a way of trying to be visible and different in a culture that seems to delight in those who are different, special, or famous. There is a strong cultural demand that we each try to express ourselves in a uniquely individual way. In the creative world, the arts that are valued are those that offer radical, fresh expression that breaks free of the old order. Innovation is everything.

This approach stands in marked contrast to the prevailing disposition within Eastern cultures.[21] In Indian dance and music, for example, expertise is measured in terms of the adherence to the subtle principles of the art, not by innovation. As a painter of *thangkas*, or Tibetan religious images, I encountered a similar view. In Tibetan the term *rang so wa,* meaning "self-created" or "innovation," is a derogatory expression implying that you just made it up and, therefore, it has no authenticity or authority. As is true of many other aspects of Tibetan Buddhism, the thangka reflects a lineage of tradition where creative innovation is considered entirely inappropriate.

Individuality will have its positive and negative consequences. It will bring us a capacity for self-sufficiency, self-reliance, self-expression, self-motivation, and a relatively stable sense of self-identity, all of which might be seen as ego-oriented. It leads to innovation and change and the reevaluation of old conventions. Conversely, it will engender insecurity, self-preoccupation, competitiveness, and all the narcissistic failings we suffer. It can lead to an overemphasis on the need to prove oneself and an arrogant self-determination—all things familiar in Western life.

We will inevitably bring this individualistic disposition, which can appear to stand in clear contrast to the Eastern view, into our spirituality. The question must be, however, do we assume that this individualism is wrong, merely an expression of egotism and self-obsession, or is it a necessary aspect of our twenty-first-century condition? Do we see the abandonment of the "delusion" of individuality and surrender to spiritual authority as a necessary ingredient of the path? Alternatively, is there a positive side to this individualism that can actually be included within the evolution of our spiritual ideals?

One of the by-products of our individualism is that we have the capacity to think our own thoughts and, as a consequence, will tend to question spiritual authority. From an Eastern perspective this can be seen as terribly arrogant. Some, however, may say this is actually a very positive aspect of our Western tendency. We are less likely to be taken for a ride by the unscrupulous. We are more likely to question traditionally held beliefs to genuinely explore their validity. A natural consequence of the need for individuality is the desire to only embark upon what feels right for us. Some may say this is just a pick-and-mix kind of mentality which takes only what is easy and safe. This can be true. Yet this mindset could also prove to be important in integrating Eastern spiritual traditions into Western life. If we are genuine in our attempts to be true to our inner call, we must at some point trust in our inner feelings of what is appropriate for us. This need not be seen just as a compulsion to be individualistic but as the natural desire to respect and validate individual differences in spiritual life.

Individualism has a near neighbor in the process of individuation. Individuation and individualism are not the same, but they do have some common elements. Where individualism can carry a dark shadow, individuation is the redeeming factor that opens up the possibility that our individuality can have a positive outcome, even within a spiritual path that emphasizes going beyond egotism.

Individuation can be seen as the positive consequence of individuality. Jung used the term *individuation* "to denote a process of becoming a psychological 'individual,' that is, a separate, indivisible unity or whole."[22] To individuate is to gradually actualize our innate capacity to live as a unique individual. It is the consequence of a process of awakening that releases our innate potential. As Jung put it, "Individuation means becoming a single homogeneous being, and, insofar as 'individuality' embraces our innermost, last and incomparable uniqueness, it also implies becoming one's own self. We could therefore translate individuation as 'coming to selfhood' or 'self-realization.'"[23]

In the same way that Michelangelo is said to have revealed David from the base stone, so too we gradually release our capacity for self-realization and wholeness. What may sometimes become confused is the distinction between the emergence of ego-identity and the process of self-realization. As Jung stated, "Again and again I note that the individuation process is confused with the coming of the ego into consciousness and that the ego is in consequence identified with the Self, which naturally produces a hopeless conceptual muddle. Individuation is then nothing but ego-centeredness and narcissism. But the Self comprises infinitely more than mere ego. . . ."[24]

As we individuate we grow to recognize our individual relationship to a universal wisdom that has a unique expression because of our particular personality. To individuate is to expand the boundaries of individual identity and personality to be rooted in our inner sense of totality. It is our growing sense of, in Jung's terms, the Self as the root of meaning and the archetype of wholeness within each of us. As we individuate we can experience our own deeper spiritual heart and then begin to express it in the world. This expression of individuation enables us to have a quality of inner authority, integrity, and knowledge of what is true for ourselves. It enables us to open to our unique responsibility in the task of our life for the welfare and good of all.

Where individuation and individuality differ is that individuality leads to separation and a sense of self-preoccupation that isolates us from others, while, as Jung asserts, "Individuation does not shut one out from the world, but gathers the world to one's self."[25] Individuation is the discovery of our own personal quality of wholeness that is intimately connected to our experience of the whole. We stand upon a threshold where the individual meets the universal yet retains a unique sense of self. This inner sense of wholeness is then open to the interdependence of ourselves with all others. I am reminded of the metaphor of there being one light though the lamps are many.

Individuation is our capacity to be true to our own center while intimately involved in relationships to others. It means we are no longer caught up in the need to conform and be part of collective consciousness. Rather, we are in a state of genuine self-knowledge that does not need collective approbation.

In our culture, where individuality is prized, it is a necessary evolution to see individuation as the healthy movement towards personal spiritual responsibility in relation to the greater good of the world. Does this in any way contradict the essential principles of Buddhism?

If we look at the Buddha's life, we discover that he had a strong disposition to learn from teachers and then move on. He must have been acutely aware that if something did not feel true, then he must trust his inner voice. In this sense he was an example of individuation par excellence. His path was in constant contrast to the collective expectations around him, from the time that he left home until he parted ways with his five companions just before his enlightenment.

The Buddha's message is to test the teachings and see if they work or fit our lives. His teachings emphasize a process of self-exploration and self-realization that does not take on institutionalized truths but rather finds inner truth. Even the essential principle of Buddha nature rests not on salvation by some outer agency or god but on a genuine awakening to our own true nature.

Where individuation comes into potential conflict with the principles of Buddhism is, firstly, in relation to our notions of the ego and egolessness, and, secondly, in relation to the principle of the guru and guru devotion.

If we consider the first of these, the ego is something easily misunderstood even within Buddhist circles. Some may equate the growth of our individual identity with the consolidation of the ego and see this as a fundamental flaw in our nature. To read the Buddhist notion of emptiness as the complete eradication and abandonment of the ego is tantamount to saying we must relinquish our individuality and abandon our ego-identity. It is true that within the striving for individuality there is a huge emphasis on what could be seen as egotism and ego-grasping. If we seek to abandon this aspect of our nature it would be wrong, however, to cast the baby out with the bath water. Egotism and individuality are not the same.

We need to recognize that from a Buddhist perspective the central problem with the ego is ego-grasping: the clinging to a sense of self as solid and self-existent. It is ego-grasping that leads to unhealthy self-preoccupation and all of the emotional reactions that evolve from it. The need for a stable focus of identity does require an established sense of "I," an ego; it does not imply, however, that we contract around this in a narrow, limiting, and emotionally defensive way, as with ego-grasping. If we recognize this distinction, then we can cut through the unhealthy aspect of the ego without having to get rid of the necessary aspect of a relatively stable sense of identity. An individual in our culture needs, perhaps more than in Eastern cultures, to retain this stable individual identity without the underlying grasping at a self as true, solid, and permanent.

When we can see through the ego-grasping that is at the heart of so much of the individualism in our culture, it does not mean we will no longer seek individual expression for who we are. Ego-grasping is a deeply rooted disposition to contract and solidify our identity around a wounded sense of self. To free this contraction does not destroy the presence of a notion of self-identity. When we see that the ego is empty of substance, we open to a more spacious, permeable sense of self. This creates a greater awareness of our fluidity and lack of permanence. It can mean we are more open, generous at heart, and less attached to who we are. Because we are no longer so contracted and self-preoccupied, we suffer less.

In the path of the bodhisattva a stable and mature sense of self-identity is crucial. This will, by its nature, lead to a stronger capacity to travel an individual path in the way that is most appropriate for the attainment of complete awakening. It will foster a strength of identity that is able and willing to engage in working for the welfare of others with responsibility and commitment. H. H. the Dalai Lama once said that a bodhisattva needs a strong ego to take on the responsibility of his or her journey. Similarly, Shantideva's *Guide to the Bodhisattva's Way of Life* repeatedly places great emphasis on strength of mind and the willingness to endure the hardships of the path—and do it alone—for the welfare of others.[26]

The bodhisattva could be said to personify the essential quality of individuation in the Buddhist world. There is, in principle, no contradiction between individuality and the bodhisattva ideal. The recognition of the lack of inherent solidity or inherent existence of the ego opens this disposition up to be more responsive and flexible, less

caught up in self-illusions and attachments to outcomes. The bodhisattva's recognition of emptiness also counters any disposition to
become inflated and overidentified with what might easily be seen as
grandiose, messianic ideals of liberating all beings from suffering.

Just as individuation implies an inner recognition of one's place in
the universal play of reality, the bodhisattva feels a deep-rooted universal responsibility.[27] While the journey of individuation calls us to let
go of the ego as the central focus of will and open to a higher intention, so the bodhisattva is acting from a place that lets go of self-will
and opens to a higher intention of bodhichitta. This intention is the
willingness to awaken to our full potential in order to benefit all beings.
It is perhaps the most refined expression of individuation, with the
ego remaining only as the relative vehicle through which this higher
intention can express itself in the world. Jung spoke of the archetypal
intent of the Self as a profound, underlying movement towards wholeness.[28] In the Buddhist context this "archetypal intent" can be seen as
the root of the bodhisattva's intense compassionate desire to fully
awaken for the welfare of others.

How do we then include the notion of surrender to a spiritual purpose or, indeed, to a spiritual teacher within our conception of individuation? Surrender to a spiritual ideal or purpose may be relatively
easy to consider, as there is inherent within this surrender the conscious recognition of what is meaningful to the individual's inner
process. Jung spoke of individuation as the surrender of the ego to the
Self, or the shift from "I will" to "thy will be done." He called this the
relativization of the ego to the Self.[29] While Buddhism does not speak
of the Self in these terms, there is nevertheless a similar notion of surrender. We could simply replace the idea of the Self with the idea of
Buddha nature. If we did, it would not be an unreasonable step to see
our relationship to Buddha nature as one in which we turn to an inner
source of wisdom and insight. This is the essence of "taking refuge"
in a profound inner way. A Buddhist may then personify this Buddha
nature in the symbolic aspect of a deity and visualize a way of surrendering or taking refuge in this archetypal aspect of our nature. This

process, practiced with great effect, is very common within the tantric path, where aspects of our true nature are personified in the form of deities.[30] These symbols of the Self would indeed offer us the means to surrender.

Surrender, as an aspect of individuation, is a profound inner process that values the individual's relationship to his or her true nature and "inner knowledge wisdom." This implies not an ego-centered sense of individuality but a stable individual identity centered in our true nature.

While the notion of individuation lives comfortably alongside the Buddhist idea of egolessness when understood correctly, we may still question the viability of individuation within the guru-disciple relationship. The relationship to a guru or teacher is one in which, traditionally, the ego and our individuality are supposed to be surrendered. Since this idea is often given such emphasis, especially in Tibetan Buddhism, it is worth considering what its implications are. The theme of the teacher-student relationship will be explored further in Chapter 16.

If we see the teacher as the embodiment of enlightened insight, then whether we understand this to be a projection from within or something outside, the relationship is important. Being able to relinquish some of our personal struggle to someone who seems to have answers can be a great relief. As a Buddhist, finding a source of inspiration and instruction is invaluable. Our ego and self-identity may indeed be greatly challenged by this relationship. Very often a teacher will provoke periods of self-reflection that dismantle much of who we thought we were. Generally this is to help us free ourselves from the limitations and traps we have created for ourselves out of ignorance and insecurity. Much of our individuality is a kind of edifice we have constructed as a strategy for our survival in the world.

The guru may ask us to surrender ourselves, but in my experience, this is not to relinquish individual responsibility and is not intended to be at the expense of personal integrity. The teachers who have taught me have always emphasized that their intention is to enable us to be increasingly true to our own inner truth, or our "inner knowledge wisdom," as Lama Thubten Yeshe called it. They have also been very aware that I had to live my own life and find my own path, with their assistance. Surrender, in this respect, was more a process of trusting in their guidance in a process of empowerment that gradually awakened inner potential. The true surrender is then an inner process where the ego gives way to an inner root of meaning, purpose, and truth.

We may call this "the inner guru," or we may call it, as Jung did, "the Self." Once we discover this inner experience of the guru, we have awakened a vital aspect of our unique journey of individuation. When we do, it will enhance our individual capacity to manifest our Buddha potential in the world through everything we do.

The bodhisattva, as the personification of individuation, discovers a unique capacity to awaken his or her potential to work for the welfare of others in whichever way most suits his or her individual disposition. When I consider my own teachers, one thing I particularly value is their capacity to be authentically themselves. They each have their unique personality and quality that is a genuine expression of their individuality. There is no contradiction between our Western need to be individuals and the Buddhist path. Buddhism does not demand that we become clones of some ideal. Rather, it asks us to respond to who we are and awaken our full potential, expressing it within our particular individual capacity. My Tibetan teachers have supremely individualistic personalities, something I love and value deeply. They respond to me as an individual with my own personality, which they would never ask me to relinquish. The fact that they were each on their own unique journey within the Buddhist path was, for me, a sublime example of the bodhisattva as an individuated person who has truly responded to the inner call to awaken.

Manjushri

T HE LEGEND of the Holy Grail begins with Parzival, the central figure, living with his mother in a secluded forest far away from any other dwellings. She fears that should Parzival wander out into the world, he will follow in the footsteps of his father, a knight who was killed in battle. To protect Parzival from a similar fate, his mother keeps him in seclusion so that he does not meet outside influences. In time, this smothering overprotection begins to trouble Parzival, who wanders further and further from home. One day, while exploring the forest, he encounters four knights in dazzling armor. He is spellbound by their appearance and naïvely asks one of them if he is God. The knight, clearly surprised at his ignorance, explains what he is.[31]

The appearance of these knights remains in Parzival's mind. He is enthralled. Gradually within him the idea germinates to leave home, but he knows that his mother would never willingly allow him to go. He must, therefore, eventually have the courage to defy her wish and run away. This act of leaving his mother's maternal cocoon is a deeply significant step in Parzival's journey. It marks the beginning of his capacity to enter the world and individuate. His quest for truth and understanding has begun.[32]

In the Buddha's life we have seen a similar theme. Siddhartha, too, was kept in an enclosed and cosseted environment, protected from the realities of the world outside. On each of four secret excursions outside his enclosure, however, Siddhartha saw things that troubled him deeply. First he saw a sick person, then an aging person, a corpse, and, finally, a wandering mendicant. These experiences profoundly affected the young man, who decided he must escape the palace and go off in search of answers. Like Parzival, Siddhartha knew that were he to ask permission to go, it would never be granted. Rather he must make the decision for himself and leave secretly.

What is the symbolic significance of leaving home expressed in these two stories? What are the psychological implications? Both stories depict the need of someone naïve to the world to wake up and see the reality he has been denied. Both lives emphasize the need to leave behind a person or circumstance that will hold them in a state of ignorance and unconsciousness. They are forced to take a step that is coming solely from their own deeply felt impulse to emerge from a stultifying home life. They perform an act of will that defies the natural pull towards security, obedience, and comfort. In essence, they are taking a step towards individuation.

In his work on the heroic journey as the path of individuation, Joseph Campbell considered the first threshold of emergence to be a crucial one. It marks the letting go of an old way of being that is fundamentally unconscious. Whether we consider the notion of leaving home literally or metaphorically, this threshold is one that must be encountered if we are to go forward and genuinely respond to the call rather than remaining relatively stuck in old habits and patterns. As we cross this threshold we must leave behind some of the safe, comfortable security that pulls us backwards and face our fears.

Emergence as a psychological step is therefore the first step in facing who we are on the journey. As we leave home, in the literal sense we leave the security of parental holding and, in particular, of the mother. To remain would be to become gradually suffocated and unconscious. We would fail to grow. Unfortunately there are those who fail to cross this threshold, but the consequence on psychological health is serious.

There is a term in Tibetan, *nge jung*, that is often translated as "renunciation," but which literally means "definite emergence." While many Buddhist teachers and teachings speak of renouncing the flawed happiness of worldly life, the term *nge jung* has implications that add another psychological dimension to its meaning.

Definite emergence is the capacity to wake up and be willing to face our life and our habitual tendencies. It is the intention, either consciously chosen or instinctually driven, to become conscious. This movement towards consciousness has at its heart the recognition that the resolution of the struggles and suffering of our life is to face them. While we may be tempted to hide our fallibility and problems and deny or anesthetize our emotional struggles, they are resolved only when we genuinely address them honestly and openly. Anything else simply perpetuates a regressive sleep of ignorance. We may put a bandage over our pain and wounds, hoping they will go away, but at some point we will need to bring fresh air to them. In our lives it would seem that almost anything may be used as a means to avoid facing ourselves and anesthetizing our awareness. We may take refuge in our material desires, our sensory stimulation and entertainment, our work, relationships, and various intoxicating substances, including food.

When we recognize the pull of sensory and material anesthetics, it may lead us to say that we must therefore have nothing to do with them, like the alcoholic who cannot control his habit. However, the problem may remain the same if our inner response does not change. I have known monks who live a celibate life, having renounced sexual relationships, but who are constantly preoccupied with sex. An emphasis on abandoning the happiness of this life found in some doctrines can, in this respect, be very misleading. From my work as a therapist it is apparent there are many ways in which this attitude can come from deep-rooted psychological problems relating to the degree to which we may be avoiding reality. The concept of renunciation can also be colored by our particular Western spiritual heritage. A puritanical Christian background often accentuates the values of purity and self-denial that require giving up pleasure as a kind of spiritual purging. This may particularly involve the abandonment of the body, the sins of the flesh, and worldly pleasures. In the extreme this can lead to an attitude that believes it is fundamentally wrong to enjoy ourselves. We may become stiff and controlled in the attempt to abandon all the things we used to enjoy that are "worldly concerns." We give them all up and throw them away. The more we enjoyed them, the more virtue there is in giving them away or stopping them. In this way we gradually tighten the grip we have on our life and its pleasures. If we enjoyed music, then we give it up; if we liked relationships, then we avoid them; if we liked food, then we become really strict about it. In this way we avoid the stimulation of those feelings of enjoyment that might give rise to attachment, which is the cause of suffering.

Aversion and fear of pleasure, however, are as much of a problem as becoming hooked on pleasure. If renunciation as a way of cutting through attachment leads to avoidance, abandonment, or self-denial as a spiritual approach, it becomes a kind of puritanical Buddhism. Indeed, one can see that within the range of Buddhist approaches there is a spectrum between something puritanical at one extreme and very liberal at the other.

When renunciation, emphasizing abandoning the happiness of this life, is taught, it remains questionable how valuable this notion is if it leads to an avoidance of life. Among my peers in India, there were some for whom the idea of renunciation seemed to confirm a depressive view that life is always disappointing, bad, or wrong. Yet we are alive and must engage with our life as best we can. Life may be suffering, on one level, but there is also great richness, joy, and value. The danger of this kind of renunciation is that it actually conveys the view that life itself is the problem. This does not sit well with many Westerners, and perhaps for good reason. Why should we see something that has such potential and such value as something to be abandoned? This attitude of life rejection can so often be an attempt to justify a negative, depressive pathology. It seems to lack the love, compassion, and courage to engage in life fully, despite its problems. This interpretation of renunciation runs counter to the heart of the bodhisattva's willingness to take up the challenge of life and live it fully for the welfare of others.

Renunciation as definite emergence is not a process of separating and running away from the world or from life but rather of changing our relationship to it. From a psychological viewpoint, emergence asks us to look at the notion of renunciation in a more subtle way than as just abandoning aspects of this life. Emergence is not an avoidance of relationship to material reality; it is an inner change of attitude towards its potential hold over us. We could see this, in a relatively simple way, as the need to overcome material attachment and its seductive hold over us. Renunciation in this sense is letting go of any expectations or hopes that reality should give us a sense of happiness; equally, it is a letting go of the cynical aversion that loathes the world for all its flaws. Things are as they are and we suffer because we become too sticky and attached. As Lama Thubten Yeshe once put it, once we have gained a sense of renunciation, "we can touch the flower"; we can enjoy the pleasure it gives because we are not turning it into rubbish through attachment. When we learn the capacity to not contract, even in subtle ways, into the things we encounter, either pleasurable or painful, we can remain open and do not suffer. The meaning of this renunciation is not giving up life; it is living it fully, fearlessly, and with openness.

The challenge of emergence is to enjoy our pleasures because we are not afraid of them, but, equally, to not become caught in them. Lama Thubten Yeshe once said, "How much pleasure can you take?" He was asking us to experience our joys and pleasures without becoming obsessive and grasping, because when we contract around them we set ourselves up for suffering. We emerge into a world where we can live fully with our joys and our hurt and allow them to pass without judgment and without expectation. When we begin to have the courage to live our life in this way, we can step out on the journey ready to face what arises.

On a psychological level, emergence calls us to look at where we still remain unconscious and fail to see reality, where the mother is a primary representation of the pull to unconsciousness. This may have been translated into various forms of material and emotional security that shelter us from the world. Many of us, particularly men, even though involved in a spiritual path for many years, may be unaware of the fundamental psychological bond that still continues in our relationship to the mother in particular. Until we are consciously able to move on from this, we will be always weakened and held back.

Leaving the security, reassurance, and emotional safety of the mother is a move towards independence and psychological maturity. If we remain bound within the mother principle, it will castrate us and we will fear separation and emergence into individuality. "Castration" in this sense can also be applied to a woman bound in the parent, whether mother or father. Neumann in his commentary to the myth of Amor and Psyche suggested that for a woman to be bound to the maternal principle is as much a kind of castration as for a man to be caught in the mother.[33] For a woman to emerge as a fully rounded woman in her own right requires emergence from being solely mothering in nature. While the process of mothering brings important qualities, finding an identity as an individual outside of the role of mother is important in the process of individuation. It may become crucial for women once children have left home, when the loss of a sense of purpose can be very painful.

While there is inevitably a difference between men and women in this respect, physically we may have left home long ago, but if we fail to emerge psychologically, we can still be caught in the power of the parent. A negative father will often create a lack of self worth as an inner destructive voice. An inner maternal domination will pull us backward into unconsciousness. Bound by its power, we may remain something of a victim, lacking the will and sense of self-determination to go forward into life. This regressive pull is personified by the archetypal black mother, the witch, or the devouring spider mother. She is the dark side of the wisdom mother and embodies ignorance and intoxication in the unconscious security and seduction of the maternal world and, ultimately, a kind of annihilation. Anyone caught in this tendency will resist demands to wake up and face him- or herself, to take genuine responsibility for emotional problems and engage in the challenges of life. Unfortunately, the spiritual path can sometimes seem to offer a means of transcending these demands in an idealism that denies reality and covers the lack of emotional maturity in a veneer of spirituality.

In our culture we create many substitutes for this need for emotional security that can be just as much a way of avoiding the struggle of emergence. The mother can be translated into matter, materialism, and the apparent security of material possessions and pleasures. It is the absorption in materialism that becomes a kind of anesthetic to soften the blows of the world. It can be reflected in the constant need for sensory pleasures and material possessions as an intoxicating cocoon to ward off the pain of facing ourselves. In the extreme, this can be expressed in the form of addictive behavior such as drug addiction or alcoholism.

Maternal substitutes can also be sought in institutions and groups that provide a safe and protected space to shield us from the insecurity and alienation experienced in a potentially hostile and stressful world. It is perhaps for this reason that the BBC has been nicknamed "Auntie." Other companies and organizations, as well, offer a kind of parental security to their employees. We can equally see how spiritual groups and communities can become a safe haven, a cocoon to protect young aspirants from needing to face the rigors and hardships of life "in the world." Once again, this could mistakenly be seen as a kind of renunciation.

It was my own experience while living in a Buddhist community that many of us were wounded and damaged in our attempts to emerge into the world. The opportunity this community provided was for it to be a place to heal and discover more about ourselves; but less positively, it became a place that was sufficiently safe to make it hard to leave and return to the world. Some of us, needing spiritual escape, could easily transform our community into a safe womb to cushion us from the demands of the outside world, even though life inside it could be very challenging. When I eventually left I was aware that I had not really equipped myself for the world; rather, I had postponed something I was reluctant to face.

Crossing the threshold of emergence requires a quality of will as we challenge the pull to remain unconscious, in a sleep of denial and avoidance. There often comes a point in our life, however, when we have suffered enough the consequences of our defenses and patterns of avoidance and are ready and willing to embark upon a path of honest self-exploration. This may lead us into spiritual practices that we believe will help us encounter or resolve our problems. We should not, however, fool ourselves. We may be able to enter states of absorption in meditation and yet still be using these as a way of avoiding who we are, of avoiding our pain and emotions by what Welwood calls "spiritual bypassing."

One of the most hazardous dispositions that emerge in the spiritual journey is that of the *Puer Aeternus,* or eternal youth. For men, being trapped in the mother leads to the Puer tendency in its most negative sense.[34] The Peter Pan syndrome, as some like to call it, means that we are caught in an unconscious avoidance of growing up. A Puer-dominated man as much as a *Puella*-dominated woman may feel an aversion to the demands of a mature engagement with life that can look very much like renunciation. It can, however, lead to a form of spiritual flight that needs more understanding. Unfortunately for some, the spiritual path can be one expression of this tendency: a kind of false emergence. To abandon relationships and children and give up possessions and the things that we enjoy to join some form of spiritual organization may look like renunciation, but it is not emergence. Likewise, flight into spiritual purity, idealism, and intellectual studies of spiritual doctrines are not emergence. We may learn many sophisticated meditation techniques, but these can so easily become a way of cutting ourselves off from our feelings and from our wounds within. We can fool ourselves into believing that because we live spiritual lifestyles in spiritual communities we have actually faced the process of emergence. Even in Buddhism one of the hazards associated with organizations that define the nature of one's life-style, the principles one should live by, and the kind of beliefs one should adopt is that they create a false sense that one has crossed the threshold of emergence. All too often this can become like a cocoon that is actually cutting us off from emerging upon a path of individuation.

In the therapeutic setting I often encounter young men and women involved in a particular Buddhist organization. One of the primary dispositions that emerges in the young men is the fear of relationships in which commitment and real emotional engagement are required. They may be involved in a relationship because they can't resist it, but there is often an underlying belief that relationships are essentially an obstacle, hindrance, or distraction to the true spiritual path they believe they are on. The women partners of such men describe how painful it is to be caught up with someone who fears commitment as the ultimate trap that will destroy their spiritual aspirations. Abandoning or avoiding family, relationships, and work in the world as an obstacle to spiritual practice is not the true meaning of renunciation. It is, however, a reflection of the pathology of the Puer type. Emergence asks of us that we face the struggles and challenges of relationship and work with courage, openness, and honesty. Relationships can be a powerful opportunity to truly test our capacity to practice, to let go, to be compassionate, and to honestly face our emotional problems.

Definite emergence as a natural instinct comes from deep within as the seed of the intention to individuate, like the instinct of a chick to break out of the egg in which it has been safely held. The transition of emergence is not an easy one, and one can become stuck. It may be tempting to just remain safe, surrounded by comfortable conditions that take away the demands to face life's challenges and individuate. Alternately, emergence into the challenges of a world measured by material wealth and work success creates an illusion of emergence. Unfortunately, in our culture the pressures of the world are very great. We do not live in a supportive environment that retains close community. The independence and individuality our culture demands lead to the chronic alienation that freedom brings.[35] Is it any wonder that we have developed highly sophisticated mechanisms and strategies to retain some of the security we fear losing? Our institutions, our materialistic culture, and our need for endless insurance policies may seem like a source of security in our individuality. Instead of genuinely emerging to individuate, however, we become caught in a constant struggle to maintain this illusion of security.

Emerging from this illusion, we take a step across the threshold, facing our fear and insecurity. This requires an inner decision: the willingness to truly wake up and face ourselves, to engage in life knowing that the source of our suffering or our happiness lies in our own minds. We are then confronted with the reality that we, on one level, choose the life we create. We could try to live in denial and remain unconscious, but at some point we must see that the solution to our emotional troubles lies within. To embark on this path requires more than trying to change the world to make it safe or comfortable, and more than trying to transcend it with "spiritual" ideals. It requires the willingness to become a warrior on the road, facing the challenge of the mind and its habits. The heroic quest begins when we take up this challenge.

The Time for Commitment 9

In 1973 I found myself sitting on a hilltop in Nepal overlooking a lakeside village called Pokara. Before me was a spectacular range of jagged peaks central to which was one nicknamed the "fish tail," or Annapurna. While I looked out across this breathtaking sight, inside I was in utter turmoil.

I had, some days before, inquired about a month-long meditation course to be held at a Western Buddhist center called Kopan, close to Kathmandu. The principal teachers were two Tibetan lamas I had never heard of, but whom many people had described as seriously evolved beings. I knew that if I enrolled in the course it would be a significant and possibly life-changing decision. I was terrified to step through this door and commit myself to something that could have such a profound impact.

I realize I am not alone in this fear. I see it in many of those I work with in therapy and during meditation retreats. In my own journey, I have had to step across this threshold of commitment several times. Each time required its own period of soul searching. A year following my first taste of the Kopan meditation course, I returned for a second time and stepped through another doorway, taking bodhisattva precepts. Again the sense of trepidation was there. Some years later, when receiving my first Higher Tantra initiation, I had the same mixture of fear, resistance, and excitement. Later still, while living in India, I met another threshold, which proved to be one I would not cross. I looked long and hard at becoming a monk.

Many of us reach a point in our spiritual journey where we recognize that we must commit ourselves, even though the process of commitment can be highly emotionally charged. We may have drifted around exploring a bit of this and a bit of that, finding much to stimulate our thirst for interesting experiences and knowledge. Then there comes the recognition that we may have a breadth of knowledge gained from different traditions, but no depth of genuine transformation. We may even have accumulated great intellectual understanding of the path and all of its permutations and flavors, but no actual inner taste. Even the great yogi Naropa, a revered sixth-century adept from Nalanda in India, was once challenged by a manifestation of a *dakini*[36] as to whether he genuinely understood the Dharma he studied.[37] It was this question that eventually led him to leave the monastery and go in search of his teacher, Tilopa.

We will almost inevitably come to a point where we are asked to take a step that truly commits us to a process of transformation. The alternative is to remain only partly engaged, even though we may have much knowledge. The metaphorical meaning of the alchemical vessel is that it is the container that holds us through a process of transformation. To step into this vessel is to commit ourselves.[38] We make a choice to no longer drift around, wriggle away from full engagement, or avoid facing ourselves.

Often the process of commitment feels like stepping off the edge into the unknown. It requires a willingness to let go of the safety of what was familiar yet limiting. Commitment may evoke the fear of a restriction of apparent freedom, seeming like a loss of options. What commitment usually brings, however, is a loss of the freedom to not be fully responsible. I recall how, when taking certain vows such as the bodhisattva and tantric vows, I felt that I was at a point of no return. Once the vows were taken, I was in it for life and there was no release. I was reminded of a visit I once made to a Christian closed-order monastery in Sussex. This was a place where monks would live in silent seclusion in cells for life. I have a vivid memory of stepping through the door to one of these cells as a monk showed me around. The sound of the heavy wooden door closing behind us sent shivers through me. This is for life, it echoed. There is no escape.

Commitment is a profound decision to take our own journey and spiritual life seriously. We alone must take responsibility for what evolves in this life, and until we step into that process with true engagement, we will be halfhearted. Commitment in this sense requires heart; it requires courage and the readiness to see that life is too precious to simply mess around frivolously. Commitment is about more than joining a club or enrolling in some external course of training: it is a dedication to our true nature or true potential.

If this is so, why does it feel so frightening? Perhaps because we know somewhere that there is no escape from the reality of our life. We are masters of avoidance and take refuge endlessly in relatively meaningless things that provide an illusion of safety, ease, and happiness. We may work incredibly hard to create this security and yet eventually see through the illusion. Commitment to a spiritual path is a deep-rooted turning around in our life to see that what leads to liberation is living with full awareness.

In Buddhism a significant threshold in the journey is crossed when we "take refuge." The term "taking refuge" in Tibetan is *kyab su chi wo*, which has been translated by Alex Berzin as "to take a safe direction." In this respect, to take refuge is to change the very nature of the direction we face in life. It is to reorient our sense of what is meaningful and what brings peace and happiness away from the conventional worldly refuges that tend to anesthetize us from our life troubles. Taking refuge is traditionally described as refuge in the Triple Gem: namely, the Buddha, the Dharma, and the community of practitioners, the Sangha. This is often translated into a commitment to a teacher and his teachings and even to a spiritual organization that we join. While an understanding of the qualities of the Buddha and the significance of his teachings is important in this process, the ultimate meaning of taking refuge in the Buddha, Dharma, and Sangha is that we turn inwards towards our true nature as the touchstone and inner resource. This implies learning to live with an awareness of the quality of our innate

Buddha nature, recognizing this as the true source of peace and liberation from our life struggles.

Part of the shift of direction that occurs in taking refuge is the recognition that, firstly, things are not what we would like them to be—they are not reliable, solid, and safe—and, secondly, that the ego does not have much actual control over reality. Our emotional need for security in a potentially chaotic world leads us to constantly try to control our environment. We have in our culture many sophisticated ways in which this control is expressed. Commitment to the Buddhist path implies relinquishing control—a kind of surrender. The ego will usually fear this surrender. It is used to getting its own way and finding the safest option to avoid suffering. Seldom would it choose a path that leads to its own demise. To commit to a spiritual process such as Buddha Dharma is, however, to ultimately confront the ego with its own demise. Although this may not be obvious, on some level we know this to be so, which is why these moments of commitment can be so disturbing. In this sense commitment is a giving up—a letting go or surrender of what we held to be unchallengeable, namely, the ego's need for control.

The intellect is one dimension of this ego control that dominates many individuals, particularly men. This form of ego control can be expressed as a kind of arrogance that believes that it is always possible to find an intellectual, scientific, rational answer that will give a sense of security. When the intellect provides a rational answer to what is going on, it creates a sense of being in control and, therefore, safe. Refuge in the intellect serves us to some degree but eventually becomes painfully inadequate. One man I know who suffered this habit was able to use his intellect to rationalize every aspect of his emotional life in such a way that he had created an intellectual armor that was almost impenetrable. His capacity to intellectually dodge and weave to avoid real contact with both his feelings and his existential fear gave him a sense of invulnerability. The challenge came when his intellectual defense began to show its limitations. As he looked through the cracks that appeared, he could see that in order to resolve his emotional and existential predicament, he would need to simply surrender his ego's precarious position. Suddenly he could see that all of his Buddhist understanding was actually an obstacle to direct experience. He stood on the edge of a precipice and knew he needed to leap. His intellectual knowledge had pushed him up to the edge and left him stranded.

This was his moment of surrender, when he knew he needed to actually let go and jump: he needed to commit himself to the process. He could see that his intellectual knowledge was a defense against real commitment. To step across this threshold, however, required that he relinquish his pride in the capacity to always find a solution that closed even the smallest chink in his reality. Essentially his intellect was finally failing him, which was terrifying. As his mind began to release its grip, rather than going insane, as he feared, he did not disappear. He felt that he began to open to a more relaxed, more present, more spacious quality that could bear the paradoxes of his existence without panic.

The threshold of commitment is a point of letting go we may encounter many times on our journey. As we go deeper, we reach new levels of commitment that can demand still more opening. In this sense our understanding of refuge goes deeper and deeper. Once we step across this threshold, something dies and is renewed, and this happens in each crossing. In the process of making this transition, we must leave some things behind. We cannot take our old habits and refuges with us. We cannot close our eyes and hide once they are opened. Sometimes people say they wish they had never started when they realize how hard it is to no longer be able to run away. It is seldom comfortable to realize that the only solution to resolve life's problems is to go further, deeper, to become even more committed and wake up.

The point of commitment can, however, bring a great sense of relief. It is the ease and openness that comes when, to use Jung's terms, the ego finally lets go of its need for the dominant position in the psyche and gives way to the Self. The shift from "I will" to "thy will be done" brings trust in a process that we can only partly comprehend, but this is part of the mystery. As a Buddhist, one can see this as a trust in our true nature as personified by the Buddha: our Buddha nature. This is not a trust in something to cling to, like a god or a savior, which from the Buddhist perspective would be to trust in an illusion. When we can let go and commit to the process, we are changed, and we do not need to try to change as much as to allow what is to unfold. This process will not be easy. When we enter the alchemical vessel we begin to cook, and this cooking brings to the surface what we must begin to transform. According to Jung the first stage of this process is known as the *nigredo,*[39] during which the Shadow is gradually revealed and transformed. Only once we are truly committed to this process will transformation fully take place. One of the hazards of any process of this nature, however, is that we may choose to go into what might be called a kind of spiritual flight.

O UR JOURNEY of individuation began with a call—a deeply felt awakening to the reality of our life's challenge. This call leads to the eventual crossing of a threshold of emergence and the willingness to embark upon a process of awakening that confronts us with our fears and insecurities. We may be willing to face these and take up the challenge to commit ourselves to the path of transformation. We may, however, fail to truly cross the threshold and instead embark upon what might be called spiritual flight.

Spiritual flight may seem like a form of emergence but unfortunately is not. It is quite possible to embark on a spiritual path that is largely dominated by avoidance or is a kind of false emergence. Flight into idealism and intellectual spiritual knowledge, combined with a yearning for purity and perfection free from worldly contamination, are, regrettably, signs of a continued psychological malaise. The disposition to avoid any involvement in emotional relationships, material possessions, work, money, and family responsibility may seem like renunciation. It is, however, most often a reflection of flight. Only when we are willing to meet with and work through life problems will the tendency toward spiritual flight be countered and a genuine, grounded spirituality begin.

In psychotherapy, possibly the single most influential archetype that shapes people's experience of "spirituality" is the Puer Aeternus, or eternal youth. The effect of this archetype has been very powerful in my own journey and among many of my friends and peers in the Buddhist world. As a psychotherapist I have found that the Puer archetype is perhaps the most familiar disposition in those seeking "spiritual" solutions to their life problems, particularly among men. The Puer disposition can be equally strong in political idealists and in the world of the arts. In the spiritual world, however, its influence is extremely important to recognize because it is particularly active in the phenomenon of spiritual flight.

In the spiritual world, Puer can be seen as the archetypal spiritual instinct: the search for meaning and creative inspiration. It is the aspiration towards transcendence, or a life beyond mortality and the bondage of matter, physicality, and the cycles of nature. As Hillman writes in *Puer Papers,* it is the archetype "that personifies ... the transcendent spiritual powers of the collective unconscious."[40] It is the principle that struggles against earthliness to become a divine being, pure and undefiled by earthly corruption. Puer in this sense is the personification of the spiritual quest—the principle of ascendance and transcendence.

Puer often carries the image of the messiah or savior who brings the message of liberation from earthly pain and death. The Puer savior can become a cult figure who promises liberation or everlasting life, if we are willing to become a devotee and give up worldly life. Almost all religions that emphasize transcendence hold this archetype uppermost, even though it may not be named as such, and clearly the figure of Christ is one of its avatars. Puer can be a divine messenger who brings the revelations and visions of the spirit. In this respect, in the West our view of spirituality is influenced by the Puer archetype of all that is uplifting, visionary, inspirational, and pure, beyond worldly defilement. By contrast, in Eastern religions such as Buddhism, the figure of the bodhisattva expresses a more grounded ideal of spirituality within the human condition.

Mythologically, almost all Puer figures are winged. The two most well-known are Mercury and Icarus. Mercury with his winged boots acts as the bringer of revelation from the gods down to earth and into the underworld. Icarus, alternatively, warns us of the hazards of the Puer disposition when ungrounded and overidealistic.

Puer brings new vision into the world and is often present at the initiation of new schools of thought, new traditions, new spiritual movements, and new political ideologies. Visionary individuals who carry the messianic nature of the Puer archetype initiate many of our spiritual, political, and creative traditions. History is peppered with an assortment of youthful icons who have been inspired and intoxicated by their visions. We see this reflected in figures like Mozart, Che Guevara, and John Lennon.

We need the Puer spirit in our lives if we are to maintain a relationship to that which gives us vision and inspiration, but those who become possessed by its power can have some particularly difficult characteristics. While being the archetype of spiritual vision, Puer carries all manner of shadowy peculiarities. Puer draws us upward, away from the earthly dimension of reality. It leads us into ideals that can be out of touch with the pragmatic needs of daily life. Puer-dominated people will tend to suffer the consequence of their flight into spirit by disliking materiality, particularly the demands of work and practical life. They will often experience the necessities of daily life as mundane, tedious, and banal, as a prison that feels stultifying and suffocating. People with strong Puer natures find anything that ties them to the practicalities of life and responsibility to be trapping and frustrating.

Commitment will give rise to deep fears that lead the Puer type to endlessly keep on the move. Travel and a transitory life-style do not demand commitment to putting down roots and staying in relationships. Puer-oriented individuals do not sit comfortably in committed relationships and will always strain to break free. They seldom want to be tied down and will feel trapped if anyone should demand that they really engage in commitment.

In therapy I have on many occasions heard women clients speak of their relationship or, perhaps more accurately, attempted relationship to men involved in Buddhist practice. One in particular I recall spoke of the man she was attracted to because of his spiritual visionary qualities and his gentle sensitivity. She felt he was someone able to meet her as no one could, provided there was no potential for anything to develop between them. He was unable to offer a sense of continuity or commitment, and would stay for a few days and then be off to various Dharma centers, where he could continue his spiritual studies free of the distractions of relationship. When he returned he would be sincere and honest with her about his feelings for her but he seemed unable to recognize the effect of his elusiveness. It was as though he offered something he could never deliver because to do so would require the ability to truly remain in relationship. He could only cope with intimacy provided there was absolutely no attempt to create something more solid. This would perpetuate a kind of romantic unreality. It would also allow him to avoid any real involvement with feelings that might not be positive. In time, this experience became increasingly painful and frustrating for my client because she needed something more real. There could never be a normalized relationship involving practical day-to-day experiences. After a while she began to feel used and degraded by the experience, eventually realizing that this was not what she needed in her life, even though he was very attractive to her.

This is a familiar story and reflects the Puer's immaturity in relationship. Spirited and flighty, the need of Puer figures is to break free of the bondage of the mother's domain, yet the mother always haunts them so long as earth is denied. The greater the binding to the mother, the greater the urge to fly, to always try to break free, yet the Puer remains caught in the habit of not turning to face the thing he fears. The Puer unwillingness to live in the world can make many of the necessities of that life hard to face. As a consequence, such individuals may never satisfactorily earn a living or deal with the necessities of paying bills and domestic chores. Ironically, many Puer-dominated men will often enter relationships with particularly earthy, practical, often motherly women who fulfill the grounding role. This can be a source of terrible frustration for their partners, who eventually become tired of the supporting role. I have seen this in a number of women whose male partners were involved in the broadcasting world. They were happy to support their inspired male partner in the pursuit of his creative work until they began to feel thoroughly used and abused in this role. One woman in particular also realized that her Puer-inspired partner was living out her own creative side because she was afraid to risk doing so.

In my early years as a Buddhist practitioner I recall how much I resented the need to deal with the necessities of earning a living and found that the ability to receive welfare payments was a useful means to avoid what I really did not want to face. I could justify it by saying I was a Dharma practitioner and the state should support me because what I was doing was so worthwhile. I am well aware that much of this was because I did not wish to be caught up in such a worldly sullying of my "pure practice." I wanted to have the freedom to follow my visions and ideals of spiritual development. Little did I understand that these visions become real only as they are grounded in the material world. I was also sufficiently naïve or arrogant to think that I was renouncing a world that I judged as bad, and yet I relied heavily upon this world to support me.

The Puer vision is a great gift, but if we are unable to make the ideas and dreams materialize into practical reality, little is achieved. The Puer type of person will be heard describing wonderfully plausible ideas with great enthusiasm, but will often leave a feeling of doubt that these will ever really come to pass. Dreams and ideas do not demand the toil and exertion of making things materialize or concretize. Puer fears that his or her visions will never be as good once they are made "real." The nature of the materializing process invariably means that as our visions are brought from the ideal to the concrete, they will become imperfect as they form. For some, this imperfection is too painful to accept. As a consequence, some potential artists dominated by this archetype never actually create anything. Their lives become profoundly unsatisfactory and unfulfilled as they struggle to avoid putting their dreams into reality and therefore potentially having them tested and evaluated.

For many Puer-dominated individuals, their spirituality or artistic endeavors are felt to be the most important aspect of their lives. Spirituality will often be the one thing they can commit to, as it will be one aspect of life that will seriously honor and venerate their visionary aspirations. Their attention to spiritual matters, however, will often be to the detriment of all else. Their relationships and family will be secondary and often seen as an obstacle to spiritual progress. I have known a number of Puer-dominated men who fear having children as deeply as any other danger. Having children, they feel, would be the most limiting trap imaginable. It would mean becoming involved in the demands of money and work to support a family, which they see as death to their spirituality. The Puer type will feel that the most important thing in life is to engage in spiritual matters and that money is a contamination of those ideals. Often this leads spiritual organizations to have peculiarly naïve, idealistic attitudes towards financial matters.

When a man or woman dominated by the spirit of the Puer meets a spiritual tradition such as Buddhism, Puer pathology flavors the outcome. The powerful and inspiring ideals of the Buddhist path with its promise of liberation and everlasting happiness are irresistible to the Puer spirit. Often, many of those who meet this tradition are severely wounded Puer types in the first place. The Puer's natural avoidance of materiality and the demands of being in the world fit somewhat pathologically with notions of renunciation. The Puer's natural inclinations turn the notion of renunciation into an expression of spiritual flight, because there is no true understanding of what in the Tibetan tradition is called "definite emergence." If the Puer views earth as mundane, unclean, impure, and stultifying, without meaning or value, the prospect of a liberation that takes one away from this painful world may seem irresistible.

The bodhisattva's renunciation, or definite emergence, is not an avoidance of the world, life, relationships, or work, but Puer pathology may see it that way. Rather, it is a willingness to engage with the realities of life and wake up to their challenges, while recognizing that they do not hold ultimate meaning. If renunciation is an abandonment of attachment to the material world, the Puer type turns this into an avoidance of the material world. Puer's fear of ordinariness, mundanity, and emotional discomfort will drive Puer-dominated individuals towards a transcendent intellectual and spiritual idealism that can take them further away from the reality of living. Often the result is that reality bites back and, at some point in life, the process of grounding will have to be faced.

For those Puer spirits who have spent the first half of life aspiring towards spiritual ideals, a life change will often confront them with the need to become more grounded. It was the Greek craftsman Daedalus, the father of Icarus, who fashioned wings to fly and said to his son, "Do not fly too high or too low." Icarus's failure to heed this warning inevitably led to his fall. Someone dominated by this tendency may be very resistant to putting their spirituality into the real world. As I myself discovered, I was more comfortable spending long periods of time in retreat because I felt it was meaningful; the challenge came when I returned to the West and began to put this experience to some practical use. Puer's healing comes with the gradual grounding of spirituality in practical life—in beginning to apply and materialize what has been an ideal or vision. This may involve the materializing of some creative vision, or as H. H. the Dalai Lama is always stressing, making spiritual life practical in the service of the community.

Puer values orient strongly towards ideals of purity and holiness and can lead to a veneer of spirituality cut off from body, emotions, and feelings. Again, the influence of the Puer archetype on Western attitudes to spirituality is different from that of Buddhism, in which the split between spirituality and the body and feelings is not so apparent. Behind Puer's controlled and seemingly pure and pious behavior there is often a strong shadow of emotions denied for the sake of maintaining an ideal persona of peaceful tranquility and detachment. I spent many years of my early days as a Buddhist trying to convey the illusion that I never felt anger. Like all Puer-dominated people, I had an ambivalence about relating to and expressing feelings. This ambivalence leads to an avoidance of confronting emotional problems and a wish to transcend them instead, particularly through intellectual idealism. Spirituality becomes very heady. In spiritual communities, and the one I lived in was a good example, an overemphasis on disciplined, "spiritually correct" behavior leaves the Shadow lurking, repressed and unexpressed. Emotional undercurrents, moods, and resentments not acknowledged then erupt in bitter conflicts and schisms that can make these communities a torment to live in. Members may have gone there to liberate themselves from the world, and yet all the things they wished to avoid manifest.

The healing of this particular Puer pathology inevitably comes as we accept that our feelings and body have as valid a place in our spiritual life as our mind and its visions. Indeed, part of the richness of the Puer spirit comes when it is possible to blend this visionary life with a more grounded, embodied relationship. This blending may tarnish something of the idealism of spiritual correctness, but it will certainly make us more human and compassionate towards both ourselves and others.

There is a level of arrogance and inflation in the attitudes of Puer-dominated individuals that can come from preciousness about their spirituality. Creating the illusion that they are destined for great things, it will often lead to an intense striving for perfection, on the one hand, and a resistance to accepting their fundamental humanity, on the other. This inflated position of the Puer nature does not find comfort in human fallibility and so such individuals can be deeply critical of their own failings. While this inflation is usually totally unconscious, its counterpoise is a kind of over-sincere humility. I saw this in myself and some of my peers when I was in my thirties. We tended to cultivate a kind of false self that was self-negating, humble, and soft-mannered. This veneer of spiritual niceness often had a shadow that was not allowed to come to the surface. Thankfully, as I grew older, this niceness began to erode to allow through my more natural sense of irreverence.

In retrospect, I can see how my own Puer nature dramatically affected my spiritual life. I became what could almost be described as a Buddhist fundamentalist. I was genuinely committed to my spiritual beliefs and would be almost fanatical in defending their validity. There can be a fanatical shadow of the Puer which upholds ideals as though they are crucial to identity. I can see in retrospect how dogmatically I would assert a kind of absolutist Buddhist doctrine.

The Puer archetype is a potent force in the lives of many men and women alike. Despite its many difficulties and challenges, it would be wrong to damn it completely as something to be eradicated in our nature. To do so would be to lose sight of its essential quality as a visionary inspiration that leads us to awaken to deeper insights in ourselves. The test is in being able to gradually, consciously integrate and embody this side of our nature in a more grounded and pragmatic life.

Some Western psychoanalysts rather harshly judge the Puer nature. Marie-Louise von Franz, a Jungian analyst who has studied the Puer extensively, has been an advocate of work as the greatest "cure" for the Puer.[41] This cure is not always a welcome one. It is, however, one that my own teachers, particularly Lama Thubten Yeshe, seemed to appreciate. Many of his students, including myself, have worked hard engaging in the practical process of building Dharma centers. I recall hours and hours of demanding work tearing down dry-rot-infested walls and gradually rebuilding a huge priory. For four years my Dharma practice was largely as a builder and electrician.

Once it is appreciated, however, growth comes with the capacity to engage in materiality and commit to creative tasks that hold vision. The dreams, visions, and ideas that the Puer so readily follows can then materialize in ways that are often fresh, creative, and innovative. Work has, from my own experience, been an important transformational vehicle, providing it retains a sense of meaning that expresses the Puer visions. If it does not do so, work will prove depressingly unfulfilling. When we are able to marry our vision with the practical demands of crafting our skills, the results can be rich and rewarding. This crafting process can be as important in the creative world as in the spiritual one.

The Puer archetype is of great importance in many people's lives. It carries much of the inspiration and vitality that is needed in the spiritual quest. The positive side of the Puer is a wonderful inspiration that can inform everything we do in a creative and meaningful way. Unfortunately, it is the shadow side of the Puer nature that is so hard to come to terms with. Because this side is so insidious I have described at length its various characteristics. This is not, however, to detract from the value of Puer once skillfully integrated into our lives. At some point this integration requires an understanding of the Puer's archetypal counterpoint in the *Senex,* or "old man," the pragmatic principle that brings structure, order, and grounding.

This counterpoint to the Puer archetype can appear in a number of ways that will be explored in future chapters. One is within the context of spiritual organizations that provide a grounding structure; another is in the process of engaging in a task that requires discipline and commitment. Perhaps it is the latter that the Puer nature finds in the guide. The spiritual guide may offer a way for the Puer nature to engage practically in the path—to embody spirituality and skillfully ground it in life.

PART II

Encountering the Shadow

❖❖ ───────────────────────────

INTRODUCTION

O NCE WE RESPOND to the call and embark upon the journey of individuation, we cross an initial threshold of emergence after which we enter what both Jung and Joseph Campbell have described as the "the road (or path) of trials."[1] Throughout this journey there are phases and rites of passage that enable the deepening of particular experiences. A natural expression of these phases is that they will also carry their own potential pathology. It is often in overcoming or transforming this pathology that we grow and move forward. The fact of encountering problems or making mistakes is not the issue, but rather when these problems become stuck or we fail to recognize the mistakes we make. The journey is not one on which we should have no problems and no pathology; indeed, this is the manure of our transformation. Perhaps the greatest hazard is when, through blindness or denial, our errors become crystallized into a spiritual view or belief system that is fundamentally distorted.

Psychologically, this journey begins with an emergence from psychological innocence and unconsciousness. We embark, either willingly or through coercion by circumstances outside our control, upon a process of awakening. Answering an inner call, we cross a threshold, leaving behind naiveté, innocence, and irresponsibility, and embark on a genuine path of self-discovery. The call to awaken begins to draw us from relative unconsciousness. We leave behind familiar securities and experience what might be seen as a kind of death. It is the death of who we once were and the unconscious life we once led. Once we cross the threshold that leads to the "path of trials" we are unable to turn back. Once our eyes begin to open there can be no closing them, for to do so would be regression and our call would haunt us. Failure to heed the call results in a kind of psychological freezing or deadening.[2] Yet to truly commit to where we are going is not easy; it is still such an unknown land. In our blindness and uncertainty we naturally seek out significant influences to that process, which may take the form of guides and mentors. As we will see, however, this threshold of emergence can be avoided, and the path of trials is by no means simple. We will be given challenges that will awaken us if we are willing to face them; there are, however, many ways in which we can delude ourselves into thinking we have made genuine inner change.

Once we commit to the process of self-discovery and enter the alchemical vessel, it is inevitable that we will encounter the aspects of ourselves that have not been addressed or faced, or what we might call the Shadow. The Shadow is a term coined by Jung to describe the side of our nature that has been cast into the unconscious and held there in the dark to protect conscious life from what we feel may be unacceptable, either to ourselves or to others.[3] It is the side of ourselves we need to hide in order to present a positive face that the world accepts. As we bury parts of ourselves we do not wish the world to see, they gradually become blind spots, maintained in darkness through denial. The Shadow, as Jung sometimes suggested, is the unconscious itself with all its chaotic and potent instinctual aspects. These may be negative, primitive, or undeveloped, but also may be positive yet seemingly unacceptable aspects of ourselves.

On the path of trials we must begin to encounter these facets of our nature because without doing so we will remain incomplete. We will lack the integration we need for our spiritual path. The Shadow may be unseen, unhealthy, or even demonic, but it will contain the roots of our potential transformation.

The hidden, blind side of our nature is the beast in the labyrinth; the wild demon in the wilderness; the dragon that must be faced and tamed, befriended, or slain, as the case may be. This is the side of ourselves that will influence much of what we do, even though we cannot recognize it. It lives in our hidden agendas and secret intentions. As such, it will often be the aspect of ourselves that will unwittingly distort our experience of the spiritual path. While sitting in his cave, Milarepa, the famous Tibetan yogi, experienced a manifestation of his Shadow in the aspect of a demon. He had no capacity to overcome this apparition until he recognized it to be a reflection of his own mind.[4] To encounter and face the Shadow is therefore crucial both in ourselves and in the spiritual environment in which we move. To idealistically assume that all is well within our spiritual world is naïve and blind. It endangers our spiritual health. To open our eyes to potential hazards is vital, whether it entails facing our own Shadow and its pathology or facing those of our spiritual friends, our teachers, and the collective culture in which we practice.

What follows is an investigation of some of the aspects of the Shadow and spiritual pathology that have emerged over the years in the context of my own practice and my work as a psychotherapist, and in relation to spiritual groups I have encountered. Many of the apparent anomalies that come to light demonstrate many problems with the way in which a spiritual tradition such as Buddhism can emerge healthily in the West. This is not to suggest that these problems are not already being addressed and, indeed, are not also enabling us to mature both individually and collectively. Once our eyes are open, our fallibility is glaringly obvious. If our Shadow remains unconscious, the continual lack of awareness or resistance to looking at our blind spots will be our greatest obstacle.

THE BUDDHA was a being of outstanding brilliance. And all things that emanate such radiance inevitably seem to cast a shadow somewhere. One might then ask the question, Where did the Shadow exist in the Buddha's life? Although the term *Shadow* is not used in Buddhism, the principle is far from absent. In the life of the Buddha there are two figures, one symbolic and the other supposedly actual and historical, that play a curious role. One of these is known as Mara, and the other is a relative of the Buddha named Devadatta. Their role in the unfolding of the Buddha's journey seems to be that of a hindrance, adversary, or enemy, or perhaps, psychologically, the Shadow.

It is said that when the Buddha was seated beneath the Bodhi tree in Bodhgaya, India, during the last phase of his path towards enlightenment, Mara devised tests and temptations intended to distract him from his meditation. Mara plays a role similar to that of the devil in the temptation of Christ in the desert. However, unlike the devil, he is not seen as such a literal entity. *Mara* was the name given in the Buddhist world to the obstacles and hindrances that arise in our path to make us deviate from awakening. He, although gender is not specific, is given a demonic personification, as though he is a symbolic aspect of our inner saboteur that emerges when we are intent on the journey. Mara manifested to the Buddha as beautiful women, as fierce attacking soldiers, and as terrifying monsters, each intended to find a chink in the Buddha's impeccability. If there had been a hook for these phantoms to use to gain a hold, the Buddha would have failed in his intention. His impeccability was such that they could not shake his meditative equipoise and therefore became powerless. The beautiful sirens became old hags and the weapons became a rain of flowers.

Devadatta has a different origin, yet he too is vilified as the antithesis of the Buddha's purity, goodness, and perfection. He is said to have been born close to the Buddha in each of his incarnations. He is usually a relative; in the Buddha's incarnation as Siddhartha, Devadatta was his cousin. It is said that on various occasions Devadatta, who was jealous of the Buddha and all that he represented, attempted to kill him. Usually the Buddha employed some miraculous insight to foresee what would happen and avert the danger.

It is apparent that on a symbolic level both Mara and Devadatta embody a shadowy aspect of the Buddha's apparently impeccable life. One could see this rather simplistically as the struggle between the forces of good and evil. It is perhaps a little more complex.

In the case of both the Buddha and Christ, one could argue that without these shadowy characters, they would not have achieved what they did. Is Mara an inevitable or even necessary aspect of our path that manifests to enable us to grow? It is apparent from Buddhist teachings that Mara represents primarily an internal delusional force that must be faced in the process of awakening. The capacity to resist the pull or beguiling presence of this aspect of ourselves is a natural aspect of transformation. The position of Devadatta is less clear.

I have often wondered what was supposed to have happened to Devadatta, since even to contemplate a harmful thought towards the Buddha was said to result in rebirth in the deepest hell. Whenever I have asked Tibetan lamas whether Devadatta would be able to overcome this negative disposition and attain enlightenment, they have almost invariably laughed somewhat awkwardly and given no answer. It is as though he represents an enigma that seems to be overlooked or ignored.

My reason for wanting an answer to this question was primarily because I was conscious that almost all the tales of holy beings put forward as exemplary practitioners were of those who were already extraordinary at the time of their birth. In the Gelugpa tradition, for example, the life of Tsongkhapa, its founder, is venerated as that of the perfect practitioner. He was, however, already considered an incarnation of the Buddha Manjushri at birth. I wanted to know what the path was like for someone who was less exalted; for someone with shadowy faults and problems, who would struggle with heretical views and deeply entrenched negative habits.

I think one reason I found my retreat teacher Gen Jhampa Wangdu so inspiring was that he was a very ordinary person who, as a young man, had truly struggled with the monastic establishment he was part of. According to stories I have been told by one of his closest friends, he had been something of a roughneck who was quite mischievous as a young monk. When I met him and he began to teach me, I was inspired not just by the depth of his insight and the power of his presence, but also by his ordinariness. He had attained profound realization as a man, not as some sort of saintly avatar who had graced us with a perfect incarnation.

Essentially I wished to learn how to deal with the shadowy side of my nature and found this easier to learn from someone who had clearly had to work with it. How do we transform the unruly, wild, emotional side of our nature that we struggle with to be "spiritual?" How do we heal the wounded side of ourselves that we are barely able, or often unwilling, to recognize, yet which dominates much of our lives and permeates even our spiritual practice?

For Jung, to be human is to have a Shadow. One of the factors that separates us from the animal world is that animals behave in what appears to be an uncontrived and immediate way. They seem to have no fabricated identity, as we experience it, that gives rise to the need to split off unacceptable behavior and impulses. Jung saw the Shadow as that aspect of the psyche that has been repressed and denied because we have wanted to hide it from the world. He implies that as we grow, we learn what is acceptable and what is not, according to the prevailing attitudes around us. We learn to repress feelings and behavior rather than risk disapproval and being judged as bad or unacceptable. An infant, rather like an animal, has little or no discrimination of what is and is not acceptable; its responses are raw, natural, and uninhibited. Inhibition grows as the ego forms more fully in consciousness and learns to separate that which serves to maintain approval from that which does not.

One of the most powerful influences over what shapes the nature of our Shadow is the cultural and spiritual atmosphere in which we grow up. If we live in a predominantly Judeo-Christian culture, this will have a particular effect upon what is found to be good and acceptable in our behavior. Our attitudes towards the body, the expression of sexuality and the emotions, and our sense of self-value will all, consequently, be strongly affected. If we then begin to explore the practice of an Eastern spiritual tradition such as Buddhism, our existing values will influence how we practice. They will also shape the way we deal with the Shadow and what is generally contained within it.

The Shadow is perhaps the most important aspect of our lives that must at some point be addressed. To assume we have no Shadow is both to become blind to ourselves and also potentially inflated. To be human is to have a Shadow, and those who are genuinely without Shadow are rare, and indeed beyond being human. The Buddha and Christ could perhaps be seen as the rare beings who finally purified the Shadow. Unfortunately, the Shadow, being by nature a blind spot, is not easy to recognize in ourselves, although others may see it. Those in positions of spiritual authority, such as teachers, are particularly vulnerable to this blindness when they are idealized by others. Once they have become caught up in the idealized view others project, it may be tempting for them to try to hide their Shadows in order to maintain their sense of authority.

As spiritual practitioners it can be painful to discover that our spiritual identity is an illusion, a fraud. This usually happens when we have had much invested in developing an idealized spiritual identity. Adopting a "spiritual" persona can give a sense that we are special and may bring much praise and veneration from others. We can create a veneer of spirituality over buried emotional problems so that we eventually convince even ourselves that we are spiritually evolved. Unfortunately, it is just a matter of time before the illusion is shattered and the Shadow emerges. It can be a humbling, sometimes painful experience to be brought back to earth rather than succeeding in living a somewhat grandiose ideal.

For several years in my mid-twenties I lived in a Buddhist community. Many of us at that time, being relatively new to Buddhist practice, had the tendency to control and repress emotions with the assumption that this was the way to practice and be virtuous. We were receiving teachings that suggested that these negative mind-states had to be tamed and controlled. We were trying to be good, peaceful, wholesome, spiritually correct practitioners, but in a particularly unhealthy way. We learned to overcome our emotions by living in a kind of spiritual straitjacket that forced strong feelings and emotions underground. We generated a very unhealthy collective Shadow and, rather than going away, these buried feelings remained and would emerge in unpleasant conflicts, negativity, and resentments.

To deny our Shadow is to live in an unreal illusion. For many in the spiritual world the Shadow holds little more than their repressed or denied emotional bad habits: the anger, jealousy, greed, and ignorance that we all suffer. For some, there may be a deeper secret that has been shut away. This often relates to trauma we have suffered at some point in our lives. It can involve deeply distorted and wounded self-beliefs that are touched when the control falls apart in private or on bad days. The illusion of a spiritual identity may cover up or compensate for this painful truth but never heals it. Healing takes place only when we return to our wounds and accept and appreciate ourselves with them. As Lama Thubten Yeshe would say, "Compassion is not idealistic"; it is our capacity to genuinely accept ourselves with our Shadow and live without illusions. With compassion, self-acceptance, and a sense of humor, we can learn to be authentic and open about our fallibilities.

The illusion of a spiritually idealized identity is often created as a flight from the pain of self-doubt and a sense of lack of worth. I recall a woman who had become a gifted and charismatic spiritual teacher whom many people valued and venerated. Her quality and depth of insight as a teacher were unmistakable, but unfortunately, much of her identity was bound up in this place of veneration and being seen as special. On occasions she would fall through the illusion that both she and her students were creating of her. She would crash into a desperate sense of self-loathing and worthlessness. From this place she would gradually drag herself back to a more realistic view of herself. The danger was of being pulled back into an illusion, created partly by her students and partly by her own pathology. Her fear of being a nobody and having no value or identity was very painful. Healing could come only when she began to accept her humanity and value herself with both her gifts and her pains. She could then potentially heal the split between the idealized image of herself as the special child she wanted to be but never felt from her parents she was, and the unlovable person she secretly believed she was. Once she had recognized this in herself, the healing could begin.

Most spiritual traditions have ideals of perfection personified in teachers, saints, and martyrs. These figures of spiritual nobility are often the cornerstones upon which traditions are built. The psychological hazard in this culture of idealized icons is that we create something against which we can tend to judge and measure ourselves. The doctrines that then become established will often set up ideals of perfection, goodness, or wholesomeness that we *should* follow. Rather than being guidelines to aspire to, these doctrines can reinforce our belief that we are good enough only when we achieve this ideal. Psychologically, this can set up a destructive internal conflict that pushes what is not acceptable in ourselves into the Shadow.

For a while, the ideal of the bodhisattva had this effect on me. The selfless goodness exemplified by the bodhisattva was something I felt I could only shadow. I was left feeling degenerate and low quality, selfish and unworthy—perhaps how Devadatta may have felt.

The polarity of idealized self and shadowy low esteem is one of many that become evident when one faces the Shadow. The splitting off of the Shadow is particularly evident in the puritanical attitude that characterizes much of the Western attitude to spirituality. Inevitably, the Shadow's polar opposite of puritanical control and spiritual correctness is the anarchic, hedonistic, Dionysian instinct that wants to be free to indulge in and become intoxicated on drugs, sex, and rock and roll. Many of us experience such a conflict, which makes us swing from pole to pole, unable to find a satisfactory resolution. At one time we become pure, contained, and strict only to find a growing urge to break out and get stoned or have rampant sex.

An example of this was a young man who had been involved in yoga and meditation for many years. He was going through a period of intense Buddhist practice and study that brought into question how he was living his life. His tendency was exactly that described above. He would live for long periods with very strong ethical boundaries. He kept his life-style pure and contained. His diet was clean and healthy. He would spend most of his time mindfully cultivating good, wholesome behavior.

After a while, a deep urge would arise to break out of this strait-jacket and seek what he would describe as a kind of underworld life. He wanted to dance and drink and find a woman to have sex with, sometimes a prostitute. He felt that he was unable to contain a sense of moderation. He went to extremes and would be left afterwards feeling an intense shame and guilt. Before long, he would return to his strict, puritanical life-style, having taken the edge off his hunger.

When we spoke of this it was evident that living one side of the polarity would always drive its opposite into the Shadow. He would become increasingly uncomfortable and restless until such time as he would need to break out again. Within this dilemma lay a view of Buddhism that saw purity and control and the abandonment of this side of himself as the way of practice. This left him constantly feeling bad for not being able to control himself.

We may choose to suppress the Dionysian side of our nature and drive it into the Shadow, but it will not go away.[5] If we then live among Buddhists who are strongly influenced by a puritanical need to be pure and pious, this Shadow can become something of a problem. Puritanical spirituality has a strong fear of deep instinctual, archetypal forces that are wild and unruly—of the side of our nature that is potent and passionate and often seeks intoxication and sexual expression. When it takes us over we have little capacity to contain its demands for gratification. In the West, this unruly side is tied to nature gods such as Dionysus[6] and Pan, who have both become associated with the Christian Devil. To the puritanical part of ourselves, this aspect of our natures must at all costs be constrained or driven out. Unfortunately, or fortunately, depending on one's perspective, the god does not go away but remains in the Shadow. There it may feed on denial and become increasingly demonic. In time it will break through our superficial control and take us over, with sometimes devastating consequences.

Inevitably, those who live within strong moral constraints will at some point be confronted with this demon from the unconscious. Living a polarized spirituality, though, will seldom resolve the inner conflict that then ensues. The challenge of the Shadow is unavoidably one of containment and transformation. As Jung once said, the Shadow and morality are two faces of the same psychological dilemma. While we have these powerful forces within our natures, we must live with some form of ethical or moral boundary that prevents us from merely acting out our instincts. How can we live with the Shadow without forcing it into a suppressed and increasingly unhealthy place?

This dilemma has been present on my own path as a Tibetan Buddhist and has not been easy to resolve. As I have a somewhat passionate emotional nature, my spirituality tends to be more oriented to my feelings and my instinctual sense of devotion to the sacred. This devotion has been intrinsically bound up with nature and sexuality. I am well aware of the Dionysian side of my nature. The resolution has come in my exploration of Tantra, which, probably more than any other aspect of Buddhism, offers a means to understand and integrate this shadowy side of our psyches.

Perhaps this is the real challenge to our Buddhist practice. Facing the Shadow is no easy task, and different Buddhist traditions will view its challenge in different ways. For some, Mara is the manifestation of circumstances that provoke uncontrolled delusions. If we avoid these circumstances, we will not be troubled by the result. This is akin to the alcoholic avoiding pubs or bars. For others, Mara is to be encountered with a quality of awareness that could be seen as a sublime indifference. This approach is to develop a quality of detachment that can simply observe and disengage. It may be very effective; its only detriment is that it does not acknowledge the value of the forces at work in the Shadow and can lead to a tendency to be emotionally absent. The emotions are allowed to dissipate into emptiness rather than being harnessed for creative use. This detachment, however, may bring a lack of emotional engagement with life and relationships.

To the bodhisattva in the Mahayana tradition, the intention is to remain firmly engaged in the world. The Shadow is an inevitable part of that encounter and is addressed with courage, compassion, and wisdom. Whenever circumstances give rise to the shadowy sides of his or her nature, the bodhisattva seeks to transform them into the path. The aim is to recognize the challenge in any circumstance and to face the inner process, reflecting on the positive value of overcoming obstacles in order to maintain a compassionate and open heart. The Shadow is like a test to be regarded with diligence and mindfulness, never letting its nature mar the clarity of the intention to work for the welfare of others. Whatever arises is a creation of the mind and may be overcome by a change in attitude.

In Tantra, or *Vajrayana* as it is also called, the approach to the Shadow is different. The wild, potent, unruly instincts and passions are seen as the manure from which certain enlightened qualities and powers arise. The tantric approach as I have described it in *The Psychology of Buddhist Tantra*[7] is to recognize the essential nature of the Shadow. Rather than being demonized, it is recognized as a quality of energy that can be given a channel or vehicle for transformation and integration. In Highest Yoga Tantra the deity is at the heart of this potential to transform our wild nature and its forces. These forces are dark and demonic only because they have no means to be experienced with clarity and integrated.

To integrate the Shadow we need a safe container within which transformation can occur. This puts a different emphasis on our understanding of morality. Rather than being a process of constraint, repression, and denial, morality is the clear awareness of boundaries within which the forces of the Shadow arise and transform.[8] Often a meditator will experience powerful passionate energies that need to be harnessed so that their potential can be used in a creative and dynamic way. The question will always be, How is this possible?

For those who find themselves caught in this dilemma, the only option may be to respect the wild god that runs through their psyches. Simply compressing it into a spiritual straitjacket does not heal or transform it. Finding a path that provides a means of transformation is vital if the Shadow side of our nature is not to become a growing source of psychological ill health. As Jung suggested, there are gods in our psychological diseases.

For those who have a strong Dionysian aspect to their nature, the purity and piety of spiritual correctness will always feel like an anathema. Rather than becoming alienated by spiritual mores laid down by those who live a controlled, pious, and abstinent life, it becomes important to find a spiritual way that fits. For some, this may be the unorthodox following of the gods of intoxication and spiritual ecstasy. There have been many such mystery traditions in both the East and the West. The Shivaite tradition of the Hindu Tantras and the practice of particular deities of Buddhist Tantra provide a way to bring this aspect of the psyche back into the temple rather than repressing its nature. There, it can be venerated in its particular way as a profound means of transformation and awakening.

In India, the tantric approach was particularly associated with a group of Indian Buddhist adepts known as the eighty-four mahasiddhas. These were tantric yogis who were renowned for the power of their realizations. Their biographies[9] show that many of them were rejected from the monastic tradition because they would not conform to the expectations of the institution. Their behavior led them to be cast as the Shadow of the institution and, as such, scapegoated for their lack of complicity. Their ejection from the monastery, however, served to bring their hidden qualities as remarkable holy beings to public attention.

One such example was of a monk at Nalanda, a famous monastery in India established soon after the Buddha's time. His name was Virupa and he spent many years practicing a particular Tantra, which he felt was not giving him results. In despair one day he threw his ritual implements into the toilet. That night he received a vision of a dakini who initiated him into the Hevajra Tantra. With only a brief practice he attained the quality of Hevajra, and from that time onwards he was heard to have female voices in his cell. This caused the other monks to question his morality. They accused him of breaking his vows and began to revile him as a degenerate. In disgust one day he said it was clear the monastery no longer wished to have him there, and he simply walked through the wall and left. The monks were angry with him and threw stones at him, which transformed into flowers and settled around him.

Virupa wandered away from Nalanda and came to a land where the population had a reputation for drinking alcohol and having no spiritual life. He entered a shop that sold alcohol and began to drink. He impressed the locals with his capacity to consume vast quantities. When asked to pay, he said he would do so when the sun's shadow passed a certain place. He continued to drink, but the sun's shadow failed to move. The locals, in amazement, realized this man was very special. Eventually he was asked to explain his spiritual qualities, and he began to teach. Virupa became the originator of the Tibetan lineage known as the Sakya.

There are many other examples of famous adepts in India who did not conform to the traditional ideals of spiritual behavior and who thus came into conflict with society's need for purity and piety. Despite this, their unorthodox practice demonstrated that the Shadow contains energies and forces which, when harnessed through intense practice, give rise to extraordinary realization.

Vajrapani

IN 1985 I returned from a period of five years of living in India and began to train to become a psychotherapist. This training gradually confirmed for me that our Western psychopathology was sufficiently complex to require quite sophisticated understanding for its potential healing. It also confirmed my growing sense, through many years of connection to Buddhist centers, primarily in Europe and India, that many of us attempting to practice Buddhism often fail to address some of our key emotional difficulties. We may be genuinely trying to do so, but we do not seem to shift some of our fundamental emotional wounds.

When I eventually began to work as a psychotherapist, frequently those who contacted me wished to enter therapy because their personal problems were blocking the integration of Buddhist practice. Most wished to look at emotional issues they felt were deeply rooted in their childhoods and which were difficult to unravel. Many felt that the complexity of their problems was not resolved by their meditation practices or by the doctrinal views that tended to be generalized approaches to how to deal with the mind and emotions.

What emerged in these therapeutic encounters reinforced a concern that had been growing for several years–that it is surprisingly easy for us to distort and color our spiritual understanding through our own individual psychopathology. I use the term *spiritual pathology* to refer to the way in which our emotional wounds and beliefs have the power to influence, shape, and distort the way we practice and view our spiritual path. Of particular importance is the fact that we are often blind to this side of ourselves, since these wounds live in the unconscious as our Shadow.

Although the term *Shadow* comes from Jung and not Buddhism, its recognition is nevertheless crucial to Buddhist practice. If we do not do so we will remain blind not only to our failings but also to many aspects of our natures that are outside of our conscious awareness and yet influence our lives. The Shadow, far from being something to be suppressed, contains much of the manure out of which we grow. Failure to face the Shadow will have one significant consequence: namely, that we will tend to distort our spirituality through our Shadow's particular pathology and, because the Shadow is our blind spot, we will be relatively unaware of what is happening.

For the most part our Shadow is held in the dark by denial and a wish to maintain the status quo. It may be, however, that our emotional patterns are deeply rooted and form the very core of our identity. They may be so inaccessible to consciousness that it is virtually impossible to take responsibility for them. They may equally be formed through a survival necessity that requires much understanding before we can willingly change. Our lack of awareness makes it extremely difficult to see what we are doing. If we were to wear colored sunglasses all the time, we would eventually become used to the tint they give to the world and no longer realize that all colors were distorted. So too our lack of awareness of the Shadow blinds us to the ways in which we construct and distort our spiritual beliefs. Sadly, when we create such distortions without examining ourselves, we are living an illusion and using our spirituality to validate our own pathology.

My work as a therapist has brought to my awareness many ways in which this occurs. For example, a woman whose approach to Buddhist practice had a strong puritanical edge feared almost compulsively any so-called negative behavior. She constantly monitored her actions of body, speech, and mind so as to live as purely and correctly as she could. In principle this may have accorded with certain teachings she received on "thought training," but the psychological place this compulsion came from in herself turned it into a constant re-wounding of her sense of self-worth. She was never good enough, and she had to bury her real sense of herself. Another example was a woman who would continually sacrifice herself to look after others. On the surface this looked like a genuine, compassionate selflessness. Her inner experience, however, was of a deep despair arising from the belief that she was acceptable only if she always gave herself up to others' needs. Far from being a way of practice that brought her joy and peace of mind, it was simply deepening her depth of despair and self-loathing. Her self-sacrifice was a form of self-abuse.

Individually, we have responsibility for our spiritual distortions and self-deceptions and must at some point address the consequences of our actions. One example of an individual's capacity to turn pathology into a religion became extremely painful for me when I was in my late twenties. I was in a relationship with a woman who made friends with a man who was an experienced practitioner of Tibetan Buddhism. He was very charismatic and lived with his wife and two children, having turned his home into a kind of Buddhist center. He was an enthusiastic follower of the Indian saint Padmasambhava, who brought the Dharma to Tibet and who had two consorts, one called Mandarava and the other, Yeshe Tsogyal. My partner went to study with this man, who had offered to be her teacher. She was very attracted to his rather theatrical charisma and gladly took up his offer. She went to stay with him and, over a period of time, started to learn more of his practice.

It was on her return from one of her visits to him that I learned that part of the nature of her stay with him was that she would also be his lover. He had convinced his wife that this was important because the relationship he had with my girlfriend was so special it was a deeply spiritual experience. Although it was painful for his wife, she agreed that part of the time he would sleep with my partner and part with her. When I began to ask my girlfriend what was going on, she told me that I should accept it as part of her practice, in the same way that Padmasambhava had two consorts. They both tried to tell me that I could never understand the spiritual heights to which they would go in their sexual relationship and that it was so pure there could not be any fault in it. My problems, they insisted, were because I was so attached and should really let her go to this higher love. I was told that she saw him as her guru and, this being the case, she must be with him, irrespective of the pain it caused his wife or myself; after all, pain comes through attachment.

At some later point the man, who gradually grew more extreme in his self-presentation as a "lama," wearing exotic robes and the regalia of a yogi, came to visit us. I was shocked and hurt one day when he came to me and said that he was going to sleep with my girlfriend and that I should allow it, as it was good for my practice of generosity. If I should object it would show that my practice of bodhichitta, the aspiration to always work for the welfare of others, was hopeless. I was sufficiently young, naïve, and feeble to take all this seriously and found I had no grounds to question the validity of what he was saying. He tried to convince me it was best for my practice, and that his love of my partner was so pure that what they were doing was right.

I tell this story because it is typical of the kind of delusion we can conjure around our self-beliefs, one sufficient to create the conviction that we are entirely right in what we are doing. The grandiosity of this man, for example, made him utterly blind to the delusion he was caught in and the consequences of his actions. I was somewhat intrigued several years later when the same man came to me devastated because my former girlfriend had left him for another man. He wanted someone to talk to in his distress and was surprisingly apologetic for the way he had treated me. I did not find it easy to contain my sense of vindication.

It was Freud and, later, Erich Fromm who spoke of neurosis as a private form of religion and stated that the power of religious movements and cults is that they give a collective validation to our personal neuroses. There can be little doubt that for many people the spiritual or religious culture they inhabit or generate around themselves reflects the nature of their personal pathology. This is particularly evident when we consider the power charismatic cults have to lead their members to perform extreme and often self-destructive acts in the name of their beliefs. The mass suicide of cult members at Jonestown in Guyana and the gassing of the Tokyo subway by the Aum Shinrikyo cult in Japan are two prominent recent examples.

When faced with the degree of alienation many experience in modern life, a religion or cult that offers some kind of refuge in a higher spiritual authority is very seductive. If we grow up with a sense of alienation, insecurity, worthlessness, or powerlessness, turning to a guru or a religious movement that offers security or salvation can be very comforting for a while. Unfortunately, all too often there are those who are willing to exploit the weaknesses and vulnerabilities of others in the name of spirituality. The fanaticism expressed by some religious fundamentalists is a terrifying outcome of individual fears and insecurities being swept up in collective hysteria under the guise of religion.

One could equally say, therefore, that the spiritual institutions and belief systems we create for ourselves are often a rationalization of our personal neuroses. This is not to say that spirituality *per se* is always an expression of pathology, but that, unfortunately, our inner neurosis is often more powerful and less known to ourselves than we realize. Indeed, it can be so strong that even the most clear-sighted and authentic spiritual traditions can become subsumed under its domain. We can turn Buddhism into a reflection of our personal confusion and distort its essential principles. We can rationalize away our personal distortions and justify them to the point that we convince both ourselves and others of their validity.

An example of this occurred during a discussion on the Buddhist view of reincarnation at Sharpham College in the UK. One of the participants fiercely held the view that the principles of Buddhism could be practiced without any need to believe in reincarnation. In principle, he was right. What was particularly noticeable, however, was the emotional ferocity of his beliefs. His argument was very convincing, but behind it there was a level of emotional charge that seemed to be more significant. It was as though the rigidity of his belief was a defense against something very threatening. When asked how he might feel if he were to consider that reincarnation were true, he admitted that it would be very frightening. It was clear that his rationalization was a means to avoid having to deal with strong feelings of fear around death and whatever may happen thereafter.

Spiritual pathology is therefore both a collective and individual phenomenon. Individually, we may be drawn to collective circumstances that unconsciously collude with our pathology. Collectively, we may create institutions that have deeply rooted and extremely unhealthy pathologies that have become normalized so that we cannot see the extent of this malaise. It is tempting to suggest that the existence of patriarchal religious traditions is a vivid example. The unquestioned power and authority of patriarchal figures and institutions, even within Buddhism, is a manifestation of such a pathology validated for the maintenance of tradition and political as well as spiritual power.

When we look at the institutions created around spiritual teachers, often the underlying emotional culture echoes the pathology of the dysfunctional family, which, to outsiders, can be glaringly apparent. The idealization of teachers combined with disciple rivalry, jealousy, and vying for favor reflect strongly the psychological roots in parent-child dynamics. These may become critical only when some event occurs that causes disciples to actually question the nature of a teacher's role in the collective culture. This can be seen most strikingly when a teacher in some way abuses his or her position, at which point the underlying pathology often explodes the collective myth.

Collectively, therefore, hidden pathology leads to a cultural malaise that can be sustained for long periods until some process shakes its foundations. The cracks that then begin to appear in the veneer of health often cannot be plastered over without a collective purge. Whether this purge leads to health or merely scapegoating is dependent upon the willingness of the community to address its Shadow. Sometimes the disintegration of what has sustained a spiritual community does not enable it to survive. It could be said, however, that this is the healthiest thing that can happen, as there is ultimately little benefit in spiritual institutions that are founded on some fundamental delusion.

Spiritual pathology has many faces, some of which have become glaringly evident in recent years. No religion is immune to this shadowy tendency, and it would seem that the potential for us to engender collective prejudice, hypocrisy, and even sectarian hatred in the name of religion is limitless. It seems to be a tragic fact of life that when we scratch the surface of religious movements, we find beneath all kinds of pathology that have been hidden.

The institutions of Buddhism are unfortunately not immune to these failings, and individually we are also part of this problem. Unless we are willing to face the reality of our disposition to distort our spirituality into a shape that suits our personal pathology, we can easily perpetuate delusion in the guise of spirituality. It would be wrong to cling to the idea that Buddhism has some immunity to this tendency, because it does not. Buddhism is as reliant as any other religion on the individual's integrity and willingness to look at him- or herself, face the Shadow, and take responsibility for it.

We can live with integrity so long as we seek to uncover our emotional blind spots and challenge assumed beliefs and accepted practices. We can trust the integrity of spiritual communities so long as we search for the places where we have created institutions that have become corrupted by narrow-mindedness and dogmatism or have simply become havens that collude with our pathology. We can begin to trust our spiritual guides so long as we are willing to challenge teachers who have become inflated by power or blind to their fallibility, and so long as we are prepared to wake up to self-deception. To do anything less is surely to break the very heart of the Buddha's search for truth.

◆ ◆

IN WORKING WITH the Shadow and personal pathology, our relationship to feelings and emotions is of critical importance. They
are fundamental aspects of our response to the world in which we live,
and they color the whole of our lives. When we are unable to cope
with our feelings and emotions, our lives can be an unbearable struggle. The fundamental experience of suffering emphasized so much in
Buddhist philosophy can be seen as being largely determined by our
capacity to deal with this feeling aspect of life. While the problems
and challenges our lives throw at us give rise to painful emotional
responses, the crucial factor is not how to change the world but how
to change our minds. If we have clarity and spaciousness in the mind,
the pain and stresses of life do not cause the same level of suffering.

When we learn to respond more healthily to the emotions and feelings that arise, we can radically change the quality of our lives. One of
the greatest disappointments I felt in growing up was that no one ever
gave me help in dealing with emotions. The experience must be
extremely widespread, because as a psychotherapist possibly the main
aspect of my work is helping people discover how to live with their
feelings. No doubt much of what attracted me to Buddhist psychology and meditation is the attention given to working with the emotions. The different Buddhist traditions may approach emotions in
subtly different ways, but their management or transformation remains
a priority.

In exploring the management of the emotional life, I have found it
useful to bring together two threads of my own background, one

drawn from my experience as a psychotherapist, the other from my experience as a meditator. When I first began to work as a therapist I was conscious of a difference in these two styles of dealing with the emotional life. Initially, psychotherapy seemed absorbed in looking at the origins of our emotional habits and talking them through, while Buddhism seemed to be more interested in taming and controlling the emotions in order to achieve a state of mental quiescence. Over time, my understanding of both methods has deepened and become more subtle, and I now find that the reflective and contemplative approaches complement and inform each other, both in my work as a therapist and in my personal life.

This exploration has, however, highlighted a particular concern: namely, the potential for those who develop meditation practices to use them as a means to avoid feelings rather than to transform them. Welwood aptly calls this type of avoidance spiritual bypassing.[10]

When spiritual practice is genuinely integrated in daily life, this is reflected in how we are, moment by moment and day by day, with our feelings and emotions. Some who claim to have a great experience of meditation may still display strong emotional problems. Others equally experienced in meditation show signs of having repressed their capacity for feeling and emotions in quite unhealthy ways. The question then arises as to whether someone who is developing deep insights in meditation should be free of emotions and emotional reactions.

I have often been amused by people who say, when I honestly express how I have emotionally reacted to something, "But you're a Buddhist, you shouldn't have any emotional problems." Evidently they think that Buddhist meditation practice is supposed to eliminate feelings and emotions. My answer to this is that the intention of Buddhist practice is not to become emotionally sterile but to have the capacity to respond to emotions in a healthy way. In this respect, once again, it is not the fact that we have feeling or emotional responses to the world that is the problem, but exactly how we are with them.

When an emotion arises we can respond to it in a number of ways. We may become completely absorbed in it or, to use the psychological language, "identified with it," so that all we feel is the overwhelming power of the emotion. If we are hurt we may become so utterly absorbed in the hurt it is as though we are the hurt. At this time it can be unbearable and all-consuming, as though there is no other reality. Furthermore, we may respond directly and instinctually from the place of hurt. We may break down, strike out, or become defensive. In this identified state there is little awareness of the emotional process unfolding. We are not able to witness the experience because we have become lost in it.

When we are so lost in our feelings and have no awareness that can witness them, it is as though we are unconscious. We will also be unable to observe the underlying process that has occurred to give rise to the emotional state. If we could slow the process down, so to speak, we might see that this emotion began in a relatively subtle feeling that grew as we intensified our contraction around and into the feeling. Eventually, it became the full-blown emotional response.

I am reminded of the time when I was in retreat in the Himalayas in India. I would spend each monsoon season high up in the mountains with a staggeringly spectacular view of the sky in all its moods. I would often sit outside my stone hut looking out towards the plains below. Suddenly within the intense blue sky, I would see the emergence of a speck of white cloud. It would wisp around in the air currents and gradually grow. Within the space of perhaps an hour I could watch before me the germination and growth of what was gradually becoming a powerful cumulus cloud. As it grew and billowed up into the stratosphere, I would begin to see its dark core of a critical tension of forces. Flashes would begin to manifest from this core. Rumbles of thunder could be heard as the tension grew to the point where something had to break. Suddenly I would see below the cloud an immense downpour falling out of the heart of this dark mass. Having spent many years in India I knew only too well what it was like to be in that drenching storm. The volume of water that gathers in these cumulus clouds only to fall in such a short time is truly a natural wonder.

From my vantage point I could watch the guts of the cloud spill onto the land below, emptying and releasing the tension. The heart of the cloud would collapse, expended and discharged. The natural forces would slowly diminish, having released their energy, and the conditions that supported the cloud would dissipate. The cloud slowly shrank to a mere wisp again, slowly circulating in the currents. Finally, the last vestiges would vanish and the sky would be pristine blue once more.

Many times I reflected on the parallel between the nature of the mind and the emotions and this cloud formation I witnessed from my retreat hermitage. Only when I could slow my inner processes down and witness them in an increasingly subtle way was I able to see that the similarity was remarkable. Our emotional life originates on the level of relatively subtle responses to the environment, in what Welwood, and others have called a "felt sense." These subtle responses may be triggered by other senses, like sights or sounds, or even by brief thoughts. The Tibetan term *tsorwa,* literally "feeling," can refer to body sensation and also to the domain of the emotions. It is a subtle relationship in the body of a feeling or sensation that is present all the time in relation to our environment. We are picking up information all the time that rapidly gives rise to feelings and concepts about those feelings, but this process is usually so subtle that it goes unnoticed and therefore remains "unconscious" to us. These somewhat diffused, subtle felt experiences give rise to the more specific feelings that then become more accessible and focused. This is akin to the wisps of cloud emerging out of the blue moisture of the sky. Slowly, those feelings intensify until, at a certain point, they become the center of our conscious attention. They will also have provoked a thought process that is probably aggravating the effect. As we feel with greater intensity, we tend to contract around the feeling as a relatively instinctual reaction to intense dis-ease. This contraction intensifies the experience still further until we are almost driven to act in some way to relieve ourselves of the distress. At this point we will experience the cloudburst, so to speak, and probably splash our emotions into the environment around us. By then we have lost control.

This release may bring some relief so that we can gradually quiet down. But the question arises whether this has in any way been healthy or was just an acting out of our emotional distress.

There are some who, from a psychological perspective, would see this discharge as beneficial, but many in the therapeutic world see it as only a temporary solution. From a Buddhist perspective such a discharge would generally be considered as simply perpetuating the process of karma by reinforcing the habit of unconsciously, uncontrollably acting out our emotions.

What, then, is the solution? How might we respond to this emotional process differently? The solution is not to have no feeling or emotional life, for this would be to deaden our natural feeling capacity. Neither is it to endlessly act out and discharge our emotions.

From a conventional therapeutic position, the beginning of the journey of living with our emotions comes with what is called disidentification. This refers to our capacity to step out of the center of the emotional cumulus sufficiently to be able to witness its arising. There are various approaches to this. Some choose to simply name the emotion, for instance by saying, "I am feeling really angry about this," rather than just spitting abuse from within the anger. Others may use an approach that is akin to naming the inner sub-personality of the emotional state. This would be like acknowledging to oneself that one is being a tyrannical, angry, hurt child, or a domineering, bossy patriarch. Giving a sub-personality face to the emotional state can provide a sense of understanding of the larger picture of what we become like when particular sets of emotions arise.

These methods can enable us to step outside the intensity of the emotional turmoil so that we are not taken over. It may be that in doing this for the first time in our lives, we actually feel as though we can be relatively stable and yet still feel the emotions. So often when people speak of their emotions, they describe how they feel utterly powerless to do anything about them. They feel out of control and dominated by the force of the emotional eruptions. Disidentification when emotions occur suddenly brings a sense of still being in control—and this does not mean controlling the emotions—even with the presence of powerful feelings. In the therapeutic setting it is often after many months of struggle that suddenly a client will say, It happened again the other day, but this time I did not get lost in it. The sense of relief and renewal of self-trust is immense.

Disidentification is the first step towards what in the meditation world leads to an altogether new possibility. At first, meditation actually strengthens this capacity to disidentify, as the witness awareness becomes more acute. Disidentification is very difficult if everything happens too fast. Before we know it, we have been taken over once again. What meditation facilitates if it is practiced skillfully is the capacity to watch feelings and emotions arising from a conscious and increasingly subtle place. By holding the mind's awareness in a clear, relatively thought-free state, it is possible to be mindful of the arising of feelings and emotions with greater and greater skill. The mind is not easy to tame and as a consequence will be easily blown around by whatever thoughts, images, and feelings arise, as well as by sounds and other sensory influences from around us. As we learn to settle the mind into a relatively quiet state, witnessing what is passing through its field of awareness becomes more and more possible. We will begin to notice the little clouds before they become huge storms.

If we can cultivate a disposition that is not sticky—that is to say, does not get caught up in passing experiences—then witnessing them becomes more stable. From a meditation point of view, the most powerful capacity of mind that can relate to the emotions and feelings in a fresh way is one that is clear, non-judging, open, and spacious. That is, clear in the sense of being free of the conceptual clutter the Tibetans call *namtok* that worries and fantasizes around emotions, making them even more solid and fixed; spacious in that the mind does not contract around and try to interfere with our feelings so as to do something to them to make them go away. This is a state of complete acceptance of what is arising.

In the practice of Mahamudra, one of the main Tibetan meditation practices, as we gradually settle into a clear, spacious quality of present awareness, feelings and emotions are allowed to arise and pass without interference. When we do not interfere by contracting around them or pushing them away, the energy of these feelings can pass through without so much disturbance. We may feel them intensely, but they pass through rather than becoming stuck. It is not the strength of emotions or feelings that is the issue but whether we are simply remaining open and allowing them to go where they need to go. This does not mean acting them out or even discharging them. It is more the capacity to remain fully in the body, aware of the arising of the feelings and allowing them to move through without obstruction. The underlying energy of these emotions can then become an extraordinary invigoration of vitality that rushes through our nervous system but is not obstructed in its flow.

If we deepen our capacity to remain present with our emotions and feelings without interfering, it is crucial that we do not use our meditation to split off from them. There is a big difference between the process of meditation that remains present and open in relation to feelings and one that splits off and disconnects from feeling. For some meditators this is a tendency that has to be guarded against. Some meditation teachers may even tend towards teaching a meditation style that becomes disconnected from both the body and feelings. In such cases we need to take a serious look at whether the practice is genuinely transforming our emotional life or whether it is simply bypassing it by placing a veneer of mental quiescence over layers of suppressed emotion.

At the heart of a contemplative style of working with the emotions, whether in the therapeutic setting or in meditation, is the need to remain present and in relation to both the body and the feelings. Only by slowing down the process, so to speak, so that we are able to develop a more sensitive yet spacious quality of presence, will we be able to transform our emotional life.

Transformation is a step beyond the disidentification process that happens when we just allow the energy of our emotions to be as they are without interference. This quality of acceptance of them as they are heals and transforms in a profound way. Feelings we may have struggled with for years are transformed only when we utterly accept them without judgment and without contraction. This does not mean our feelings disappear, but we become able to live with them in a very different way. Emotions arise but are able to pass through without becoming stuck.

Our emotions are possibly the greatest challenge we ever encounter. It is central to Buddhist thinking, however, that the resolution to life's problems comes through a change within the mind. This is certainly true in terms of our felt relationship to the world. As Shantideva writes in the *Guide to the Bodhisattva's Way of Life*:[11]

> Likewise, it is not possible for me
> To restrain the external course of things;
> But should I restrain this mind of mine
> What would be the need to restrain all else?

There is, in this sense, no outer problem that will not be resolved through a capacity to change the way we relate to our emotional life. When we come to terms with this truth, there is a sense of liberation.

One of the practices of the bodhisattva is to transform adverse circumstances into the path. This is possible for Buddhist practitioners only if we have some capacity to relate to our feeling and emotional lives in a fresh and healthy way. If we do not, we can simply put a positive front over a deep distress. Transforming our lives is about more than just being positive all the time: it is the capacity to feel things fully, either in pleasure or pain, but to remain spacious and open. This spaciousness in our experience is not about making life positive; it is just being open, engaged, and authentic to what is. In the practice of Mahamudra our emotions become naturally liberated into their innate vitality and pristine awareness when we learn to remain open and clear. The bodhisattva's capacity to transform life circumstances is born out of this profound inner openness to feeling. For this transformation to happen, it is essential that the individual is able to remain embodied and present within the richness of the feeling life.

◆ ◆ ——————————————————————————————————

S PIRITUAL HEALTH must at some point be gauged in terms of our capacity to be embodied. Spirituality needs to be practically grounded in the world but, equally, it needs to be grounded in the body, particularly if we are to have a healthy relationship to feeling. Embodiment is also an important aspect of the natural expression of who we are. We may embody who we are instinctively and naturally, or it may be something we have to learn consciously. Animals, one could say, are naturally embodied. They do not have to practice it or think about it. They move in a way that is instinctively a healthy expression of their essential animal nature. Only when animals are severely badly treated do they potentially lose this capacity. I recall in Spain seeing a tethered donkey rocking its head from side to side in a distressed manner because it had been left this way for so long. Embodiment, therefore, does not have to imply conscious embodiment. If, however, our relationship to the body has become damaged, conscious embodiment may be necessary.

Babies and infants instinctively express who they are through the body. Emotions and feelings are embodied and pass through with relative ease, so long as they are allowed to express themselves. As we grow, our relationship to that natural process of expression tends to become distorted and frustrated by both internal and external constraints. In adulthood our capacity to naturally, healthily embody how we are has often become damaged. When this is so, we may require skillful re-learning to free ourselves of the armoring and constriction that locks us in.

Our body, whether we are comfortable with it or not, is the vehicle of our essential relationship to the world. Once we accept this, we can realize the importance of maintaining a healthy relationship to this vehicle. In the practice of Tantra this is vital, as the body is seen as a fundamental place of creative transformation. To ignore it will dislocate us from the very source of the vitality that is at the heart of the tantric path. This includes our sexual energy and our relationship to the environment around us.

Perhaps the most familiar example of disembodiment is of those who seem to live entirely in their minds or in the head. While this tendency is most apparent in men, it is not exclusively so. If we are stuck in our head, mind, or intellect, our relationship to spiritual practice and meditation in particular will be shaped by this pathology. We will often be out of relationship to feelings and unable to remain present in body sensation.

I am reminded of a friend who has significant spiritual insights, a considerable knowledge of Buddhist philosophy, and who has done a great deal of meditation practice. Even so, he is ordinarily barely conscious of his body. He acknowledged that as a consequence he has not readily listened to its needs and therefore has not responded to the signs suggesting his health is at risk. In a recent conversation I learned that his health was waking him up to the importance of attending more closely to the body's needs.

A lack of connection to the body often entails a lack of awareness of the feelings, which may lead to a difficulty in relationships. We may fear being in the body with its potentially overwhelming emotions and feelings, but as the body is the vehicle through which we incarnate our spirituality, inhabiting it is nevertheless vital. If we do not there will be a tendency to be ungrounded—practically or spiritually stuck in the head.

In the West our relationship to the body is somewhat ambivalent, and most of us suffer some degree of disembodiment. We often emphasize the body's appearance, and we may use and abuse it as the thing that works hard to keep us going. Even those who are athletic can fail to be genuinely in touch with their bodies except as tools to be developed. We often fail to be aware of or listen to the signs the body gives us as to its well-being. If these are our tendencies it is not surprising that as we embark on the practice of meditation, we will perpetuate the tendency to remain disembodied. This disembodiment often arises because of a lack of understanding of the principles of meditation. Whatever its causes, if disembodiment is perpetuated in our spiritual life, we are missing a crucial point. For the sake of our overall health, we need to resolve the split that can occur between spirituality and the body.

Disembodiment occurs through a number of causes. Possibly the most severe examples are of those who in early childhood have experienced some trauma that has caused a splitting off from the body. This may have been through extreme trauma such as sexual or physical abuse. In such instances, splitting away from the emotional and physical experience was probably the only way to cope with the trauma. One could see this as a potentially healthy mechanism in an intolerable situation. Later in life, however, this tendency begins to become a problem. If someone who has suffered in this way then chooses to restore his or her relationship to the body, the long-buried trauma will almost certainly reawaken. This trauma then needs considerable time and skillful support to gradually re-integrate. For someone with this kind of wounding, meditation may be a mixed blessing. It may reawaken traumatic experiences too rapidly, causing a potential re-traumatizing. Alternatively, some may actually use meditation to remain split off from the body and its sensations and feelings. This practice can maintain a safe distance from the body and emotions, but it does not thereby enable a process of healing or transformation to take place. Meditation then becomes a way of bypassing, rather than resolving, emotional problems.

There are those who in early infancy experience the environment as unsafe or hostile. In the process of beginning to incarnate in the physical body, something can start to go wrong. Having seen the process that occurs in my own children as they gradually inhabit their bodies, I am aware that this process is a very subtle one. When something goes wrong it will often lead to a growing difficulty with being present in the body. This may manifest in poor balance and coordination or a sense that they are not really there. If parents are equally disembodied, it will be very easy for a child to grow up alienated from the body and caught in the head.

The personality type described in psychoanalytic theory as schizoid fits into this pattern of disembodiment.[12] The schizoid tendency is initiated when an infant in distress can no longer cope with the emotional pain it is in and actually dissociates, or splits off from being present. An adult who has this tendency will sometimes seem to be not really present. I see this sometimes with people who go into a slightly glassy-eyed state in which they may be just gazing into space or out of a window. They seem to have just gone. This can be somewhat disconcerting to be around because it leads to a feeling of not really being met. The person is not present in interactions.

Again, this disposition of disembodiment leads to a distortion of the experience of practices such as meditation. These people may well be able to develop quite deep absorption in meditation. The danger is that it will also be split off from relationship to being present with what is arising. They will be out of the body in a mind-state that has little connection to feelings and body sensations, even though it could be quite a blissful, peaceful state to be in.

In the therapeutic setting I have also encountered those who suffer from what could be seen as profound resistance, reluctance, or fear, not just of being in the body but of being in this life. As we have traced deeper their sense of being here, a deep resistance to being alive and in this life gradually emerges. This is not just the expression of someone unhappy or depressed with his or her life. It is far more fundamental to how they inhabit themselves on a core level. The feeling is pre-verbal and vague and therefore hard to articulate, but they know they do not want to be here. It is profoundly distressing to those who feel it and will often manifest in a tendency to withdraw from really engaging with life. A further common ingredient is the sense that they are aware of some state of being prior to the entry into the womb that they long for or have lost.

When someone with this tendency looks to spiritual life as a means to resolve his or her emotional struggle, some curious side effects can be present. Not engaging with life is often validated in spiritual doctrines. Transcending the body and materiality in favor of some state that is peaceful and free, yet dissociated from the world, is a powerful longing. Meditation practices can take people into deep experiences that draw them further away from reality rather than keeping them present within it. Letting go of a sense of solid self is almost the most natural thing to do so as to merge with oceanic feelings of oneness. The question is whether these experiences are a move towards awakening or a regressive pull back into a primary state of unconsciousness.

It could be said that disembodiment is something most of us experience to some degree, particularly in the West. Whatever the form or degree of this tendency, the solution is a gradual return to the body. This journey may require careful and skillful support from experienced guides. The process of incarnation and embodiment is not always a comfortable one. It is, after all, some form of distress that has usually led to disembodiment in the first place. As Levine makes clear regarding working with shock trauma, restoring awareness and healing trauma in the body is something that must be done gradually.[13] If someone has suffered relatively severe trauma, it is vital that internal resources be built up and external support be available before any kind of healing can begin. If the process of re-embodiment is done too quickly, it is very easy for re-traumatizing to occur.

Meditation, when learned skillfully, can enable a return to awareness of the body, our sensations, and feelings. When we are not given specific guidance to ground our meditation within the body, however, meditation can easily perpetuate a disembodied spiritual practice. This is accentuated if our view of spirituality sees the body as some kind of problem to be transcended. Unfortunately, this view can prevail even within the Buddhist world, despite being counter to the essential principle of mindfulness and presence. When, however, we cultivate the capacity to remain present in our felt experience within the body, our relationship to ourselves changes. We can begin to feel more grounded in our life and more stable in our identity.

Engaging in a disembodied spirituality is no solution to our life demands. It may be a way of experiencing states of mind that can be very seductive, even addictive. Seldom does it address the roots of our emotional problems. Transformation comes when we are willing and able to restore or develop a sound relationship to our body in a healthy way. With many Buddhist practices, such as Tantra, this is essential, for the body contains the vitality that is the heart of our innate creative potential.

Embodiment therefore implies a full engagement in life with all of its trials and tribulations, rather than avoidance through disembodied spiritual flight. The value of meditation is that it can enable this engagement because it cultivates the capacity to be present and remain open, not grasping at or rejecting what arises. When meditation emphasizes presence rather than transcendence, this openness is a natural outcome.

Power and Will 15

A s we respond to the call and face the challenge of the Shadow, we must inevitably confront our relationship to power. Power is perhaps the most consistently misunderstood area of human nature in relation to spirituality, as its most familiar face, in many religions, is patriarchal. Most established religions are steeped in the patriarchal need for power to establish and maintain authority, hierarchy, and the tradition. This makes power one of the most contentious aspects of religion and, by association, of spiritual life.

In my encounter with spiritual organizations, principally in the Buddhist world, I have seen much confusion about vital issues relating to power. There is seldom an acceptance of the reality of personal power; it is rarely spoken of openly because it evokes fears and uncertainties and seems to carry an unconscious taboo. Our ability to assert our personal will or individual truth is viewed with great ambivalence, as though it touches a critical boundary of something dangerous and forbidden. Personal will and the power to act and fulfill individual wishes are sometimes shrouded in guilt and confusion about being selfish. The ability to assert personal boundaries clearly and firmly can be either limited or absent, and it is often impossible for people to say no.

Our ability to relate appropriately to personal power often seems to evaporate when we are trying to live a so-called spiritual life. As a result, power becomes unconscious, shadowy, and potentially destructive. What is not lived consciously becomes distorted and confused but is nevertheless present as underlying pathology. Personal difficulties relating to power are then often reinforced by spiritual traditions that have an ambivalent attitude towards it.

Power pathology may have some crucial consequences for those involved in Buddhist practice, both personally and collectively. Disciples often have unaddressed power issues in relation to their teachers, a theme I will pick up in the next chapter. When we endow traditions and their spiritual leaders with power and authority, we unwittingly give away a vital aspect of our individual responsibility, at great cost. Organizations often have underlying patterns of power and control that make some disciples remain relatively disempowered and dependent, while others actually become the agents of the teacher's parental authority. Denying and disowning personal responsibility for our power is welcomed in charismatic religions where devotion to the teacher is paramount. The dangers of this process, however, are that we leave ourselves open to abuse, exploitation, and dependency.

Reclaiming responsibility for personal power is vital if we are to grow and individuate, but the path is fraught with confusion. Many of us fear our power because we think it will be destructive and dangerous if released. Perhaps one of the simplest manifestations of ambivalence towards personal power is a confused relationship to assertiveness. In its absence people can often manifest a disposition to be deferential and submissive, fearful of asserting individuality. When someone asserts her own wishes and needs or firmly stands by her own "truth," this assertiveness can easily be viewed disapprovingly as selfish and ego-centered. This in turn can lead to intolerable feelings of guilt. Those who suffer the sense of disempowerment that results from a failure to express their truth often find that their assertiveness lies buried in anger and resentment. Anger consistently originates in feeling disempowered or incapable of asserting ourselves appropriately. Frequently, however, there is also some confusion about how those engaged in spiritual practice should relate to anger.

Some Buddhist teachers accuse the therapy world of promoting and cultivating anger. They will often deny any validity to anger, viewing all anger merely as a cause of suffering to be overcome and controlled.

This view, however, can deprive us of a vital resource that needs to be understood more deeply. The simplistic view of anger as a cause of suffering fails to take account of the complex nature of the origins of anger. We lose sight of its underlying psychological significance and deprive ourselves of a potentiality that has often become lost within the experience of anger. When anger is understood more deeply, it is possible to discover the underlying root that may require a more straightforward, creative, and effective way of expressing itself.

As long as we live with the view that anger is to be condemned, we can easily fall into the habit of repression. We will also fail to hear what truth lies behind it that is not being voiced. When we ask questions such as, "What do you really want to say?" or "What are you really wanting that is not being heard?" we will begin to hear what is at its root. This becomes a healthier way of living with anger, rather than creating a regime that fears it and tries to disown or suppress it. If our capacity to be assertive or to feel heard has become blocked and distorted, when we listen more deeply to what lies beneath or behind the anger, we will often discover some inner truth that needs to be asserted more clearly and creatively.

From a psychological perspective we may describe a range of experiences that could all be seen as in some way living under the umbrella of anger. Rage, outrage, resentment, frustration, and aversion are all familiar expressions of very different experiences of anger. There are also more passive manifestations that are often not recognized as manifestations of anger, such as some kinds of depression, passive aggression, and even boredom.

The origins of anger are complex and cannot be simply controlled and repressed. Sometimes anger is the raw acting out of the emotional need to attack or punish someone for our not getting what we want, or for getting what we don't want. However, for many who are unable to assert themselves and who feel disempowered and ineffective, anger may be the only expression possible. Anger can be the first stage in a process of regaining and restoring self-confidence, self worth, and the power to be effective in life. The passive victim who feels unable to make choices and just accepts his or her lot with hopelessness manifests an inability to claim personal power. Anger may be the beginnings of a shift towards no longer being a victim. The sense of disempowerment and ineffectiveness some people experience in life is overcome only by regaining a relationship to their potential power. Those who have been abused and disempowered may find this only when they can access their buried outrage. This may lead to the courage to stand up and say no.

When our potential effectiveness or assertiveness has been damaged, it can turn inwards self-destructively and result in depression and feelings of despair, hopelessness, and even a desire to harm oneself. I could see this in the experience of one of my clients who had little or no capacity to assert herself either in her marriage or with her family. She would spend a huge amount of time complaining to me about her lot, without any capacity or willingness to change what was happening. On occasions when she was again repeating her sorry tales, I could feel a growing anger and frustration in myself which, I could feel, wanted to bully her into doing something about her situation rather than remaining a victim. When I reflected this back to her, she said it was very familiar to find her friends pushing and angrily bullying her to do something. The anger and bullying she was provoking was the anger and assertiveness she refused to own in herself. This is very common in the person who holds the position of a victim, and reclaiming this anger is the first step towards reclaiming personal responsibility for the power to no longer be a passive victim of life.

While anger is one manifestation of a poor relationship to personal power, another is the incapacity to create effective boundaries. When we are unable to say no and create clear boundaries around ourselves, the effect can be dramatic. For some, this inability will result in angry resentment. For others, it will lead to formlessness, or the lack of a clear expression of individual identity. Those unable to say no are then potentially open to abuse and manipulation through others' demands.

Unfortunately, this is a familiar occurrence in organizations that rely upon the goodwill of others offering their services. I lived in a community where people often felt a conflict between an obligation to serve and the need to preserve a space for personal needs. I used to suffer feelings of guilt if I did not constantly offer to serve the community and instead chose to do my own work. Some of my close friends who found it impossible to say no gradually came to resent being exploited or taken for granted. Others seemed to endlessly sacrifice themselves and became exhausted by the constant demands placed upon them, which they felt unable to refuse.

Asserting limits, saying no, and standing up for our inner truth with firmness and courage do not imply that we have become egocentric and selfish. It is more likely a healthy self-protection needed in certain circumstances for us to retain our self-identity. For the first time, we may be able to stand in our own power and authenticity, true to ourselves, and state what is important for us. It may be a vital step in protecting ourselves from being abused and exploited—protecting our life energy and spiritual needs, without turning our powerlessness into anger and aggression.

This need became particularly apparent in a woman artist whose work was growing in demand in the commercial art world. Art galleries would put great pressure upon her to produce work to order and then expect her to deliver as though she were a production line. She increasingly felt this was alien to her natural creative instinct. She felt that her work was something sacred that had a deep spiritual undercurrent needing careful nourishing to unfold. Her problem was that she was not used to saying no to those who made demands of her. She found it very hard to really feel she had a right to look after her needs, and she failed to appreciate the nature of her own creativity as something that needed to be protected. Her background left her sorely inept at creating boundaries around what was and was not acceptable to her. As a result, she had become somewhat over-compliant, which had left her extremely vulnerable to the pushy demands of gallery owners. Through her work in therapy she began to feel stronger and more assertive with her boundaries. She saw that it was perfectly valid to protect the sacred nature of her art and to make sure that others respected that. Although her new attitude was not welcome at first, gradually she came to feel that her needs were being respected because she made it clear her priority was her art, not the marketplace.

In Tibetan Buddhism there are three central deities that embody essential qualities of Buddha activity. The most familiar of these are Chenrezig, the embodiment of compassion, and Manjushri, the embodiment of wisdom. Less familiar but of vital importance is Vajrapani, the embodiment of power. If we consider Vajrapani as an aspect of our true nature, he represents the power to assert our sense of value and purpose clearly and with great will and determination. This is strength and confidence that will not be taken advantage of and will overcome all obstacles to accomplish what is necessary. Vajrapani embodies our ability to truly stand in our power and be unshakable. Power is neutral and can be used either for good or ill, depending on our motivation and whether we are being consciously responsible for it. Many problems arise when people relate from a place of power but do not really take responsibility for that fact. The deity Vajrapani embodies the essential nature of power that, when expressed consciously, can enable us to be effective in a much cleaner and more open, caring, and compassionate way.

Wrathful deities in the Tibetan tradition exemplify a powerful, wrathful compassion free of the petty, limited, defensive ego-grasping that wants to retaliate, hurt, or punish. There may be times in our lives when we need to use such conscious expressions of power to forcefully express boundaries when others are being irresponsible or abusive. Just as a parent would use "wrathful compassion" to state clearly and concisely to a child in danger what must be avoided, someone who has suffered the abuse of power by another needs to have the inner strength to assert, "No, stop, you will no longer abuse me." For Buddhist practitioners the recognition of the emptiness of self does not mean that we will not be able to assert a clear "no" when something is wrong.

When we develop an authentic sense of our inner power and begin to trust ourselves with it, we will not need to use our power in a destructive way to disempower others. This is not the "power over" of the patriarch but simply the power of being true to oneself and living with self-confidence. If we are in touch with our power we can accomplish what we wish more cleanly and effectively, without the tendency to be controlling or domineering.

A further aspect of our personal power that also seems to be easily misunderstood in the Buddhist world is the nature of our will. Once again, many of us have a poor relationship to will, which can range from having an almost obsessive willfulness to being like a leaf blown around by the wind. There may be those who see the will as something to be avoided in Buddhist practice because they think it is just an expression of ego and the creator of the karma that leads to suffering. From this viewpoint it may be thought that if we relinquish will and settle into a kind of passive detachment, then whatever happens, we will not create causes for suffering. It may be true that many of us need to learn to let go and accept more, rather than trying to maintain control; however, to disengage our will can be merely to avoid taking responsibility for our actions or indeed, our lives.

Understanding will in relation to the Buddhist path leads us to yet another paradox. This is a paradox that anyone who embarks upon the practice of meditation will at some point encounter. We may require a level of determination and discipline to engage in meditation, but the actual practice requires a level of surrender. *Trying* to meditate can become the greatest obstacle to the experience of meditation, like trying to relax. Nevertheless, having a healthy will is important for normal life as well as for our spiritual practice. If our will becomes overbearing and obsessive, however, it will become destructive and ultimately turn us away from the natural unfolding of experience. The ego dominated by a need to push, strive, or control loses relationship to our true nature and will often create the conditions for some form of crash.

As we grow up, our will is an important aspect of the development of a sense of identity as a separate, self-sufficient individual. We gradually cultivate the capacity to engage our will and take responsibility for our life choices. The absence of self-will at this time can be very detri-mental. For much of our lives, the right use of will enables us to engage fully with what we do in a creative and individual way.

At some point in this journey, however, there needs to be a shift in our relationship to this will. This often happens naturally as life forces us to open to the influence of a deeper sense of meaning and purpose that is unfolding us. We encounter the paradox that willful striving is not enabling us to accomplish what we wanted. The individuation process is demanding that we begin to align or attune our personal will to what might be called a kind of divine will or, to use Jung's term, the will of the Self. This becomes most acute during the period of mid-life, when there can be a natural shift from the position of the ego's will to the will of the Self. This transition often demands that we let go of control and experience a kind of giving up, during which life seems to live us and we have no choice but to follow its bidding. When we open and surrender to the will of the Self and trust in the unfolding of our life, it is an act of faith. This implies not passive fatalism but a harmo-nious participation in the process.

While at first this idea may seem alien to the Buddhist with no notion of a Self or divine principle, it does not require a great shift of under-standing to see it at the heart of the bodhisattva's life. An aspect of the bodhisattva's intention of bodhichitta is a quality of will that dedicates life to a higher purpose. This is sometimes known as the "Great Will." The bodhisattva learns to surrender personal intention to the service of a higher goal, which acts like a deep undercurrent in all he or she does. In the bodhisattva vow it is written, "in order to eliminate the suf-fering of all sentient beings, I offer myself immediately to all the Bud-dhas."[14] Surrendering personal will with this deeper sense of purpose opens the bodhisattva to a quality of vitality and power that is totally transformational. This is not a passive position, however, but one where personal will engages with an essential intention so that we live as a vehicle for its expression—something the bodhisattva does to great effect. Learning to engage our will yet remain open to what unfolds is no easy task. When we get it right, however, we may feel profoundly in harmony with our journey even though it still demands of us that we courageously go through the pain of living it.

Once we reclaim our power consciously and align our intention with that of the awakening mind of bodhichitta, our potential for transformation is extraordinary. As we surrender the ego's will to this greater will we experience a profound sense of purpose, even though we may not know exactly where it is leading us. That, however, is part of the mystery of individuation. When the ego allows the path to unfold without struggling to control where it goes, we will also be able to embody power fully, without having to self-consciously impose it on the world.

◆ ◆ —————————————————————————

IN ORDER TO AID CLARITY and understanding, I have chosen to look at the teacher-student relationship in the context of the Shadow not because I see it as something inherently problematic but because this relationship is complex and worthy of close psychological scrutiny. I feel this is especially necessary in view of the difficulties many Westerners have when relating to teachers. I do not claim to have solutions or some special insight into this subject, but having spent much time discussing people's experiences, I have found that certain important factors do emerge.

Many people have a strong desire to seek a spiritual guide. They may be searching for a friend who can give spiritual support in difficult times, or for someone like a mentor who can be a source of knowledge and insight. They may be seeking someone who will be a model or inspiration for the journey they wish to follow, someone who seems to embody the spiritual values and experiences they aspire to. Sometimes the search for a spiritual guide is for someone to surrender to and trust as a refuge in a fundamentally alienating and hostile world. There are also those who feel complete aversion to the very concept of a spiritual guide, often because they would under no circumstances give up their own volition.

Since the nineteen sixties, interest in Eastern religions and spiritual guides has grown rapidly in the West. In part this has been a response to the apparent absence of genuine examples of spiritual evolution; it has also been a reflection of a growing disillusionment with established approaches to theistic spirituality, where there is often an absence of a practical path to self-realization or self-transformation. The result has

been a dramatic increase in the number of Western followers of Eastern spiritual traditions, particularly Buddhism.

While the teacher-disciple relationship can be an invaluable and
fruitful experience, the process of relating to spiritual teachers also has
its hazards. This is in part the result of naïveté among Westerners as to
the nature of the teacher-student or guru-disciple relationship. It is
also partly the consequence of a lack of understanding on the part of
Eastern teachers as to the nature of the Western psychological makeup.
Added to this is the apparent tendency of a few Eastern teachers to
actually exploit the relationship. With the advent of a growing number
of Western teachers it is becoming necessary to really address the
underlying psychological and ethical basis for this relationship. Too
often there are potential abuses of this relationship, particularly confusion around boundaries.

In the East the tradition of the spiritual guide has been present for
centuries, even millennia. The long cultural familiarity with the guru has
meant that there is often greater ease with the relationship, even though
it may be full of prescribed patterns of behavior. In the Buddhist world
this relationship varies from one tradition to another, and nowhere is
its importance more stressed than within the Tibetan traditions. In the
Theravadin traditions the teacher is a valued and honored mentor worthy of great respect—a model and inspiration on the path. In the
Tibetan traditions, however, the teacher is viewed as the very root of
spiritual realization and the basis of the entire path. Without the
teacher, it is asserted, there can be no experience and insight.

In the teachings known as "stages of the path to enlightenment," or
lamrim, Tsongkhapa,[15] says that the guru is the root of the path and
source of realization and should be viewed as an embodiment of the
Buddha. Only through skillful devotion to the guru will the disciple
receive the blessings of the realizations of the path. In Tibetan texts
great emphasis is placed upon praising the virtues of the guru and giving thanks for his (they are usually men) kindness. In the tantric teachings this is carried further still by repeatedly generating visualizations
of the guru and making offerings and reciting praises. This devotional

practice, known as *guru yoga,* is seen as one of the most profound ways to cultivate the qualities and results of spiritual practice. In the tantric tradition particularly the teacher becomes known as the *vajra guru,* the one who is the source of initiation into the tantric deity. Having made this relationship, the disciple is asked to enter into a series of vows and commitments that ensure the maintenance of the spiritual link. Some teachers even stress that to break this link is the most serious downfall anyone could make.

How are we as Westerners to receive these principles of the guru-disciple relationship? Is the guru so crucial, or are we simply seeing the dogma of religious orthodoxy? What is the value of the teacher-disciple relationship? Furthermore, how can Westerners make sense of this relationship when there can be so much room for confusion? These are not simple questions to resolve, and yet they are important to explore so that we can truly understand the value of this relationship as well as recognize the dangers involved.

The position of the guru in Eastern religious traditions carries with it many factors that could be highly questionable when transported to the West. The patriarchal nature of most of the dominant Eastern religions has an impact on the way in which a teacher's power and authority is viewed and then maintained. Teachers are often brought up in a medieval culture that invests them with both spiritual and political power. We may need to consider the psychological consequence of a teacher brought up in a rarefied prescriptive world, viewed as some kind of special being, moving to a culture that does not have the same social and ethical base. The tendency of Eastern religions to place women in a secondary or inferior position can also have a considerable influence on the way female students are treated by male teachers.

There are Eastern teachers who make the transition from one culture to another in a clear and skillful way. Others, unfortunately, do not do so and tend to retain a perspective within the West that can be thoroughly inappropriate. All these considerations may require that we question and re-evaluate the doctrine of guru devotion in modern times. I am aware that to certain Tibetan teachers in particular, this seems like a challenge to possibly the most hallowed principle in Tibetan Buddhism. Nevertheless, we should not be afraid to ask these questions. Indeed, there are certain Tibetan teachers, H. H. the Dalai Lama being one, who are well aware that there is a need for skillful reflection on the relationship to the guru so that we are better able to avoid the possible pitfalls.

The concept of a guru is not inherently problematic. Problems arise in part because we do not understand the meaning of the guru as a factor in our spiritual path. Additionally, we have too many romantic expectations and fantasies regarding the nature of the guru. If we have a strong yearning for a teacher, we can easily become caught in an idealized illusion of what the guru is.

Many people naïvely assume that the one they call the guru is going to be perfect and infallible. The teachings of Tibetan Buddhism, for example, tend to reinforce this view by insisting that we see the guru as Buddha and, therefore, free of any faults. There may be an emphasis on testing and evaluating the teachings, but the authority of the lama remains unassailable. The requirement or desire to view the guru as enlightened can lead to a profound awakening of insights and experiences that occur because of the state of openness it creates. It may also lead to great confusion if we begin to see that the guru has a human side that is still fallible.

How, then, do we come to terms with this twofold nature? Is it possible for us as Westerners to come to an understanding of the guru as an embodiment of profound insight and awakening while not falling into the illusion that this person is without fault? The teachings on the guru within the Tibetan tradition offer some important insights toward making sense of this apparent contradiction by considering the guru on outer, inner, and secret levels.

THE OUTER, INNER, AND SECRET GURU

The paradox of the guru as enlightened yet possessing human fallibility is one that can be resolved only as we understand the concept of the guru more deeply. In the Tibetan traditions the guru is viewed on three levels, called outer, inner, and secret. Usually our first experience is of the outer guru, who can be a vital source of insight and inspiration. He or she may act as an example of the practice and needs to have the compassion and genuine lack of self-interest to respond to a disciple with care and support. When this relationship begins it can be truly wonderful, like finding the lost and longed-for friend we can trust with our innermost secret and who can lead us in the dark. The connection to the guru opens us to a sense of our true nature. He or she is the catalyst that makes this possible and helps us to deepen that experience. The guru may also be instrumental in guiding the development of this experience.

Our relationship to the outer guru may change and evolve with time. While it often begins with a kind of falling in love, in time this changes into more of a working relationship. The guru, as Lama Thubten Yeshe once said, "can shake our heart." He or she may have the capacity to get through to our core in a way that few others can. The consequence of this experience is that the outer guru can be in a position of great power. Indeed, the very nature of seeking guidance is that we are investing someone with that power. With the spiritual guide, this connection comes from the heart and is therefore of great importance. The practice of guru devotion asks of us that on some level we surrender some aspect of ourselves to the teacher so that we are able to open to our true nature. The power given to the guru requires that he or she must be someone whose integrity we can trust. Inevitably this carries a great risk, but when we find someone who is genuine, the value of such a relationship is extraordinary.

Gradually, as the relationship grows, it begins to lose some of the idealistic glow and becomes more real. In this respect, the relationship matures and requires greater authenticity. The teacher may test the disciple but, equally, it may be important for the student to check out the teacher. To fail to do so, as H. H. the Dalai Lama once said, may spoil the teacher. He felt that too much deference did not challenge the teacher and was a mistake. Whether teachers are willing and able to take up this challenge is another matter. Some clearly are, and others are not so comfortable with it.

Perhaps one of the important ingredients in a skillful teacher is the capacity to genuinely empower students to question and find their own way. The outer teacher is crucial in enabling students to discover their own innate potential, even if this means going beyond the teacher's jurisdiction. The outer guru's role is to lead the student to an authentic experience of the inner guru. Once they do so, the nature of the relationship can evolve still further. In the tantric tradition in particular, the outer guru is the one who initiates an experience of a deity as an inner expression of our Buddha-nature. It is this deity that begins to hold an experience of the guru in a very different way. The deity becomes known as *yidam,* or "heart bound," to signify a heart connection to the inner guru symbolized as the deity.

The relationship to the inner guru is therefore initiated by the outer guru—sometimes explicitly, sometimes not. One of the most important gifts of the outer guru is the reminder that the real guru is within us. As my own guru, Lama Thubten Yeshe, would constantly say, "We must learn to trust our inner knowledge wisdom," our inner guru. He always wanted his disciples to recognize that their independence and autonomy as individuals was dependent upon finding and trusting their inner experience. The inner guru is a deepening trust in our own knowledge, understanding, and truth. This may be the root of a sense of our own individual integrity, authority, and self-reliance. In the Tantras this inner wisdom is facilitated by the relationship to a deity. This deity, inseparable in essence from all the Buddhas and the outer guru's inner nature, is to be awakened within each individual as an experience of the sacred or the divine within. Our inner relationship acts as a kind of lodestone or touchstone that can be there as a reference when we need it.

In guru yoga, the essential practice is to be aware that the essence of the outer guru, our own innate nature, and that of all the Buddhas is inseparably unified as the deity. In the tantric tradition in particular, the guru's personification in aspect of a deity occurs in two ways. One is when a historical figure, such as Tsongkhapa, Milarepa, or Padma-sambhava, becomes deified, and the second is when deities such as Manjushri or Vajra Yogini are seen as personifications of the inner guru.

As the inner experience grows and deepens, we may be able gradually to let go of the emphasis and dependence upon the outer guru. We may also recognize that an inner quality of clarity and wisdom can inhabit a relatively human and fallible outer form. These two dimensions of our nature can coexist, both in the teacher and in ourselves. We may nevertheless still be unable to fully embody our true nature, as it is veiled by the obscurations of our fallible human conditioning.

When we see this duality we are able to more comfortably reconcile the paradox of someone being both primordially pure and yet shrouded in human fallibility. Once we understand this we can relate to the outer guru in a more real manner. He or she may indeed have profound insight into the nature of reality or have deep experience of his or her own deity nature and yet still show signs of human fallibility. This shift of understanding can be a great relief to students, as it opens up a far deeper potential for a real relationship to the outer guru, free of some of the confusing contradictions. When we can hold this paradox of the outer guru being relatively fallible yet a vehicle for something primordially pure, we can go beyond idealized illusions.

The outer guru leads us to recognize the nature of the inner guru. The inner guru is then like a gateway or threshold to the secret guru or the ultimate nature of the guru. The inner guru is still a relative manifestation of something that gradually awakens. It is the finger pointing at the moon. Increasingly, as we open to the innate clarity and spaciousness that lie within, we can shift from relative forms and appearances to an experience that is beyond such duality. We likewise gradually move from reliance upon relative truths and relative wisdom to something far deeper. This dimension of the guru is the direct experience of our mind's innate clarity. It arises as a quality of pure presence that opens to the empty nature of all reality. In the Tibetan tradition this innate wisdom of non-duality is known as *dharmakaya*.

This is sometimes seen as the ultimate truth or the ground of being out of which all appearances arise as the play of emptiness. Dharmakaya is a profound inner realization inseparable in nature from the omniscient mind of all the Buddhas. In this experience there is no person and no duality: it is the experience of totality.

If we perceive and understand the nature of this ultimate guru, we need no longer be held to any notions of the relative forms of the guru. The implication of this is far reaching. If we recognize that all phenomena arise as the play of emptiness, or dharmakaya, and see that this is the ultimate meaning of guru, then effectively any phenomenon can be seen as a manifestation of the guru. For example, we might relate to some object or event in such a way that we recognize its significance and meaning to us. If some thing or experience awakens deeper understanding and insights, we could see this as a manifestation of the guru. This does not mean the relative outer guru but the ultimate guru as emptiness and nonduality. The outer guru can also be seen as the ultimate or secret guru manifesting in relative appearance for our benefit, and this is so whether or not he or she has fully awakened

The outer guru has an important role as the catalyst for this inner experience to be awakened in the disciple. His or her human fallibility need not hinder this process. To understand how this relationship takes place, it is useful to consider a more psychological understanding of the guru-disciple relationship.

The Psychology of Transference

To understand the manner in which the guru-disciple relationship develops from a Western psychological perspective, it is useful to look at the notion of transference. This can lead to a greater depth of insight into the power of the relationship as well as the potential dangers contained within it.

In its simplest sense transference occurs when unconsciously a person endows another with an attribute that is actually projected from within him- or herself. Counter-transference occurs when unconsciously the other takes on this projection and lives it out, thereby projecting in return a counter-attribute. This process occurs in most relationships but becomes most problematic when the projections are particularly negative.

Jung recognized in his exploration of the psyche that what we are unconscious of, we tend to project into the world around us.[16] This, he saw, was particularly true of the inner masculine or feminine, which he named *Animus* and *Anima*, when they are projected into our relationships. The effect of this projection is well recognized, as we fall in love and become completely enthralled by the appearance of the loved one. This romantic projection endows the beloved with all manner of wonderful attributes that may lead us to feel he or she is the special "soul mate" we have longed for. We may suddenly feel that in this union we have become whole. That we gradually see through this projection to discover the "real" person is in part to our benefit because the relationship grows, but partly a cause of great conflict if, as a result, we experience dissatisfaction and disappointment.

This process of projection occurs in relation to other archetypal aspects of the psyche, and the guru is one such phenomenon. Jung recognized that each of us has as an inner archetypal aspect of what he named the Self, which can manifest in the form of the teacher or guide. This may be expressed in a number of forms. It may be symbolized, for example, as the old wise man,[17] the messiah-like youth, or the wise woman or crone. One may perhaps add to these an attribute that for many Westerners is Eastern and exotic. I do not think it is mere coincidence that so many Westerners think of the guru as coming from outside Western culture. The image of the Eastern teacher perhaps offers something that is free of the Western preconceptions and worldly profanities that blur or obscure the potential sacred nature of the symbol. When this archetypal need is constellated in a particular person, that person will carry a charge or numinosity for us because he or she embodies a deep inner quality.

When we encounter an individual who draws out our projection of the archetype of the guru, the effect can be dramatic. I recall the first occasion on which I met the lama who became one of my principal teachers. I was stunned by the experience. He entered the crowded meditation room and I could hardly see him. When we sat down and I was eventually able to see him seated upon a high throne surrounded by colorful Tibetan thangkas, I stared in awe. He looked utterly radiant and beautiful. I had been somewhat primed by the sense of excitement and anticipation in the hall; nevertheless, his presence in the room was strikingly palpable.

As we transfer the inner archetype onto the outer person we may see him or her as truly awesome. We may fall in love with the wonder and inspirational quality we are seeing. As we do so, that person begins to have a powerful effect on our psyche. They are helping to constellate this inner archetype in the conscious world, raising all of its power and potential from the depths of the unconscious.

We have unconsciously imbued the outer person with an inner, archetypal quality that carries an immense power and presence with it. The outer person may indeed have some extraordinary gifts, but if this projection did not occur, the effect would never be so dramatic. In the same way, a man may see a beautiful woman and not be greatly affected; however, should the projection of his Anima occur, she will hold a magnetic attraction for him. So too with the guru: if we see a lama and there is no transference, little happens. If, however, we do transfer the unconscious inner guru—and this is not something we can consciously determine—then the effect is very dramatic.

When we transfer an inner quality onto a person, there will be a number of consequences. We are giving that person a power over us as a result of the projection. In the case of the guru one could say, in Jungian terms, that we are giving the power of the Self away. This carries with it the potential for great insight and inspiration but also the potential for great danger. If we give this power over to someone else, that person will have a certain hold and influence over us that is hard to resist; we become enthralled or spellbound by the power of the archetype. This may mean we surrender personal autonomy for a while and are willing to follow everything that person asks of us. We may trust him or her implicitly because we are seeing our own inner reflection, and why should we question it? We may be completely unaware this is happening. Consequently, when people talk of their first encounters with the guru, they do so in highly romantic, idealized terms.

The romance begins and the disciple has found a longed-for sense of wholeness as reflected by the guru. This person may indeed have the capacity to truly empower the disciple with an experience that is in accordance with the projected ideal. The effect of this positive aspect of the transferred archetypal quality onto a teacher is a profound opening to multiple levels of insight and experience. The skillful teacher gradually enables the disciple to recognize this process and helps to awaken the inner experience. In time, the nature of the relationship can become more real and mature. There can then be a growing dialogue between teacher and disciple that is not so bound in the projected idealization. As this happens, the disciple can draw back some of the projection and become more autonomous and individual while retaining a profound, loving connection to the teacher. The romance may be long over, but deep respect and trust can remain.

THE HAZARDS OF TRANSFERENCE

Unfortunately, a teacher may not be entirely impeccable in how he or she carries the projection of the guru. The danger of having endowed another with so much power and authority is that they can use it as they wish. If they have integrity and are genuine, caring, and honest, they will carry it skillfully. The outer guru may be aware of the influence he has and honor the trust that is being placed in his hands. Conversely, the guru may be quite aware of his power and yet unconsciously use it for his own ends under the auspices of helping the disciple. Most often, problems arise when a teacher is unaware or even in denial of the subtle motivating forces that cause him to use this power for his own ends, thereby actually abusing his disciples.

This abuse occurs when a teacher begins to enjoy the seduction of students' projections. If there is any remnant of a narcissistic need in a teacher, even if it is totally unconscious, this can be problematic. This can particularly occur with male gurus who find that some inner need is satisfied by the projections of women disciples. The instance of teachers becoming sexually involved with women disciples is regrettably common. We may see this in the world of Western teachers who become involved with their students, but it is also not uncommon with Eastern teachers. There have been some well-known recent examples of Tibetan lamas who did not have clear boundaries around their own sexuality and failed to honor the trust involved in the guru-disciple relationship. In the case of one lama in London, women disciples were apparently selected for their attractiveness and told that a sexual relationship would be an aid to their practice as a kind of initiation or blessing. This would have been very seductive to some women, particularly if they were sexually abused as children, as they may have had no experience of healthy sexual boundaries.

This leads to another significant aspect of the process of projection. We may project the inner guru onto the teacher, but this will often carry with it much of our unresolved parental needs. It is very familiar to hear disciples speak of their guru as though he were the parent they always wished for. His or her unconditional love and kindness seems to be something many of us thirst for. When we project this need onto a teacher, the result can be extremely healing if the teacher treats the relationship with integrity. The boundaries in this kind of relationship are crucial, however, and disciples must trust that the teacher knows how to hold them.

Unfortunately, some teachers do not seem to have this understanding and do not recognize the damage that can occur when boundaries are unclear. When a teacher crosses that boundary and invites or seduces a student into a relationship that becomes sexual, this is a gross abuse of trust and of power.

When such an abuse of the trust and integrity within the guru-disciple relationship occurs, there can be a number of symptoms that reflect the confusion it creates. Perhaps foremost of these is the need to collude in an atmosphere of silence and denial. As in all abusive families, keeping the underlying abuse protected in a cloak of silence is the only way to cope. Public declaration is far too risky to those who are caught up in it, and for those around it is hard to cope with the shock of disillusionment. Some will choose to deny its reality, while others will feel horribly betrayed.

Another symptom of the dysfunctional nature of the community around a teacher is reflected in the vying for favor and specialness that goes on in relation to him or her. Who is the favored child? There can be an immense short-term sense of inflation in being the special student. Sadly, this is an extremely precarious position because usually someone else will take the special one's place, leaving the one who is demoted devastated and abandoned. In the example of the Tibetan lama I spoke of earlier, I knew two of his "consorts" quite well. In one, the pain of being brought into an intimate relationship and then held at a distance when another woman came along was terrible to see. This woman was like a child waiting for her father's favor to return, unable to move forward.

Whether the guru-disciple relationship has father-daughter undertones or carries projections of a divine lover, the abuse of trust is just as destructive. The trust and openness that a disciple may place in the teacher's hands is a precious and vulnerable thing and requires much care if it is not to be abused. When students project an inner need for the perfect parent onto a teacher, this may be very powerful, and if treated skillfully, can be very healing. I am aware of having done so with one of my own Tibetan teachers. His capacity to respond to this projection in a healthy way gave me a sense of approbation and understanding that I never received from my own father. What he did not do at any time, I felt, was to exploit the implicit trust I had in him, which was particularly important given that I had invested him with great power and authority over my life.

In many Tibetan prayers and teachings that describe the relationship to the guru, it is familiar to see the guru depicted as a loving parent. In the East this is a very comfortable notion, as the parent-child relationship is held to be very sacred. Here, we frequently have a considerable ambivalence towards parents. In part, we have often suffered the psychological consequences of damaging parents and dysfunctional families. There is also far more reaction to any notion of trust in another's authority. The Western belief in individuality requires that we break free of the constraints and influence of parents and become autonomous and self-reliant. Even so, very often our wounding around parental difficulties leaves us with a deep-seated need for the perfect parent. When this is unconscious, inevitably it is projected onto the relationship to the guru as the loving, longed-for, ideal parent.

The hazards of this projection are that we must be alert to the possibility that the guru will not carry this projection particularly well. He may not know how to handle the degree of intensity of emotion that will be part of the relationship. He may also find the depth of need some disciples express either frightening or irresistible. Often when disciples have a history of damaged parenting, the emotional need for parental love is so great it becomes unbearable. If this is not understood—and many Eastern teachers will not understand the depth of damage some suffer in the West—boundaries can become confused. Teachers may unwittingly cross those boundaries, unaware of the nature of abuse that that will bring to the surface. Someone transgressing those same boundaries under the guise of helping never heals abuse that occurred in childhood.

DISILLUSIONMENT

In projecting the guru and parent archetype, we are putting outside of ourselves the root of our own potential autonomy and individuation. It may be extremely beneficial to allow ourselves to be guided. There may be much we can learn from this outer relationship if it is nurtured with care and respect. Problems often arise, however, when the disciple begins to take back something of his own autonomy, or starts to question the validity of the outer guru's authority. A teacher who has nothing invested in holding on to his power and position of authority will be happy to see his disciples growing in independence and responsibility. The less secure or more traditional teacher, however, may find this unacceptable. In the Tibetan world, for example, there are those teachers who gladly give their students autonomy and let them go. There are also those who follow a hard line that demands that their authority be unquestioned. They become tyrannical and disempowering towards anyone who tries to challenge them or break away. Fear of recrimination and guilt at challenging an ultimate spiritual authority are powerful weapons to use against the student who does not toe the line.

In the East as in the West, orthodox religions have a powerful patriarchal basis to their authority structure. This permeates the very roots of the guru-disciple relationship in practice and has also become encoded in the heart of doctrine. Within the hierarchy, teachers have a clear knowledge of their place in the lineage of power, and usually any infringement upon this structure is treated with great disapproval and even hostility. The consequence of challenging this line of authority is extremely difficult to handle for those who do so. They will often be vilified and scapegoated. Once cast from the structure of power they will have no basis for their practice. I have known a number of Tibetan lamas who chose to challenge this religious order in their own tradition. They were not "bad" lamas; their only crime, so to speak, was to be unorthodox and not follow the party line. The consequent scandal made their lives very difficult. In the case of two lamas I have known, their decision to disrobe and get married left them alienated from their own culture for some time. Eventually, however, they found that living and teaching in the West was more fulfilling to them.

The patriarchal nature of most religions does not readily welcome dissent or individual autonomy. The transmission of empowerment is given only on the condition that one uphold the authority of the patriarch and not step outside of it. Unfortunately, this patriarchal disdain for autonomy can deeply affect the way Eastern teachers view their position. In their own world they know their place: they pay allegiance to their teachers, and their disciples must do the same to them. It has even been written into doctrine that to break this code is to commit a most heinous crime, with devastating consequences. In the Tibetan Buddhist tradition, for example, there is supposed to be a special hell where those who criticize the teacher will go. If there were such a hell, I suggest it is the hell of guilt, fear, and torment a disciple is likely to suffer for his challenge to the authority of the teacher; a hell inflicted often by the social hostility that can come from threatening the established order; a hell that is also born out of the pain and confusion of disillusionment and the need to break free of patriarchal dominance.

However, it is not just the patriarchal nature of the teacher's role in established religions that is at issue. Whenever the relationship between student and teacher goes wrong the result is very distressing, particularly for the student. It can wound very deeply. In my work as a therapist I have had the occasion to see a number of Buddhist practitioners whose relationship to significant teachers has broken down for a variety of reasons. In almost all cases, the main distress was a deep sense of betrayal, disappointment, and grief at the loss of trust. Often a key problem was that there was no one to talk to about the confusion and disillusionment they felt. This would inevitably alienate them from their peers, who would generally not receive criticism of the teacher with openness.

In the experience of those who spoke to me, the most important factor was that the teachers tended to refuse to acknowledge that they had made a mistake. It was as though the fault would be placed back into the lap of the student for failing to practice properly. In many cases, the recognition that the teacher was fallible was a painful but maturing process. Invariably, once the student had been able to speak about and digest some of the suffering the rift with the teacher had caused, there was a renewed sense of personal validity. As in the dysfunctional family in which a child is abused, the inability to speak is the cause of much pain.

Ultimately it would seem that the disillusionment that occurred in these relationships could actually be turned into something positive. This leads me to suggest that for some, disillusionment is a natural process on the path. It is the antidote to the illusions and idealized fantasies we create around gurus and their spiritual power and authority. Disillusionment causes us to bring back our projected ideals and begin to face reality. As we do so, we may for the first time begin to see more objectively the person we have idealized. This may be very painful at first. We may feel angry and even begin to demonize the previously idealized person. In time, this will enable a more balanced view to emerge.

Disillusionment may also be part of the shift in emphasis from outer references for acceptance, approval, and authority to an inner resource and a sense of inner authority. In order to genuinely shift responsibility onto the inner guru, drawing back the power of projection is important. The awakening of the inner guru is connected to a growing sense of inner authority. It also marks the beginning of trust in ourselves. This brings greater personal responsibility, with the compassionate understanding that sometimes we will make mistakes. Strength, self-reliance, and individuation can be born out of disillusionment as we grow to discriminate between inner wisdom and emotional confusion. One thing that my teacher Lama Thubten Yeshe would always emphasize was that the capacity to trust in ourselves and to discern truth from self-delusion was crucial. He also knew that this would not grow from his constantly solving our problems for us and telling us what to do. In this respect he was the loving parent who allowed his children to find their own way in life, knowing that sometimes they would make dreadful mistakes. He was able to empower his disciples with a real sense of their own inner wisdom. This led to a relationship that did not go through the same degree of disillusionment, perhaps because there was less illusion in the first place.

INDIVIDUATION AND THE GURU

Here we can look again at the question, Is the guru-disciple relationship fundamentally compatible with the principle of individuation? I believe it is, but this question does not have a simple answer, as it inevitably depends on the individuals involved. The Buddha, whose life is a good example of individuation, entered the guru-disciple relationship several times. He followed the teacher's instruction until he reached a certain point of development and then realized he needed to move on. Did he go through some sense of disillusionment, and was he disappointed that each teacher could take him only so far? Did he suffer a sense of uncertainty when he parted and moved on? These questions we cannot answer, but I would not be surprised if he did.

There are many examples of Tibetan lamas—though they are by no means in the majority—who in the course of their journey had to go off on their own and follow their individual path. They would retain a close connection and devotion to their teachers, but their path was a particularly individual one. My own retreat teacher Gen Jhampa Wangdu was a good example of a disciple faithful to his teacher but a very strong individual in his journey. He was never someone who would just follow the collective norm.

In the West today two ingredients make the situation for teachers and students very different. First, there is great emphasis on individuality, and second, there are few opportunities for practitioners to be supported in the way that monks are in Tibetan monasteries. Generally the individual must find his or her own livelihood and, largely, find his or her own way practically in the world. The guru may be of some help in this, but the guru's role is more appropriately in the spiritual domain. I have often been surprised at the inappropriateness of advice given by lamas regarding the worldly lives of their students, particularly concerning relationships.

Individuation has at its core the discovery of an inner relationship to a sense of personal integrity, authority, and wisdom. Individuation is a process of self-actualization. This is not incompatible with the need for guidance and spending periods of time with a teacher or mentor. However, we must learn to become self-sufficient and discover the inner reference to the guru as our inner resource. The fact that the outer guru can teach and guide us need not detract from retaining a sense of our own inner truth.

Problems arise if a teacher in any way damages the relationship to our inner truth. If we become over-dependent, or give over our personal responsibility to a guru, we are in danger of losing our way. If for any reason a teacher supports or cultivates this dependency, the situation may become counter to the heart of individuation. This is the kind of problem that arises in any spiritual culture that becomes fundamentalist or cult-like. In cults where devotees maintain the unquestioned supremacy of the cult leader's authority, the relationship of the devotees to the leader is regressive and essentially infantilizing.

This could potentially happen within Buddhist organizations, as much as in any other organized religion, if it is the disposition of both the teacher and disciples. In this respect it is easy to turn religious organizations into a collective reflection of personal pathology. When organizations become prescriptive and narrow in their definition of what is acceptable, those who remain true to these prescriptions are often venerated. Those who challenge these prescriptions can receive considerable subtle pressure to toe the line. In this way Buddhist communities can have a subtly undermining influence on the individual's need to individuate.

Leaving the culture created in such an organization is often very painful. Members may see such a departure as an affront to the principles they uphold and can become defensive and even aggressive. A common factor that seems to arise is that the defector will often be persuaded to stay. This may take the form of an attempt to give the impression it is the person's problem, not the organization's. In the case of one woman I know, this persuasion was gradually undermining her own sense of her truth. She was losing the capacity to trust her own judgment about what she needed or believed to be true. Her need to leave was fundamentally a healthy movement towards individuation—something the organization she was caught in was not readily able to appreciate.

The guru-disciple relationship does not need to be anti-individuation unless some unconscious pathology causes it to be. A teacher with integrity, who genuinely has disciples' interests at heart, will not restrict the individual's journey. Possibly the most valuable asset on the journey, as we struggle to find our individual way, is someone who can be there as a reference. We do not need to relinquish our own integrity and personal responsibility in the relationship to the guru. In many ways this will require the willingness to cultivate a more straightforward and honest relationship, one that can allow for challenges in both directions. As the Dalai Lama said, we spoil our teachers with too much deference.

THE CHANGING ROLES OF THE TEACHER

We have much to learn as Westerners about how we view and relate to spiritual teachers. We may choose to follow the Eastern way with teachers, but this can be thoroughly misleading, as our cultural and psychological differences are so marked. With teachers who come from the East, we may have no choice but to follow their expectation of how students should respond. This may lead to much confusion and misunderstanding, and only a few may readily settle into the relationship. Westerners may challenge the approach of the Eastern teacher, and some may be willing to change; for others, such challenges may be entirely inappropriate.

There is much to suggest that teachers at this present time must be able to bridge Eastern tradition and our Western psychological and cultural nature. Some Eastern teachers find this relatively easy to do, while others do not. What often makes this bridging possible is a greater degree of honesty, openness, and authenticity about personal experience. In the East the guru seldom expresses personal feelings or difficulties. The guru is kept at a distance that maintains a sense of mystique. His or her private inner world is totally out of reach. This may in part arise from the disposition of Eastern people to not speak as we do of their inner experiences. The effect, however, is often to place gurus in an inaccessible and remote place where their humanity is not available to scrutiny. They will not often welcome personal inquiry and will also tend to cloak their fallibility in a shroud of privilege.

One consequence of this may be, as H. H. the Dalai Lama once said in Dharamsala many years ago, that ultimately it will be Westerners who bring the Dharma to the West. With Western teachers, however, hiding behind the traditional mystique of the guru is seldom healthy. In the West the teacher needs to be more real than this.

To counter the tendency to idealize the guru a straightforward and honest relationship, without deceptions and illusions, is required. It may be tempting for Western teachers to also indulge in people's idealizations, but ultimately this leads to a deception that serves no one. To be able to remain real and honest with regard to human fallibility is the best way to keep the fantasizing idealism at bay. So long as students are thirsty for spiritual validation and to have people they can turn into icons, both teachers and students are open to deception. Icons may have some value, but we must be able to ground our spirituality in genuine experience that is not clouded by romanticized illusion.

There are two contexts in which the teacher-student relationship evolves. One context is the formal teaching setting, and the other is in one-to-one relationship. Within the group setting, where teachers may remain somewhat distant, the potential to mystify and idealize is relatively easy. It can often be in the one-to-one setting that the teacher-student relationship becomes problematic. This is the setting in which the potential for boundaries to become confused is most evident. Teachers who make sexual advances upon students usually do so in this setting. Equally, this is the place where teachers can resort to a secure role of the authority figure who is still distant.

It is within this one-to-one context that a teacher may learn from the world of counseling and psychotherapy. A counselor or psychotherapist learns to skillfully respond to clients in a way that is principally "-person-centered." The emphasis is upon the client's psychological process and well-being, and the counselor or therapist keeps his or her own needs outside the relationship. This is often in stark contrast to the disposition of teachers in the one-to-one setting, who tend to place their own authority and knowledge of the doctrine as central. The stu-

dent comes to ask for guidance and advice. The teacher offers his or
her experience and knowledge.

Having spoken to many people who have experienced problems in
their relationship to teachers, I have found that it is often because the
teacher stays in the place of authority and then gets it wrong. They
may speak with great authority, telling the student what to do, but do
not really respond or listen to their actual psychological needs. This is
to say, it is not person-centered; it is authority-centered. I do not think
we should assume that our teachers know how to counsel us or, indeed,
how to guide us, and there may be great benefit in teachers learning to
do so, even from their students.

My experience as a workshop facilitator and psychotherapist leads
me to believe that there is a place where the teacher's one-to-one role
can benefit from more of a counseling style. This would shift the
emphasis, placing the student's process as central. The teacher might
then listen more to what the student is experiencing and actually elicit
what the student needs for him- or herself rather than giving advice.
Very often my own lama, Lama Thubten Yeshe, would respond with,
"What do *you* think?" whenever I asked him questions. It was as though
he recognized that when I came to my own understanding of something, it helped me to discover my own inner resource of insight. This
was very empowering.

I believe there is a great deal more that needs to be explored before
the role of the teacher/mentor/counselor is fully appreciated in the
West. Gone are the days when a teacher can maintain a mystification
through distance. There may also be some for whom the role of
teacher becomes a kind of protection, when more personal relationships expose their actual inability to relate authentically. There is a term
in Tibetan, *gegen,* which is often translated as "spiritual friend" and
refers to an individual who, as an experienced practitioner, becomes a
guide or companion on the path. This role may include some aspect of
a teacher, as one who imparts specific knowledge and instruction into
the spiritual practices of the individual. The primary ingredient in this
process, however, is that the *gegen* is there to respond specifically as a

support for the individual needs of the practitioner in his or her personal journey.

Gen Jhampa Wangdu died in 1984, but while he was alive he became one of the most important figures of my spiritual life. In many ways he was as important as Lama Thubten Yeshe, my root teacher, and some of the lamas from whom I received empowerments and formal teachings. He was my friend, my guide, my counselor, and an important model of someone attempting to live the life of a Buddhist practitioner while being thoroughly human and authentic. He was never grand and distant despite his profound realization and considerable reputation as a meditator. Compassionate, humble, and down to earth to the last days of his life, he was an inspiration to me.

Recently I was fortunate to meet a lama in his fifties who has lived in the West for the past twenty-five years or so. Because he is a *tulku*, or an incarnate lama, within his own culture there is inevitably great formality around him. In the West he has grown to live as a Westerner in a family. It was refreshing to discover a man who, as a lama, was willing to talk about his experiences, and not just in a somewhat monitored Dharma language. He is genuine and authentic in his openness about himself, his joys, and his struggles. His way of being is a true validation of how I have always felt Dharma teachers can be in the West.

Individuation or Institution? 17

A s the journey of individuation continues, a crucial question must be addressed. What becomes of our relationship to the institutions within which we learn our Buddhist principles and practice? Is there a fundamental conflict between our need to individuate and our relationship to institutions and organizations? The development of Buddhism in the West increasingly reveals a division between those who wish to practice within an organization and those who attempt to follow a more individual journey. Many people I have met through workshops, meditation courses, and therapy express a now familiar question: is it possible to develop a Buddhist practice without taking on the culture, personality, and style of one of numerous organizations? This dilemma seems to reflect a need to retain a sense of spiritual individuality while learning a system of practice. It echoes a deeper dichotomy: that individuality, creativity, and the development of organized religion do not always sit comfortably together.

To make sense of this dichotomy it can be useful to return to the archetypal paradigm of Puer and Senex spoken of earlier. This paradigm can affect both men and women, and wherever one polarity appears, somewhere its opposite will live as a counterpoise.

As we have seen, the archetype of the Puer is one of the most potent influences on the expression of spiritual aspiration. The spirit of the Puer is associated with divine inspiration and optimism, visions, ideals, creative ideas, and dreams. Puer brings us into contact with the transpersonal, numinous side of our nature and can seem like a spark of light that flashes into the world through its visions. Prophets, creative geniuses, and visionaries throughout history have almost certainly been influenced by this archetype. They have often been the visionaries who have been the originators of what have subsequently become religions and institutions.

The visionary inspiration of the Puer finds its polar opposite in the earthy pragmatism of the Senex. The process under which the ideas, visions, and images of Puer begin to crystallize or solidify into form is the realm of Senex. The craftsman (or woman) who has gradually mastered the capacity to bring his creative ideas into reality is the most fundamental expression of Senex. Senex is the archetype of practical structures and systems, which begin to shape and order the world around and within us.

Senex in our society is particularly expressed through systems, laws, and institutions that attempt to shape and organize society. Senex seeks to create and maintain organizations and systems that give a stable, ordered basis for control and authority in matters such as administration and education. In the domain of religion, Senex manifests in the creation of ordered spiritual systems and in the organizations that are developed around them. Even the Buddhist tradition has become organized and structured under the aegis of Senex.

Through Senex we also enter the rigors of spiritual discipline. This principle is at work in the boundaries and limits of the apprentice or novice studying under a master. It brings us into relationship with the demands of commitment and the need to engage in work and endure the hardships of gradual mastery of ourselves into the art, craft, or spiritual practice we embark upon. Senex teaches us by experience. It is an aspect of fathering that earths us in a realism that cannot ultimately be ignored.

The vision, inspiration, and idealism of the Puer archetype and the order and realism of the Senex archetype bring us to a significant and uncomfortable dichotomy. Although Puer and Senex do not easily live alongside each other, to develop they need each other. In fact, they can be seen as two polarities of the same archetypal principle.[18] Puer's vision is brought into reality through the vehicle of Senex, though the two are often unconscious and at odds with each other. Behind the Puer disposition one can often hear a shadowy Senex that is morally rigid, dogmatic, judgmental, and authoritarian. The struggle between the two, however, is an attempt to reconcile the inevitability that they are part of the same archetypal dilemma. This dilemma is how to bring creative ideas into reality or spirituality into practical, earthly life— spirit into matter. It is also an expression of the potential conflict between spiritual individuality and institutional form.

The Puer/Senex archetype is constantly at play in the development of spiritual organizations. Often, as in the case of Buddhism, the seeds of a tradition emerge in the insight of an individual who experiences a new spiritual vision. The Buddha's spiritual insight was like a creative spark initiating what gradually developed into a system and tradition that grounded it in the realm of Senex. Many of the lineages of Tibetan Buddhism, especially within the Tantras, originated with some-one whose personal spiritual insight or vision inspired a new lineage of practice. In time, the initial vision became shaped into an intricate sys-tem of instructions and techniques for practice.

The gradual shift from Puer's initiating vision towards the structure and system of Senex is natural, archetypal, and present in all creative processes. It has resulted in a great diversity of approaches within Bud-dhism, many of which are still living traditions and lineages, preserved and passed on from teacher to disciple. To be able to study and prac-tice within the structure and discipline of one of these traditions can be a profound and vital part of the spiritual journey. At a certain point on the path it may be important to commit to a process of transfor-mation that needs structure, discipline, and boundaries. A spiritual organization may offer this kind of environment until an individual is able to provide it in him- or herself.

The influence of the Senex archetype over the maintenance of sys-tems and organizations unfortunately has a dark, unconscious Shadow. At its most shadowy, Senex becomes rigid, dogmatic, and ruthless, tending to disenfranchise and control any who question its authority. When Senex forms and structures begin to ossify, they become dry and stale, closed to the potential for change and flexibility. In religious organizations and systems this leads to doctrinal rigidity and dogmatism and an increasing tendency to control and constrict disciples. When organizations become increasingly patriarchal and authoritarian, they are seldom able to recognize the degree to which they disempower and deny individual freedom of self-expression. When a system or form becomes too solid, it can gradually destroy the essential vision that gives it life and inspiration.

While the establishment of orthodoxy comes under the aegis of Senex, reformation and regeneration come under the aegis of Puer. Individual creative expression also comes into being through the Puer archetype, and in an organization, this can often threaten established order. Teachers may resist questioning or changing established orthodox practices and thereby unconsciously prevent students from developing their own experience and autonomy. Paradoxically, the vision that originated most spiritual traditions was often an individual's creative experience, and yet organized, established religion can become resistant to that same creative process. Those who choose to follow their own inner truth can often find themselves in conflict with a tradition that is trying to preserve the authority of a lineage.

As Buddhism becomes integrated in the West, we must consider that Westerners have grown up in a culture that emphasizes individuality and creative innovation. Established religion does not comfortably accept personal innovation. In Tibetan Buddhism, for example, great emphasis is placed upon retaining the purity of the traditional teachings, and innovation is often frowned upon. Some Eastern teachers and their Western disciples are extremely protective of the sanctity of tradition, which may be vital in preserving the purity of a system. It may not, however, allow objective assessment of its effectiveness or relevance, particularly for Westerners. Fear of questioning or evaluating a religion's principles, however, leads to dogmatism and can be as present in Buddhism as in any other religion. Those who question the tradition may then be cast as heretics, even though the meaning of the term *heretic* is literally "one who makes a choice." Fortunately, Buddhism has a history of profound developments arising from those cast as heretics.

How, therefore, do we balance the necessity of systematic Buddhist teachings and organizations with the growing recognition that Westerners are extremely individualistic in their spiritual needs? If we are to be true to our inner spiritual potential in a creative way, how compatible is this with organizations that have formulated ways in which spirituality is to be expressed?

Developing a spiritual practice within an organization can give one an important foundation of understanding. To an "apprentice" it can provide a structured, disciplined, and contained environment in which to learn and practice. To a member of a spiritual community or Sangha, such an organization is often the most supportive environment to practice in, among people holding shared values. However, as we become more in touch with the nature of our own spiritual journey, we sometimes find that it begins to deviate from or become incompatible with the organization we have grown up in. When this happens, it can give rise to feelings of conflict, guilt, and fear. When people find that their personal journey begins to conflict with the authority of a teacher or the prescriptions of an organization and they then try to leave, they may find themselves subject to pressure and even hostility from those who seek to maintain the security of their system. I recall attending a conference of members of various Buddhist organizations in the UK and a senior member of a well-known Western Buddhist organization saying that they were concerned that some people were leaving the organization. He was wondering what they should do to resolve the problem. My response at the time was to ask why this was a problem, when perhaps the most beneficial thing a person may need to do is to leave in order to follow their spiritual path, to grow and move forward. Who are we to judge?

For some, leaving the security of systems and organizations and going out into the world alone is a time of being true to an inner wisdom, an inner guru. The Buddha remained true to an inner voice and repeatedly moved on to pursue his journey alone. Historically, most of the great teachers were individuals who discovered their own inner experience and then expressed it in a fresh, creative way. Often these individuals found it necessary to free themselves of the constraints of an organized system. Many of the mahasiddhas, for example, were expelled from their monasteries for their nonconformity. Even Shantideva, the revered eighth-century composer of the *Guide to the Bodhisattva's Way of Life,* was expelled from Nalanda for his unorthodox practice.

This more individual journey, however, is no easy task, as there are often no clear maps of how the path unfolds. It will demand a combination of sustained vision and insight grounded in a pragmatic, self-disciplined life-style that brings together the polarities of Puer and Senex. This path outside the context of spiritual organizations is not something everyone wishes to follow; however, in our Western culture, there is sometimes no choice. Considerable self-determination is required to sustain practice alone in a world that has little or no understanding of what we are trying to do. This self-determination can easily fade to nothing. The support of a spiritual community or Sangha is then very important in a journey that is challenging and hard to maintain.

Increasingly, however, there is a shift towards "Buddhist individuation" both in those who remain within an organization and those who may have passed through a tradition and then pursued their own journey. This creates a new kind of spiritual community of individuals whose meeting point is that they respect each other's individual journey and do not cling to prescriptions or judgments concerning how to practice. Our spiritual journey is personal and individual, whether we are within or outside of traditions and institutions. As we awaken our innate Buddha potential, it is for each of us to take responsibility for how this may be expressed creatively in the world for the welfare of others.

PART III

The Path of Individuation

✦ ✦ ─────────────────────────────────────

INTRODUCTION

ALTHOUGH THE TERM *individuation* does not appear in Buddhism, it describes an important aspect of the psychological journey that is charted by Western psychology. "Individuation," Jung writes, "is an expression of that biological process—simple or complicated, as the case may be—by which every living thing becomes what it is destined to become from the beginning."[1] One can see the journey of individuation as an inner psychological process that is not specifically addressed in Buddhist psychology yet inevitably runs beneath the traditional ideas of a "graduated path," or path of gradual awakening.

As a journey of self-actualization, the gradual awakening of our inner experience of wholeness has many correspondences within the bodhisattva's path. It is therefore in relation to the path of the bodhisattva that I wish to focus on the intention to individuate within Buddhist life. The urge to individuate is as powerful within us as many other impulses. It is an archetypal intent that may be experienced as irresistible. It may require that the journey of individuation is made more conscious, but the impulse will still be an expression of something fundamental in our nature.

Jung recognized that there is a natural process of individuation that emerges as we pass through our lives. Whether we are conscious of it or not, there is a natural unfolding of our innate capacity to grow and mature through the phases and stages of life. One could, however, distinguish between this natural individuation and an individuation process consciously lived and actively participated in. To then understand how Buddhist practice may relate to and support this conscious process is important. It can enable us to recognize where we might place ourselves in relation to the Buddhist path at different phases in our lives. It may also enable us to recognize what the hazards can be in our understanding and integration of Buddhist practice.

The psychological journey, as we have seen, begins with the call to awaken. This leads to a growing urge to cross a threshold of emergence into the journey, the path of trials. We then take up the challenge of facing the demons and dragons that are our fallibility, our weaknesses, and our Shadow. As we go forward on this journey, we are able to take up the further challenges that cultivate the qualities we may need as the bodhisattva's path unfolds. In particular, we must face the challenge of going beyond the limitations of the ego and our self-identity. This process leads us directly to the experience of death and descent, during which these limiting self-beliefs, attitudes, and conceptions are stripped away. Only once we have learned the lesson of giving up, of surrender, can we enter the sacred place of our innate clear nature. Our Buddha potential is always present, but the ego will never see itself crowned king.[2]

Once we pass through the veil of the illusions of reality, we can let go of the aspects of our limited nature that prevent awakening. Being fully open, we can then return to the world in a way that truly embodies our spirituality in a meaningful participation in life. We cross yet another threshold, this time one that brings us back into relationship with the challenges of everyday life. The return asks of us that we truly embody our spirituality rather than remain in some disconnected, detached space that does not deal with the world and others' lives.

The journey of individuation continues into old age if we are fortunate enough to experience it. Even through this part of the journey there are lessons to learn as we inexorably move towards our final days. Death, from one perspective, need not be an ending but rather a recognition of the continual unfolding of the journey. While some

Buddhists do not consider the notion of reincarnation as valid or useful, there are others who hold it to be a fundamental element of Buddhist psychology. The process of death and rebirth may be something we cannot directly know; nevertheless, it will be another rite of passage we must face either literally or psychologically as we continue on our journey.

A Meaningful Task 18

IN THE PSYCHOTHERAPY SETTING I have heard many people describe a painful sense that they cannot find what they want to do in life. It is usually accompanied by feelings of pointlessness or chronic frustration. This disturbing state seems particularly pronounced at certain phases in life, such as the late twenties and early thirties. It may equally emerge in mid-life—late thirties, early forties—when what a person has undertaken feels hollow or fruitless or loses meaning. For some, there may be a deep-rooted feeling that there is some task they are here to do but which they do not yet feel they have found. Where this restless, disquieting feeling emerges from may be a mystery, but it would seem to be an aspect of the psyche that cannot be ignored.

A clear example of this arose in a woman client I saw who, from an early age, had learned to be responsible. This began in relation to a younger brother and was amplified when she was eleven, when her mother had another child. As she grew up she became a dutiful daughter and a conscientious student, eventually training to become a medical doctor. In her thirties she felt unfulfilled by this profession and would describe a deep sense of melancholy and sadness that centered around never having really listened to what she needed for herself. She had worked hard and become something her parents valued, but she still felt deeply dissatisfied. It was apparent the she was not "following her bliss," to use Joseph Campbell's expression, and needed to allow herself to find a natural expression of who she was that was not caught up in the pattern of her childhood. She felt she needed to get out of the medical world and find something that would free a sense of joy and inspiration that was entirely lacking in the way she had driven herself to study and work. Letting go of the prescriptions that had shaped her life, however, was not going to be easy.

Our yearning for something that engages and inspires us can take time to satisfy. We may take on tasks and responsibilities that have arisen from outer influences and expectations that do not awaken our inspiration and passion. For a life task to truly engage us, it needs a number of ingredients that enable it to be transformational. Without them, we may find it difficult to put ourselves wholly into the process. It needs to be something that feels "right" so that we can commit ourselves to it. This will give our life the vitality and focus that is often missing. It needs to hold us in a process that helps ground our ideals and visions in a meaningful way. It can then bring a sense of joy and creative inspiration that recognizes the intrinsic value of our life.

Possibly the most important aspect of our life that needs to have these attributes is our work. When it does, we can feel the potential for transformation in what we do. Work is particularly important in the life of someone with spiritual aspirations and, as I have said in Chapter 10, it would be no surprise for the Puer or Puella type to be told that the "cure" for their urge to flight is work. It may not be a welcome observation but is one that is hard to avoid. The nature of this work, however, may be interpreted in a variety of ways.

The Great Work, or *magnum opus,*[3] of the alchemical tradition referred to the alchemist's task of transformation that required total dedication and great perseverance to accomplish. While the popular notion considered the alchemist to be seeking the means to transform base material into gold, the true goal of alchemical work was a transformation of the person. Alchemists may not have used psychological language to describe their experiences, but as Jung pointed out, what they were engaged in was a psychological process.[4] The key ingredient of this process of transformation requires placing oneself entirely in the alchemical vessel under the guidance of a master.

In the twelfth and thirteenth centuries, the various Grail legends translated the task into the quest.[5] The quest required total dedication to the journey and a willingness to face the challenges involved. One can see in the Grail legend that Parzival was dimly aware of his quest for the Grail castle and the sacred Grail.[6] In the process of this journey, he was to encounter the trials and tests that would mature him psychologically. Once again, even though the psychological language we are familiar with today was not used, the intention was personal transformation.

In many folk tales, the heroic quest is the search for some sacred or special object that is needed to heal the problem at home. In these tales there is a consistent theme. The home has become troubled; often the king is dying or the kingdom has become barren. The insight that a particular object will heal this malaise may come through a vision or be given by a special being or guide. In "The Firebird," for example, the hero, the youngest son, goes in search of this magical bird and eventually, after many challenges, returns and becomes the new king.[7]

In the Jungian world, folk tales have been studied extensively to unravel their meaning. The king could be seen as the embodiment of a psychological state that has become sick and barren. He represents the ego structure that, as the dominant element in our conscious life, can become unhealthy and needs to be healed, or indeed to die. The youngest son, or sometimes daughter, may be seen as the naïve, innocent, idealistic spirit of renewal that can emerge and respond to the call. This is the Puer or Puella who can become the savior in the family crisis. It is not uncommon for one of the children in a family to be the one who goes in search of a healing solution to the dysfunctional family. In the wounded healer, the wound coexists with the heroic desire to find a resolution to this inherited malaise.

At certain times in our lives, the challenge to take up the task or quest is an important rite of passage to face. If we cannot find the inner resources and courage to take up this challenge, it may lead to an inability to truly engage in life. Sadly, there are those who, instead of engaging in the task, escape into unreal dreams, drug use, or ungrounded spiritual idealism, where little resolution is found.

However we interpret the notion of the task, whether as work or quest, it is in part the search for healing and wholeness. This may be, in particular, healing the inherited family dysfunction. The task or quest must be embodied on the material plane, not just remain some inner imagining. Work must be engaged in the world. Little comes from dreaming the journey and imagining the task or work but not doing it. In this respect, there is an important relationship between the task or work and what is spoken of in the Buddhist world as practice.

The Tibetan word for practice is *laklen,* meaning to take to hand or, perhaps, to get a grip of something. The hands could be seen as symbolizing the means whereby we engage in the task and the vehicle through which we craft ourselves. As Hillman observes in *Puer Papers,* the Puer struggle with the material world may also be reflected physically in the form of eczema and dermatitis, particularly of the hands and feet.[8] The hands and feet are the part of ourselves that makes contact with the world. In my work as a psychotherapist I am surprised at the number of Puer-/Puella-oriented clients who do suffer from eczema of the hands. What *laklen* implies is that to integrate the philosophy of Buddhism, we need to embark on a process of work that turns theory into experience.

In the Tibetan tradition there are many examples of tantric practitioners whose primary practice was to carry out incredibly arduous tasks for their teachers in order to clear the ground for spiritual realization. Perhaps the most famous was the Tibetan yogi Milarepa, who was repeatedly asked by Marpa, his teacher, to build and then rebuild towers of stone. He was required to shift this stone on his back across the mountainside time and time again, suffering terrible sores and nearly fatal exhaustion. He took on the task with courage and devotion to his teacher, eventually attaining buddhahood in one lifetime.

My own teacher, Lama Thubten Yeshe, was always keen for his students to work as a major part of their practice. It was this intention that brought many of us to begin the process of building Dharma centers as a means of working our passage, so to speak. I lived in a Dharma center for nearly four years, and most of my time was spent helping restore the building. I became the community electrician and was responsible for re-wiring a huge priory. It was challenging and hard work, but throughout this time, I felt I was devoting my capacity for work to something truly worthwhile.

Our spiritual yearning is for healing and wholeness. The work, service, or creative task we embark upon is often inspired or initiated by a vision of wholeness. The need to then actively engage in the task is vital if we are to ground vision in reality. Very often the point of engagement is the greatest challenge. This is the first dragon that must be slain. Making a decision and committing to the task or journey is hard but necessary. For the Puer type this can be particularly daunting in that it raises fears about being trapped in something that cannot be gotten out of. It brings up the fear that work will become mundane and boring, and also the fear that one may fail or not be good enough or adequate for the task. Being tested and made accountable for our capacity to engage in the world is not easy. Taking responsibility for our actions and their effects faces us with the realization that we create the reality we live within. Whether we live a chaotic, unhappy mess or a rich, joyous, and fulfilled life is up to us.

In order to meet the difficulties our life throws at us as a result of our karma, we need a heroic attitude. To see the problems of our life as something we can grow from and overcome gives confidence. If we habitually run away from hardships and obstacles and fail to face them, we will increase the tendency. Later in life, particularly drastic circumstances are then required to counter the habit. The older we get, the more ingrained the disposition becomes. I have seen this in one man in particular who had spent most of his life running away emotionally. He had a lot of interest in Buddhism and would read a great deal. Whenever he was offered an opportunity to turn his habit around and really begin to take up the challenge of both work and Buddhist practice, he could not face his fear. He could not overcome his habit and continued to avoid taking up the opportunity his life gave him. One of the ways that this avoidance was possible was through addiction to alcohol and drugs as a means of anesthetizing his pain.

The heroic attitude and willingness to take up the challenge of the work is at the heart of the disposition that overcomes the temptation to avoid and become unconscious. The hero is a symbol of the courageous ego and the emergence of a particular attitude in consciousness. The hero will cross the wasteland alone, face the monsters of his own psyche, and retrieve the treasure hard to attain.

We may doubt the validity of this heroic metaphor in our path. Why would we continue to seek heroic challenges to overcome? To establish the ego? Isn't this counter to the very root of what Buddhist thought tells us? This may seem so, but we must also recognize the innate need for the ego to develop before we can discover its true nature and thereby go beyond it. Those who have no stable identity and who have a poorly developed ego suffer the consequences. When the ego fails in its function, we will struggle with some key elements in our life. In its normal function, it acts as the focus of our relative, conscious world. Standing on the threshold of consciousness, it acts as the guardian at the gateway to the unconscious and is the creator of boundaries. It is needed to give a capacity of self-assertion and acts as the centralizing focus of will. Without these capacities, psychologically we would be extremely handicapped in the world. We would be incapable of expressing boundaries and holding a clear sense of form and direction. We need this capacity, not as some rigid dogmatic defensiveness or obsessive willfulness, but as the capacity to engage.

In the *Guide to the Bodhisattva's Way of Life*, Shantideva provides an image of heroic endurance that stands clear and firm in its will to engage in the path:[9]

> Therefore, with a steady mind,
> I shall overcome all falls,
> For if I am defeated by a fall,
> My wish to vanquish the three realms will become a joke.
>
> I will conquer everything
> And nothing at all shall conquer me!

I, a child of the lion-like Conqueror,
Should remain self-confident in this way.

Thus in order to complete this task,
I shall venture into it
Just as an elephant tormented by the mid-day sun
Plunges into a cool, refreshing lake.

Reading Shantideva's verses, it is not hard to recognize that he is asserting a strong, confident, and courageous sense of self-identity. He has no tolerance of ego indulgence or ego-grasping. He is not asserting that the ego is to be seen as the goal. A strong sense of self-identity is certainly implicitly necessary as the vehicle for the bodhisattva's strength of mind. When we fail to grasp this fact, we can easily remain in a somewhat formless, wishy-washy state, lacking will, direction, and boundaries and with little capacity to focus. We may lack the strength to truly take up the challenge of the path and overcome its obstacles. The path is not for the weak-hearted.

On one level, the task we must commit ourselves to is the work of practice. It is noticeable how many people are interested in Buddhist philosophy who value the effects of meditation but cannot commit themselves to the depth of practice often advocated by teachers. Often we want to keep it light and not make things too serious or demanding. So long as we are allowed to do a bit here and a bit there, we are happy. If someone were to suggest that we need to commit ourselves to practice and just do it day after day, enduring the dissatisfaction and boredom, we would shy away.

Have we lost our capacity to practice and work at it? Do we expect results and realizations without effort? Some would say we are enlightened already but don't recognize it. Those teachers who glibly say there is no need to practice, just to recognize your enlightened nature, which is present now, often fail to declare how long it took to get where they are.

The spiritual quest is work or, as Robert Bly put it, "emptying the lake bucket by bucket."[10] This needs to be engaged in with care and sensitivity, but there is no substitute for effort. Our effort depends upon our willingness to truly engage in the task with devotion, love, and dedication. This motivation requires one of two things: either a powerful inspirational yearning or a strong pain. Perhaps what made Milarepa, the Tibetan yogi, such a powerful practitioner was the strength of his pain and regret at seeing what he had done in killing thirty-five of his relatives. It is often said that those who have suffered most or who have the greatest problems work hardest to overcome them. I recall a friend once telling me how his life as a soldier in the Israeli army had changed his life completely. He could not bear the fact of having killed other men. He eventually became a deeply committed Buddhist monk. In my own life, I cannot ignore the fact that overcoming anxiety was one of the greatest motivators of my journey.

Those whose lives are relatively easy and secure often have little motivation unless some other inner distress drives them. Pain motivates us when an inner vision does not. Without some sort of vision, however, we will not have the faith and confidence that something can be different. If we do not believe we can be healthy, sickness can be very hard to bear. The Buddha, in his four excursions from the palace as a youth, was confronted with three images of pain, but his final vision was of the mendicant, serene and untroubled. This vision gave him the inspiration to go out and face what had to be faced.

The path of the bodhisattva as a journey of individuation is one that requires a deep sense of commitment, which arises from the two sources of pain and great vision. Having a deep understanding of personal pain leads to an empathy with and compassion for the pain of others. This empathy is vital in giving us the willingness to seek a solution and work for the welfare of others who suffer just as we do. A vision of wholeness shows us the potential each of us could awaken were we given the right conditions and support. When we understand and feel these two deeply in ourselves, we will be ready to take the step of truly embarking upon the task, the work of transformation.

I T IS NOT UNCOMMON for people, during mid-life, to begin to question the place in which they find themselves. A level of maturation is achieved when we have the capacity to commit to and take responsibility for our lives and work over a long period to bring our visions to practical reality. Taking up the challenge of the path through work can enable us to accomplish many things in a practical and creative way. At a certain point in that process, however, we may begin to feel that the original vision and inspiration has become obscured in the demands of the task. In mid-life, it is not uncommon for people to suddenly ask themselves why they are doing what they have devoted themselves to. This question may arise suddenly or it may creep up on us slowly. When it comes, the effect is often very disturbing.

For those whose lives have been preoccupied with the responsibilities and demands of family or work, this questioning often brings a crisis of meaning. I know a businessman whose work, which he pursued for many years, demanded full involvement and dedication. He was also supporting a family in the process. In mid-life, he encountered a typical jolt when he realized that he had lost touch with his wife, his own creativity, and his sense of what he valued about his life. His crisis of meaning took him into the world of Buddhist studies to rekindle of a sense of direction and value.

The crisis will be of a different nature when we consider someone whose life has been preoccupied with so-called spiritual matters. A spiritual way of life can become equally stagnant and bring about a period of painful self-searching. In my own journey, much of my early

Green Tara

life was devoted to spiritual practice. I was fortunate enough to have the motivation and the opportunity to spend time studying Buddhist psychology and then to enter into a prolonged period of retreat in the East. For me, a crisis occurred when I eventually returned to the West and realized I had to find a way of earning a living and supporting myself in the world. This culture shock brought me sharply down to earth as I began to see that I was virtually unemployable. How was I going to survive? Mine was a crisis of meaning, but in a way that was the opposite of the crises of those who had worked and had families. I had already fulfilled a desire to go off in search of spiritual meaning; my challenge, therefore, was to achieve a practical embodiment of my spirituality in the world.

For some, the crisis arises through the loss or lack of spiritual vision and meaning. For others, the crisis can be the lack of a grounded embodiment of spirituality in the practical necessities of life and work. Whichever direction we are moving toward, the challenge can be very hard to resolve.

It is not uncommon during retreats for people to express how difficult they find it to integrate their spiritual practice into their lives. There is often a sense in this question of how to integrate that there is a split between spiritual aspiration and vision and the demands of material life. Perhaps this can be seen as a spirit versus matter split or, indeed, as the struggle between Puer visions and inspiration and the materializing principle of Senex. If we were to reflect upon this question in terms of the Puer/ Senex paradigm, we could say that it is fundamentally unhealthy for one polarity to be abandoned for the sake of the other. These two faces of the archetype of spiritual and creative life must be brought into healthy resolution.

The consequences of losing sight of, denying, or suppressing the visionary, inspirational side of our nature can be very disturbing. We may experience a lack of vision and a deadening of the aspect of ourselves that needs to be free to create and inspire. Most of us have felt what it is like when we have become so bound up with the material demands of life that there is no vision and inspiration. We can feel dead and stuck, without a real sense of why we are grinding away just to pay the bills and maintain the upkeep of the home. Work can then become a prison.

One of the unfortunate consequences of an overburdened and responsible work life can be a profound loss of meaning and vision. One might see this as the deadening of the Puer archetype. This may precipitate a period of depression and lack of vitality as we enter a sort of wasteland. At such times, we may be tempted to patch up the cracks and anesthetize the sense of anguish that arises. Ultimately, this is of little use. It may merely serve to exacerbate the situation as we fail to address the crucial issues of our life. Emergence from this wasteland may take time and only truly begin when there is a renewal of vision. Then, the vitality that was lost begins to return.

When this occurs, particularly in mid-life, the crisis of meaning and purpose often precipitates a shift of emphasis in an individual's life as the necessary missing ingredient is sought. Some will abandon their jobs and head off on an adventure or quest. Others may seek the spiritual nourishment they need through participating in meditation retreats, joining in local classes and groups, or going into therapy. Some search for what is missing by diving into a romantic affair. However we respond to this spiritual crisis, or crisis of meaning, its repercussions can be dramatic. The power of an inner call or impulse is also often hard to resist.

When we enter such a period of transition, we may experience a growing restlessness or frustration. This may precipitate a yearning to be free, with fantasies of travel and exotic pilgrimages. The Puer archetype is emerging again as the renewal of visions that seem irresistible but also disturbing. This return of archetypal intent may herald changes that will upset the status quo. Revolution and the reformation or transformation of the old in order to begin anew comes through the archetype of the Puer.

Those who have followed a working material life and have established a pragmatic stability may well be challenged by the renewal of Puer restlessness. If, alternately, we have been dominated by the Puer spirit, our challenge will be to face its polar opposite. That which becomes established and ordered in clear and definite form lives under the aegis of the Puer's archetypal polarity, Senex. Senex could be described as aged, as the old man either wise or cynical. The feminine form is *Seneca,* or the old woman, the crone, and may manifest as either a wise old woman or a negative old hag.

Our capacity to materialize and establish a practical base that grounds our visions and ideas or ideals comes through the archetype of Senex/Seneca. The master craftsman or craftswoman carries something of the positive Senex as the one who has refined and crafted the capacity to materialize his or her visions. Both Senex and Seneca are states of being that have been established though the slow, grinding experience of time. Senex governs the establishment of laws and systems, of order and structure. It could be seen as the reality principle that requires that we be practical, pragmatic, grounded, and responsible. Senex has a strong relationship to the father as the old wise man who has gained wisdom through gradual experience. Seneca relates to the mother as the earthy old woman who is wise in natural lore and has deep inner knowledge through experience. In this respect, they have a slower, more measured, and less idealistic view of the world. The difficulty with both Senex and Seneca is that their negative tendency is to become stuck and rigid. There are many similarities in the relationship between Puer and Senex that are echoed in the Puella/Seneca polarity, but for the present I will focus upon the former.

Senex, as the archetypal root of the need for order, structure, and authority, appears in both the secular and the spiritual worlds. It is found within the world of bureaucracy as well as in spiritual institutions. Its negative and destructive tendency is then found in any institutional establishment that fears and disenfranchises those who seek to be radical, innovative, or individualistic. Senex can be seen in its most destructive manifestation in the example of the Tiananmen Square massacre, where Senex embodied in the Communist Party leaders demonstrated ruthless determination to destroy the threat of the students' Puer vision of freedom and democracy. Senex is often negatively manifested in the relationship between a father and son. It is the harsh, disdainful voice that demands that the son abandon all his dreamy spiritual idealism and get a job and earn a living. In this respect, the Senex can be seen as opposing the Puer's need for individual expression, ideals, and visions.

Puer and Senex are therefore the two poles of a significant archetypal paradigm that runs through our lives. When we are unaware of these influences, they tend to dominate us unconsciously and, unfortunately, are often at odds with each other. Puer and Senex rarely live in a harmonious relationship to each other without being consciously recognized and integrated. Their inherent dispositions are so contrasting that they do not easily shift from opposition and conflict to a position of mutual compatibility. This is in part because they live at opposite ends of an unfolding process that originates with Puer vision and terminates in Senex materialization.

To live with one polarity dominant will inevitably bring difficulties. It is therefore vital that we come to terms with the reality of both poles and not try to deny or ignore the problem. In the spiritual world, there are those who may seek to remain caught within the polarity of the Puer. The consequence is often unsatisfactory and, at some point, becomes painfully disturbing. The longer the Puer type postpones the inevitable need to face the reality of the Senex, the more painful the process eventually becomes. Those I have known who avoid addressing this issue until middle age often suffer greatly. The aging Puer is a sorry individual. The stage, film, and music world is a place where this Peter Pan disposition is most noticeable. In the spiritual world the aging Puer may be struggling to find a way to ground his or her spiritual life as the recognition dawns that time is passing.

The consequence of the stuck position of either Puer or Senex is a painful awakening to the need for a balance. Just as the businessman may suddenly recognize the lack of meaning and inspiration in his work, so too the spiritual practitioner may suddenly become aware of the need to earn a living and establish some roots. This was particularly the dilemma I experienced when returning to the West from India.

Archetypal Senex was demanding that I establish a material basis in my life, but I actually felt ready to take up the challenge.

While I was teaching at Sharpham Buddhist College in a year-long program of Buddhist studies, students were offered an opportunity to take time out from their normal lives to go through a period of study and self-exploration. Two noticeable factors seemed present for those who attended. Firstly, many of the students were people who had stepped out of a conventional working life because they wished to enter the search for a different meaning. Secondly, some experienced extraordinary difficulty settling into a sense of direction in their lives following the year-long course. It was this second factor that reflected the struggle between spiritual inspiration and its application in the world.

Within Buddhism, the resolution of the paradigm of Puer and Senex comes through the genuine embodiment of our spiritual aspirations within a practical application in life. If the disposition of Puer is to experience inspiration and the aspiration to attain liberation through transcendent and enlightened insights, then that of Senex is to need to ground this experience in the relative world for the welfare of others. We may look to the path of the bodhisattva as a journey of individuation and of the embodiment of spirituality in the world. The bodhisattva's way of life particularly resolves the issues of Puer and Senex, spirituality and materiality, through a profound process of individuation that leads not to an avoidance or transcendence of materiality, but to buddhahood.

The Bodhisattva's Path 20

◆ ◆ ──

T HE PATH of the bodhisattva is often considered the most profound within the Buddhist tradition. From a psychological perspective the bodhisattva could be seen as the figure that resolves the
contradictions of spiritual and material life as expressed in the Puer/
Senex or Puella/Seneca paradox. On the bodhisattva's path, one
seeks not to transcend the reality of the material world but rather to
remain within it to serve others. This is therefore not a path that seeks
ascendance or assumption away from matter—the normal demands
of the body and the trials of everyday life—into spirit. In Buddhism,
insight into our essential nature is incarnated in the world with every
creative act.

The bodhisattva may be said to hold a tension between two worlds:
the world of spiritual aspiration and that of the demands of normal
material life. By virtue of insight into the depth of his or her creative
essence, or Buddha nature, the bodhisattva taps a potent source of
vision and vital energy. The bodhisattva's Puer/Puella side, if one were
to call it such, is the vision and ideal of our enlightened potential. Without a determination to ground this vision in the world, however, it
would be possible to become absorbed in this vision alone and effectively disengage from the world. The bodhisattva's Senex/Seneca side,
however, brings a deep sense of responsibility and commitment to the
welfare of others. It is said that the bodhisattva renounces the bliss of
nirvana's release as well as any attachment or aversion to samsara.[11]

This is a paradox that is no easy position to hold. On the one hand,
the bodhisattva's renunciation recognizes that so much of our lives are

absorbed in things that are ultimately hollow, lacking in meaning, and illusory. On the other, there is the necessity of engaging with life and materiality and giving it some level of meaning.

I recall a conversation with a male client who struggled with a deep feeling that much of what he was surrounded by in his life was shallow, hollow, and futile. He also saw so much distress and confusion around that he began to feel a kind of aversion for life. When he tried to engage in things that might interest him, they felt dead and uninspiring. This was leading him to wish that he could just get out of it all: disengage and remain cynical and disillusioned. He was often told by people that this negative view was doing him harm, so he was greatly relieved when I said that perhaps his sense of pointlessness and futility was accurate. Rather than veering to a nihilistic extreme on one hand or trying to be positive on the other, the challenge he seemed to face was to remain open, present, and engaged. Could he act in the world while knowing, on one level, that things are illusory and lack inherent meaning or depth as a source of happiness? Gradually he came to see that attributing meaning and value to things could sit alongside the knowledge that ultimately they are all illusory and transitory. He began to live with the paradox.

A bodhisattva chooses to live within this paradox of knowing deeply the illusory nature of the world he or she inhabits while still being willing to remain within it. A bodhisattva's vision of awakening remains embodied and, therefore, has consequences that reach far beyond the limitations of our normal human capacity. Opening fully to one's innate luminosity and clarity has an extraordinary effect on the mind. It can generate a quality of intention that has immense power and inspiration behind it, radically changing the nature of intention. The bodhisattva, by remaining at this paradoxical threshold between form and emptiness, opens to a source of creative vitality that is channeled through intention. This quality of intention, known as *bodhichitta,* or "the awakening mind," is a quality of archetypal intent that transforms the will.

Bodhichitta has certain key attributes. Firstly, there is a deeply realized vision of wholeness that generates a supreme confidence in the innate potential of our human condition. This is a profound knowing—a knowledge of and awakening to our innate nature. The practitioner on the bodhisattva's path recognizes that the source of our enlightenment is not bestowed by some outer god that will save us, but rather is something present within our own nature that emerges through personal transformation. The bodhisattva's path is a path of self–realization or self-actualization that comes through a deep insight into the mind's true nature.

Secondly, the awakening of this vision requires a sense of responsibility. From a place of profound insight and compassion, the bodhisattva makes a deep commitment to the welfare of others. This commitment does not arise from the harsh, duty bound, dogmatic aspect of Senex, however, but from an openness and sensitivity to the reality of the suffering of all sentient beings. From this standpoint, it would be unacceptable to use our potential for anything other than an altruistic purpose.

Thirdly, bodhichitta is a quality of intention that is like a powerful river that runs deeply beneath the surface of the bodhisattva's life. Once he or she steps into this river, it is an act of surrender of the normal ego intention to the unfolding of a process that leads to buddhahood. In other words, when we align ourselves with the current of this river, it generates a sense of direction that does not require self-conscious trying or interference from the ego. We may not know where it will take us. As Shantideva says in his *Guide to the Bodhisattva's Way of Life*, "even while [we are] asleep or unconcerned"[12] this intention is unfolding.

Bodhichitta grows as we release the grip on our ego-identity with all its self-preoccupation and begin to open our hearts to the world around. As we do so we can begin to awaken the innate qualities of compassion, love, joy, and equanimity known as the "four immeasurable thoughts." These qualities do not have to be focused on an individual but can be when a relationship is there. They comprise an attitude of care and sensitivity towards others that will be able to respond when needed. As attributes of the heart, they bring an openness and compassion for others that is not bound by the disposition to be conditional, selective, and judgmental.

Bodhichitta brings a source of vitality that has creative, inspirational, and healing potential. I have seen this among certain Tibetan lamas. Of these, I would consider one of my own teachers, Lama Thubten Yeshe, to be a shining example. His vitality seemed inexhaustible even though he was a very sick man, suffering from a chronic heart condition. He seemed to have accessed a source of energy that restored and revitalized him, even though his constant generosity to his students took a significant toll on his physical strength.

In the *Guide to the Bodhisattva's Way of Life*, Shantideva describes the extraordinary quality of bodhichitta through a variety of metaphors:[13]

> It is the supreme ambrosia
> That overcomes the sovereignty of death,
> It is the inexhaustible treasure
> That eliminates all poverty in the world.
>
> It is the supreme medicine
> That quells the world's disease,
> It is the tree that shelters all beings
> Wandering and tired on the path of conditioned existence.
>
> It is a universal bridge
> That leads to freedom from unhappy states of birth,
> It is the dawning moon of the mind
> That dispels the torment of disturbing conceptions.
>
> It is the great sun that finally removes
> The misty ignorance of the world,
> It is the quintessential butter
> From the churning of the milk of Dharma.

Shantideva also draws an alchemical parallel when he describes bodhichitta as being:[14]

> . . . like the supreme gold-making elixir,
> For it transforms the unclean body we have taken
> Into the priceless jewel of a Buddha-Form.

As a quality of mind, bodhichitta is an expansive perspective on reality, one not caught up in narrow, limited conceptions and beliefs. As an intention, it is not bound by contracted, limiting ego fears and attachments. As a felt experience, it has a depth of compassion, love, and joy that is open to all beings without prejudice. A bodhisattva possessed of this disposition becomes an "awakening warrior," which is the literal translation of the term. This is one who courageously surrenders self-will to a profound sense of purpose, an experience that might be described, in Jungian terms, as a deep inner shift from "I will" to "thy will be done." One who has embarked upon this path towards the awakening of buddhahood becomes known as a "son or daughter of the victorious ones" and will, it is said, receive the blessings of the Buddhas.

Once this intention of bodhicitta begins to grow, it generates an undercurrent through our lives that informs all that we do. At first, this intention may need to be consciously recalled, but once we have developed trust in this deep sense of purpose, it will be like a powerful river that is drawing us irresistibly towards the ocean. Initially the flow of this river may seem turbulent and erratic. In time, it becomes a steadily flowing current that is deep and broad, eventually uniting with dharmakaya, the wisdom of all the Buddhas.

The figure of the bodhisattva may be seen as a model of individuation and the resolution of the duality of spiritual and material life. Traditionally, the qualities of the bodhisattva develop through the practice of what are known as the six perfections—of generosity, patience, morality, perseverance, concentration, and wisdom. To understand the bodhisattva's path as a psychological journey of individuation, one may see it as having much in common with aspects of the heroic quest. The bodhisattva may be seen as the awakening warrior but, within the psychological journey, can equally embody aspects of the wanderer, the servant, and the magician or alchemist—figures that symbolize stages one may pass through on the heroic quest. Each stage or path will bring particular challenges and enable qualities to mature that are important in the process of individuation. They will equally have their hazards and perhaps their Shadow side, when followed without awareness. While they may be seen as discrete journeys with the goal of manifesting the psychological maturity of the bodhisattva, it may be necessary to experience all of them. We may find that we have a natural disposition to engage in one in particular and that we enter the others at different times in our lives when we need to grow. Ultimately, they each enable particular qualities to develop as an expression of the process of individuation.

THE WANDERER

The first lessons of individuation may arise through the path of the wanderer. The wanderer embodies the move to individuality away from family and collective values. This journey we must undertake alone in order to gain confidence in our sense of self. What the bodhisattva as wanderer gains is the capacity to engage in the quest alone and seek independence and self-reliance. The wanderer therefore discovers that he or she can stand alone, separate psychologically from parents and other collective groups, and can follow his or her own truth.

In this process we must face our parental dragons. These are the fears and feelings of inadequacy and self-doubt that keep us ensnared in our limitations and prevent us from stepping out onto the journey. The Buddha's life demonstrates the hazard of becoming trapped in the security and comfort that hinder the capacity to set off on the journey. His need to leave home grew and, finally, he stepped out into the life of a wandering ascetic.

In my early twenties, a strong yearning arose in me to travel. This is not uncommon in young people of a similar age and suggests that the symbolic significance of the journey or traveling is far deeper than we often acknowledge. When reading Jung's *Man and His Symbols* around this time, I found a valuable affirmation of the archetypal significance of this process at crucial times of life. The fact that many of us travel in youth probably owes much to the nature of the wanderer's lessons rather than to the difficulties of traveling in later life.

The urge to wander is an impulse that cannot easily be ignored. Feeling stuck, frustrated, and restless and needing to break free often signifies that it is time to move on, either externally or internally. To enter the path of the wanderer in one's early twenties can particularly signify the need to break free of the web of dependency. Striking out on our own and discovering our capacity to survive in the world independently is a powerful lesson.

In a text called the *Thirty-Seven Practices of All Buddha's Sons,* Thogme Zangpo considers the hazards of a life in which we are caught up in friendships and circumstances that hinder growth. He describes the way in which our relationships can so often become a source of conflict and attachment that lead us into deeper and deeper confusion:[15]

Remaining too long in one place our attraction
To loved ones upsets us, we're tossed in its wake.
The flames of our anger towards those who annoy us
Consume what good merit we've gained in the past.
The darkness of closed-minded thought dims our outlook
We lose vivid sight of what's right and what's wrong.
We must give up our home and set forth from our country
The sons of the Buddhas all practice this way.

From staying together with friends who misguide us,
Our hatred, desires and ignorance grow.
With little time left to continue our studies,
We don't think of Dharma; we meditate less.
Our love and compassion for all sentient beings

THE WISDOM OF IMPERFECTION

Are lost and forgotten while under their sway.
Sever such ties with misleading companions,
The sons of the Buddhas all practice this way.

These verses clearly define the kinds of problems encountered in relationships that become destructive and misleading. This is often a particular problem of early adulthood, when we are much more influenced by others. The wanderer may need to sever ties to old relationships that have a destructive side to them. We can become caught in views and attitudes of others that are misleading and cause us to lose sight of our own inner truth. To grow, we may need to move on in order to find relationships to those who support who we are in a healthy way. This can be particularly true if we are attempting to practice a spiritual path that many will misunderstand. We may need to keep relatively quiet and contain things that could be mocked or belittled. I have found in my own life that there are very few people to whom I can divulge the nature of my Buddhist practice. This is principally because it could be so easily misunderstood by those who have little connection to that world. On the inside, so to speak, I may be a tantric practitioner, but on the outside I choose to be relatively conventional. This does mean that as a practitioner I have had to learn to be alone when there is no community around that shares this same understanding.

The wanderer leaves the familiar world and wanders alone so that he or she can be free of both outer constraints and inner confusion. So long as we are still caught up in demanding aspects of social and material life, we will continue to be ensnared in the causes of much suffering and confusion. At times on the journey these influences, distractions, and dependencies are a particular disturbance to deepening meditation. There is also greater peace and inner freedom when we are not bound in the conventions of a world of social and material expectations. This became absurdly apparent when I returned from India. While in the East I had little regard for how I dressed or looked and never looked in mirrors. When I was back in England, within a relatively short space of time a kind of self-consciousness returned about how scruffy and ill-dressed I felt in the Yuppie world of London in the mid-eighties.

From a psychological perspective, the wanderer's life could be seen as a time when we clear away the history of unhealthy relationships and emotional baggage that limit us. While we are still mired in traumatic aspects of our past, we will lack emotional stability. Once we have begun to emerge from our history, our mind is freer to rest quietly in meditation.

An important quality of the wanderer is the ability to be alone with oneself. For a meditator, this is very important. Being alone for long periods without the distraction of people can be terrifying to someone who is uncomfortable with him- or herself. In psychotherapy I have encountered many people who struggle with this aspect of their lives. Those who have never wandered may never have learned the capacity to be alone, silent, and present with themselves without the need to fill the space with activity. Shantideva's *Guide* proclaims the benefits of this discovery:[16]

When shall I come to dwell in forests
Amongst the deer, the birds and the trees,
That say nothing unpleasant,
And are a delight to associate with?

When dwelling in caves,
In empty shrines and at the feet of trees,
Never look back—
Cultivate detachment.

When shall I come to dwell
In places not clung to as "mine,"
Which are by nature open,
And where I may behave as I wish, without attachment?

To live in solitude may sound extreme to many Westerners. Yet one may see "solitude" either literally or metaphorically. Periods of isolation and retreat to stabilize the mind in meditation are extremely useful. They enable us to later "return to the marketplace" and retain a quality of awareness that is not easy to develop otherwise. These times also enable us to develop the capacity to stay relatively contained and present within ourselves so that we are not so shaken by external conditions. People and circumstances often pull us out of relationship to ourselves. We then lose the inner resource of clarity and awareness and can easily be affected by external conditions such that if all is well, we are happy, but when things are difficult, we become depressed and unhappy. The capacity to remain equanimous and not be so changeable comes through gaining a degree of separation and non-attachment.

Inevitably, there will be a shadowy side to the wanderer's disposition. Because the wanderer's path is often embarked upon in early adulthood, some of the needs of the wanderer can seem inappropriate at other times of life.

The shadowy side of the wanderer's disposition is that sometimes it is hard to stop. It is not uncommon to meet people who have spent much of their life traveling, avoiding attachment to relationships and situations. The need to move on, however, can become a habit that is no longer healthy. Those who become stuck in the archetype of the wanderer fail eventually to establish intimacy in relationships and commitment to work or to living in one place. The perpetual or compulsive wanderer often cannot stop because he or she fears that the consequence of doing so is becoming trapped. Detachment has become a form of avoidance. Such a person will fear commitment, and the prospect of "settling down" may feel horrifying.

Non-attachment and independent self-sufficiency are valuable qualities. If they become compulsive, however, we will disconnect and disengage from other important aspects of our lives. Those who perpetually travel often begin to recognize that their wandering is leaving some part of themselves dissatisfied. Constant movement also becomes a trap.

Knowing when to stop and remain in one place or commit to something that creates a sense of roots may be an important change. Odysseus was told, at the end of his travels, to carry an oar inland to a place where no one knew what it was. He should then firmly plant it in the ground.[17] Once we have learned the lessons of the wanderer, it may be time to move on to other paths.

THE WARRIOR

The term *bodhisattva* is often translated as "awakening warrior." According to Shantideva, the bodhisattva needs a great sense of self-confident self-will that enables him or her to face the challenges of the path and overcome them. Although these may be initiated by some external event, the real challenge is the inner one. If we suffer a lack of confidence and inner strength, we may be daunted by the demands and challenges that arise on our path. It is often hard to admit that life and its problems frighten us and that we fear that things may go wrong and even panic when they do. This may not be something we wish the world to know about because it would be too humiliating, but inside we may suffer its limitation. We may develop a habit of avoidance and find that we do not engage in our lives because we lack the courage to do so. We can feel impotent and disappointed because we limit ourselves by our fear and are not really fulfilling our potential. We may always take the safe option even though we know we are copping out.

The bodhisattva is one who, according to Shantideva, will face this challenge and not allow inner fears to hold him or her back. It is this inner "disturbing conception" that is the real challenge and requires great strength of mind to conquer. It also requires a level of compassion for ourselves because we may not always succeed. As Shantideva writes in the *Guide*:[18]

> First of all, I should examine well what is to be done,
> To see whether I can pursue it or cannot undertake it.

If I am unable, it is best to leave it,
But once I have started I must not withdraw.

If I do, then this habit will continue in other lives
And wrongdoing and misery will increase;
Also, other actions done at the time of its fruition
Will be weak and will not be accomplished.

Self-confidence should be applied to wholesome actions,
The overcoming of disturbing conceptions and my ability
     to do this.
Thinking, "I alone shall do it,"
Is the self-confidence of action.

Laziness and lack of engagement are an anathema to the warrior who seeks to apply him- or herself to every task. Self-confidence is not gained instantaneously, however, but through engaging in those things that we feel we are able to accomplish and building upon them. When we take up small challenges and are able to accomplish them, our confidence will grow. Perhaps one of the greatest mistakes for those of us who lack self-confidence is to take on some huge challenge because we feel it will really prove we are worthwhile. Our self-doubt will be made even worse if we are then unable to complete what we start.

When I was in my twenties, this was a difficult challenge. My lack of self-confidence led me to have many "big ideas" that I hoped would finally show that I was worthwhile and give me a sense of self-value. Unfortunately, these ideas remained dreams and, rather than helping me, tended to make me feel even more inadequate. It was only after giving up grandiose dreams that I was able to take on small things and begin to grow in confidence and capacity. I found this both in the material sense and also in my meditation practice. Only by completing short retreats was I gradually to have the confidence to enter longer and longer periods of isolation.

There are those who seem to have an immense capacity to engage in what could seem to be daunting tasks. My retreat teacher, Gen Jhampa Wangdu, was one such man. He had immense courage and strength of will, having spent about twenty-five years in isolated retreat. He finally died after a particular nine-month retreat which, he said, had been successful. I was not aware at the time that he had embarked upon a practice specifically intended to help avert a hindrance to H. H. the Dalai Lama's life. He had chosen to take on some of this hindrance by the power of his realizations, which he must have known could lead to his own death. Gen Jhampa Wangdu was one of the most compassionate, courageous, and determined practitioners I have ever met. He was a simple man with great humility and a wonderful capacity for laughter.

To individuate as a bodhisattva, we need to develop the courage and will to endure hardship for the welfare of others. A steadfast mind that faces life's challenges and overcomes them is the bodhisattva warrior's greatest weapon. This particularly relates to the ability to remain vigilant to the potential to lose mindfulness and fall into bad habits. To the warrior, the loss of mindfulness may lead to a moment of lapse when some unwholesome inner weakness could take over. The bodhisattva warrior's primary enemy is an inner one, whether this is an emotional disturbance or the tendency to become egotistical or arrogant. Perhaps one could say that the warrior's greatest fear is to be dominated by an inner weakness, particularly arrogance, laziness, or self-indulgence.

To maintain clarity and alertness to the inner challenges that can take us over is no easy task. In therapy, a lack of mindfulness plays a significant role in the struggle to resolve emotional problems. We may begin to recognize the nature of our emotional patterns and see the detrimental effect of them taking us over and ruling our lives. Without the capacity to witness the arising of emotions and to begin to free ourselves from their power, we remain helpless. Once we are able to cultivate a quality of mindfulness that can remain aware and present and not drown in our emotional life, it is not such a source of suffering.

Mindfulness enhances the capacity to disidentify from emotional patterns and habits. When we do so, we are no longer taken over by their power. What weakens our ability to disidentify is a fundamental lack of mindfulness. Before we know what has happened, we become caught in emotional reactions that take us over. The warrior's intention would be to never allow himself or herself to lose that capacity to remain alert.

The warrior's impeccability, determination, and courage are powerful qualities, which inevitably will have a shadowy side. There is a certain rigor in this attitude that may become extremely unhealthy. A businessman who came to me in therapy particularly reminded me of this. His task was to go into an organization and sort out the managerial problems that were arising. He would relish the challenge and used to say he only really felt alive when he was engaged in this process. He was glad that his managerial skills and his capacity to take up the challenge could be of benefit.

He was, however, becoming increasingly aware of the shadowy side of his warrior-like attitude to life as he began to experience it. The warrior does not readily tolerate weakness, either in himself or in others. The rigor with which the warrior engages with life and the task, be it inner or outer, can become compulsive. The impulse to go into battle and fight the good fight can become so instinctive the warrior does not know when to get off his horse, so to speak. Recognizing limitations is not easy for the warrior, and the need to stop, rest, or change direction may be seen as the greatest weakness.

The warrior may not know when to stop and listen to the inner needs of the body. Many people who become caught in the active willfulness of this way of life can find sickness or physical weakness immensely frustrating. They may drive themselves way beyond what is healthy. In my own life I have experienced this when the combination of work, house renovation, and demanding young children left me exhausted and feeling as though I had nothing left to give. I had driven myself way beyond my capacity by trying to complete building work that required a huge effort. The depletion that this brought about led to a prolonged period of illness during which I had no resistance to endless colds and flu. Eventually, I reluctantly recognized my limitations and the need to slow down and give myself time to recover.

When we enter the warrior's way of life, we need to be aware of the shadowy side of our nature. To ignore our vulnerability or our weaknesses will lead to a kind of inflation. It can lead to the illusion of infallibility. When this inflation happens, the warrior is set for a fall, and a warrior does not take defeat easily. Nevertheless, this may actually be the instance that wakes him up to his blindness.

Approaching the practice of meditation with this disposition almost always leads to problems. Applying our will to meditation seldom brings the results we may wish. As I have found in retreat, pushing and trying to gain experiences leads to a stressed mind and can even damage the energy-winds in the body. This can lead to symptoms such as headaches, heart pains, and emotional instability, all a reflection of what the Tibetans call *lung* or "wind" disorder. A young man who came to me for therapy suffered this in the extreme. He had driven himself to meditate with the kind of will he had used to study academically. His intellect was determined to succeed, but meditation cannot be approached with such force without consequences. When he came to me he had suffered chronic pain in his head and body for some time. Psychotherapy was limited in its potential because he really needed to rest and stop anything that was hooking into his trying-to-achieve disposition. Healing was going to be a long process of patient letting go, rest, and acceptance.

The willingness to commit to and engage in the task with will and determination needs to be tempered by the wisdom to recognize what is actually needed. Someone who is compulsively active does not always find it easy to be guided and to genuinely hear what is best. They think they know and want to get on with it, only to discover that they missed the point.

The cultivation of will and the capacity to face and overcome hardships or obstacles are the gift of the warrior's path. The courage and impeccability of the warrior make the bodhisattva's life full of dynamism and vitality dedicated to the benefit of others. However, it may eventually be time for those on the warrior path to shift the emphasis and not constantly search for a new challenge, a new cause to fight for, or a new dragon to slay. Becoming stuck in the warrior mode can be another trap. It may become too intense and rigorous, which may then require a willingness to relax and let go of the will as the way of dealing with life—something that a warrior may not find easy.

In the process of individuation we gradually learn to embody the strength of mind to accept the trials of the path and the maturity to transform our relationship to them. Tempering the warrior's willfulness may require cultivating the qualities that arise on the path of the servant.

The Servant

There is a time in the process of individuation when it is important to ask ourselves the question, What is my motivation? Even within the world of genuine "spiritual" practitioners, there is a point when we must honestly look at whether our practice is principally in the service of self-interest or is really oriented towards the welfare of others. While I was in India I became conscious that my years of intensive retreat were emerging from a very mixed motivation. Striving for self-realization or enlightenment does not necessarily mean we are focusing on the welfare of others. I think my own desire for meditation experience may have had a level of dedication to benefiting others, but there was no doubt that I also had a lot of vested self-interest. It was on returning to the West that I began to genuinely embark on a path that involved dedicating my time and energy to others. I could see my struggles and resistances to the path of the servant both in my work as a psychotherapist and, later, in my role as a father.

Within most spiritual traditions, selfless devotion and self-sacrifice are considered great virtues. The object of sacrifice and devotion may vary and may be a cause, an organization, a doctrine, a divinity, a person, or the welfare of other beings in general. From a psychological perspective, placing ourselves in the service of what Jung called the Self is a significant step in the journey. It is expressed in the wish to surrender self-interest to the service of some greater purpose and meaning.

In Mahayana Buddhism great emphasis is placed upon giving up self-preoccupation for the altruistic intention to work for the welfare of others with compassion and love. The bodhisattva cultivates a willingness to undergo great hardship and endure tremendous suffering to achieve full awakening for the welfare of others. The effect of someone who genuinely is able to do this is profound. Perhaps a supreme example of this is H. H. the Dalai Lama, whom I have had the fortune to meet and study with on many occasions. In his presence, one can feel the depth of love and joy that he emanates in his complete devotion to serving the welfare not only of the Tibetans, but of all humankind.

There are those for whom self-sacrifice is a very natural expression of a deep concern for others. Women seem particularly able to respond to this inner call out of empathy and a natural capacity to care for others. For those of us who are not so immediately and spontaneously disposed, the path of the servant becomes an important step in a process of learning to care for others in a way that lets go of self-interest.

The servant may be seen as one who sacrifices self and surrenders self-interest for the service of others. We may do this from a place of necessity or from a place of choice. We may do so from a place of love or of compassion. However we are motivated, this process of surrender and dedication will challenge us to the limit. It will test us to the core and bring out our resistances and resentments. If we have false motives, these will manifest glaringly at some point. It is extremely hard to follow this path and do so from a hidden self-deceiving motive.

The ability to offer oneself genuinely and deeply to the welfare of others can easily be affected by all manner of subtle motivations that may not be immediately apparent. In time, however, these will come to the surface and we will be confronted by our limitations. However, as

I have found in my own journey, this is the point. When I began to work as a psychotherapist and, later, as a parent, I knew it would be challenging. I could not have envisaged just how challenging being a parent in particular would be. It was far easier to remain in isolated retreat and visualize or imagine working for the welfare of others. To be pushed to the edges of my capacity day after day by the demands and needs of children is another matter. If I believed I had a capacity for patience, this illusion has been totally shattered by children who won't put their socks on or who endlessly empty baskets of toys when I had only a few minutes before tidied them up. If I felt I was able to let go of personal needs and give, this capacity has been pushed to the limit. There have been times when I have been desperate for personal space, knowing that I had to wait.

Some of the greatest lessons of the servant are patience, generosity of heart, and the ability to overcome and let go of resentments and judgments. If we are to serve others we must develop an even-mindedness, an equanimity, that does not project our shadowy prejudices and dislikes. The capacity to open and respond to the needs of others without becoming caught in limiting self-grasping requires practice. In Shantideva's *Guide* he expresses the aspiration of the bodhisattva to give:[19]

> May I be the doctor, the medicine
> And may I be the nurse
> For all sick beings in the world,
> Until everyone is healed.
>
> Without any sense of loss,
> I shall give up my body and enjoyments
> As well as all my virtues of the three times
> For the sake of benefiting all.
>
> May I be a protector for those without one,
> A guide for all travelers on the way;

May I be a bridge, a boat and a ship
For all who wish to cross the water.

Just like space
And the great elements such as earth
May I always support the life
Of all the boundless creatures.

The ability to give of our time and energy is something that can grow with a willingness to let go and open. I have known people whose capacity to give time to others who needed their attention seemed boundless. Most of us need to have clear boundaries with our time and energy; otherwise, we would exhaust ourselves. As we open through the cultivation of bodhichitta, this capacity for generosity will grow. This does not imply that the servant should have no boundaries and should endlessly give of him- or herself. To do so may be very unwise and damaging both to the welfare of the giver and that of the recipient. From my own experience, when I go beyond those boundaries I become exhausted and feel I have nothing left. This leads me to become increasingly scratchy, irritable, and in need of personal space.

While self-sacrifice is a necessary ingredient of the bodhisattva's maturation, the cultivation of this kind of giving requires some skillful awareness of where there is self-delusion. There is a difference between a genuine self-sacrifice that comes from a deeply rooted and healthy self-worth and the martyr-like self-negation that arises from unresolved wounds. To distinguish one from the other is not difficult for an observer, but someone trapped in this negative pattern may be resistant to acknowledging it. Someone whose way of relating is based upon self-sacrifice and self-negation may give because it is his or her only way of feeling valued. It may also be the only defense against despair, hopelessness, and self-loathing.

Such people will often be self-effacing and self-denying and compelled to look after others rather than allowing anyone to take care of them. To feel worthwhile they may even unconsciously need people to be in some difficulty so that they can help. They may automatically defer to others' needs, and it is often very hard to get them to say what they would like. They may adopt the role of passive victim and willingly enter into abusive relationships with both individuals and organizations. Their relationship to boundaries is often poor and they may be incapable of saying no because to do so would be "selfish."

The wounding that lies beneath unhealthy sacrifice may not at first be apparent but can often be sensed as a deep, underlying pain and despair. Unhealthy self-sacrifice usually has its origins in childhood in the form of some kind of chronic emotional neglect. According to Alice Miller the self-sacrifice tendency is especially prevalent in those who from a very early age have had to "look after" seriously narcissistic and wounded parents, taking care of parental needs at their own expense.[20] Wounded parents will often accuse their children of being selfish for having their own needs, so that being "selfish" becomes a terrible sin.

The willingness to sacrifice oneself for others may be born out of a deeply damaged sense of self. Sadly, I have seen a number of people, especially some close women friends, enter spiritual communities and work "selflessly," sacrificing themselves to circumstances that became increasingly demanding and abusive. The compulsion to neglect self and constantly work for others can easily be supported by spiritual ideals and collective approval. Within this "selfless" spirituality often lies a deep well of pain, grief, and self-destructive masochism that seldom can be resolved through self-sacrifice.

A close woman friend of mine suffered as a child from an abusive, aggressive drunken father and was called on to sacrifice herself to the family as a second mother, doing most of the housework and taking care of her brothers and sisters. As she felt a desperate need to please a punishing father, her only sense of value came from serving. She became involved with the Tibetan Buddhist organization I was connected to and enthusiastically devoted herself to the teacher's requests for people to work in the center. She found it easy to dedicate her life to his demand for self-sacrifice for the welfare of others. Unconsciously, however, she was re-enacting the relationship with her father in an effort to again serve him dutifully in order to please him and receive the love she yearned so much for. She worked hard in the community and was always willing to provide for others, no matter at what cost to herself.

Regrettably, she was seldom very happy and the demands put upon her exhausted her. She nevertheless gave more and more of herself to serve the teacher. Exhausted and depressed, she asked her teacher for help. He sent her to another center to become a major figure in its organization. Initially she was happy to have received this recognition and acceptance; it was like a blessing. In time, however, she began to again fall into the same despair. She worked constantly, exhausting herself to serve the teacher, who seemed to have no appreciation of the pathology that was being triggered by his own actions.

It took considerable courage and desperation for her to begin to look at what she was doing to herself. To begin to change and trust what she felt she needed seemed to go against the teacher's wishes. It meant confronting the guilt she felt at not dutifully obeying her father whose love and acknowledgment she so badly wanted. This was compounded by the spiritual values she had adopted, which also demanded dutiful self-sacrifice. Rather than being on a path of liberation, she was constantly being re-wounded. It was difficult turning away from the spiritual authority she had so long devoted herself to and beginning to trust what she needed for herself.

Another form of sacrifice I have seen in a number of very caring women is the tendency to take on a kind of earthy, supportive, motherly role in relationships with relatively immature, Puer-dominated men. They become the grounding principle so seriously needed by some "spiritual" men. One woman I know was prepared to sacrifice much of her own journey and self-determination to support an emotionally weak and immature male partner. Sadly, this was even reinforced by Tibetan teachers. What was particularly disturbing was the degree to which the man would regress into an infantile, abusive, and mildly sadistic treatment of the woman. Her willingness to endure this abuse was due to her capacity to sacrifice herself to another's needs, partly from some deep sense of duty, partly because of a lack of self worth, and partly because she could not say no to his weakness.

This kind of self-denial and self-sacrifice is not a healthy basis from which to engage in the bodhisattva's selfless service. There may be a time on the spiritual path when self-sacrifice is a natural next step in the process of our evolution, but not if it is enacted from a place of fundamental wounding.

The path of the servant needs to be based on a healthy sense of self. The lesson of the servant is the active engagement of compassionate bodhichitta in the service of others. As we are able to surrender, we will deepen the sense of meaning and fulfillment this gives to our lives. This surrender requires that we let go of the ego and its self-preoccupations, but not in a destructive way. So long as our sense of self-worth is still damaged, sacrifice will only compound the hurt. When we are ready, however, the willingness to serve and work for the welfare of others will become a source of great joy and boundless energy.

THE MAGICIAN OR SIDDHA

The fourth path of individuation is not easy to name, as the figure of the magician is part healer, part artist, part shaman, part mystic, and part alchemist. The bodhisattva embodying this dimension of the path is particularly found within the world of the esoteric tradition of Tantra. In ancient India there was a group of practitioners who manifested this capacity as tantric yogis and yoginis. They were known as the eighty-four *mahasiddhas*, or as Dowman calls them, "masters of enchantment."[21] The term *siddha* usually refers to those who have accomplished certain powers, or *siddhi*, some of which are considered worldly powers and others, supreme powers. Worldly siddhi are capacities such as clairvoyance, while supreme siddhi are stages of enlightenment and buddhahood. A particular aspect of the siddha's path relates to the power of transformation and of manifestation.

One could see this as the transformation or manifestation of power.

A bodhisattva's power of transformation is sometimes described as being like that of a peacock, which is said to have the capacity to eat poisonous plants and transform their toxins into the beautiful colors of its feathers. This simile emphasizes the capacity of the bodhisattva to transform whatever circumstances arise into useful experience; to learn from circumstances that might, for some, be intolerable and even destructive.

There is something fundamentally pragmatic about the bodhisattva's ability to transform adverse circumstances into the path. Perhaps Nelson Mandela showed the most extraordinary example of this power in recent times. His period of imprisonment on Robin Island, far from harming him, had cultivated an extraordinary quality of compassion and equanimity. His ability to transform such adverse circumstances into a source of wisdom and strength is a testament to the power of the mind.

The bodhisattva recognizes this power and has come to realize that our reality and everything we experience within it is fundamentally based on the mind. To gain control over the mind is therefore to gain control over the process of creation of our reality. There is nothing magical in this; it is a natural reflection of a quality of insight into the true nature of the mind and, therefore, the root of our reality.

The eighty-four mahasiddhas, who lived in India soon after the time of the Buddha, were yogis and yoginis who were recognized masters of transformation. This was in part because they were practitioners of Tantra, through which they developed extraordinary powers of creative transformation, or siddhi. The supreme siddhi of the mahasiddha was the experience of Mahamudra, the unification of form and emptiness that enables a creative manifestation of Buddha activity spontaneously in each moment. Many of the mahasiddhas were craftsmen, and it was through their particular craft that they were able to generate their awakened quality. They exemplify the potential each of us has to utilize our own creative potential in the process of transformation. Through our particular talent we can manifest our true nature and thereby embody the transformation of our innate vitality, our potential power. On the path of the siddha, the bodhisattva's actions of body, speech, and mind become progressively empowered to create whatever is necessary for the welfare of others.

The bodhisattva siddha stands between worlds: the relative world of appearances and the empty ground of being. One could say that they stand on a threshold of creation. Through the power of concentration and subtle insight gained in meditation, it is possible to become immersed in the process of creation as the reality we experience manifests in each moment. This is the place where relative forms and appearances are experienced as the play of emptiness. To stand in this position requires the capacity to remain utterly present in the natural clarity, luminosity, and openness of the mind itself. The mahasiddhas, as masters of the practice of Mahamudra, were able to act from a place of pristine clarity in a fresh, dynamic way in relation to the creative vitality present in each moment. With the intention to benefit sentient beings, the siddha then creatively engages in a play of manifestation. This manifestation may be the role of a healer, musician, artist, or teacher, or in some cases, behavior that is bizarre and incomprehensible. The purpose is to tame and transform the wildness of sentient beings' minds in whatever way is most meaningful.

The threshold of awareness between the natural clarity of nonduality and the appearances of our relative world is a place of power—not personal power but the innate power or vitality present in the manifestation of life itself. This vitality is an aspect of Buddha nature that is present for each of us. We may have many different ways of naming it to make sense of it. For some, it may be spirit; for others, it may be some divine energy that lies at the heart of our reality. In the Tantric path of Buddhism this imminent source of vitality is often personified in the forms of deities. These provide a focus or channel for this quality, enabling the siddha to manifest its capacity creatively. The siddha comes to embody a dimension of Buddha nature called *sambhogakaya* (literally "the complete enjoyment body") or subtle energy body. This powerful body of extremely subtle energy-wind (Tib. *lung*) is present even now within our nervous systems and, with practice, can gradually awaken.

As a bodhisattva's awareness deepens, the capacity to open to this power grows. In Buddhism the root of this power is our own innate Buddha nature. It is our own inner potential, which Lama Thubten Yeshe once described as a source of limitless, blissful energy. As we awaken this inner vitality we become a vehicle for its creative expression in the world. This brings about the power to manifest and thereby deeply affect others and the world around, to influence, to heal, or indeed to harm. It is therefore crucial that we recognize this power rather than fear it. Once it is acknowledged, we must take responsibility for it, which is why the ethical basis of the bodhisattva is so well defined. As our inner power grows, it is vital to skillfully channel it.

The shadow side of the siddha is the desire for power. This leads to the potential to be possessed by it and then abuse it. A state of inflation arises usually because someone is blind to the danger. Jung spoke of the mana-personality as one who had become possessed by the power of the gods and then used this power unskillfully. The figure of Darth Vader in the *Star Wars* films is a vivid personification of the struggle to embody power without becoming taken over by it. Whether we call this the struggle between good and evil is questionable. From a Buddhist perspective, there is no notion of an absolute evil, although someone possessed by power and lacking any sensitivity of the danger of his or her actions may well seem evil.

To a Buddhist the dichotomy is not between good and evil *per se* but between ignorance and wisdom. To the bodhisattva as a siddha, ignorance is the greatest danger, as it will lead to frivolous abuses of power. In particular, one can see this ignorance as blindness to the nature of our own Shadow. When we fail to recognize our power, it will be as dangerous as becoming obsessed by it. If we deny our power, we are liable to act irresponsibly. We may be blind to the effect we have and not realize how our power influences others. False humility is as much a fault as being inflated. Unless we take responsibility, we are a danger to ourselves and to others.

The past decade has seen the emergence of countless therapists and healers, people who attend a few workshops and then call themselves masters or experts, hoping to draw people to receive their particular cure, their wisdom, or their path to self-actualization. Where does this need to be seen as a healer or teacher come from? While the motivation of many may be completely genuine, there is a danger that the cultivation of spiritual powers is the reflection of a wounded identity seeking spiritual affirmation, to be seen as special, to be looked up to as spiritually evolved. When there is so much of it about, how do we differentiate what is valuable and what is not?

One thing I appreciated about the Tibetan lamas I have studied with was their desire to keep their spiritual powers secret or private. It was very apparent that they had extraordinary qualities, one could feel it in their presence, but they would never proclaim it. The tradition set up around the lamas tends to contain this power because they are always accountable to their own teachers. There are safeguards in this system that potentially keep the individual in check. Dangers arise when Western teachers, therapists, and healers have no one to answer to, no accountability.

I have seen this in the situation of a Western Buddhist teacher who held a position of great power as the principal teacher in a Buddhist center. As the primary authority, essentially answerable to no one, she could use her power without being aware of its autocratic nature. Unchallenged by her students, who would always defer to her authority, she would easily dismiss any who might question her. Despite being a highly insightful teacher, she remains blind to her Shadow to this day.

The power to manifest has many faces. It may be as artist, musician, writer, healer, or shaman. It may equally be as a carpenter, bricklayer, or gardener. We should not become caught in the grandiosity of thinking that only what are considered sophisticated arts are noble or able to bring transformation. When we awaken the power to manifest, this can be expressed in the most basic experiences, because we understand the vitality and creative potential in each moment. It is not the exotic nature of what we do that is important; rather, it is the quality of mind present in the process of creation.

The mahasiddhas of India understood this in their craft, as do the Zen artists, whether this understanding is expressed through martial arts or the creative arts. Essential to this was their knowledge of the nature of *lung* or *chi*, the innate vitality present in reality. They knew how to remain present in this creative vitality and live its power impeccably. Perhaps the bodhisattva's most challenging task is to take full responsibility for his or her capacity to manifest creatively in the world for the welfare of others.

Whether we learn through the path of the servant, the wanderer, the warrior, or the siddha/magician, the challenges that must be faced and the qualities gained are important aspects of our process of individuation. One thing that each of these paths can do is bring us to a point where our essential identity is challenged to its core, where we are pushed to our limits and beyond. Whether we pass the test, so to speak, will depend upon our capacity to open and go beyond the ego. Only then will we truly be able to bring together both wisdom and skillful means, a union that is at the heart of a bodhisattva's realization.

THE DESCENT

Whatever the nature of our path, there will almost inevitably be a time when our essential identity begins to be challenged and we are taken through a process of death and transformation. We may descend into the pain of spiritual crisis, called by Christian mystics the "dark night of the soul." These periods of depression and disintegration can be profoundly significant when we understand their meaning. Surprisingly, these psychological processes are seldom, if ever, described in traditional Buddhist teachings. The attainment of qualities and insights that arise as the fruits of practice are not spoken of in terms of the subjective emotional or psychological process that occurs. In my experience, however, any insights that emerge often follow a painful journey rather than a blissful awakening. While I was spending time in retreat, periods of depression would often lead to very deep experiences and occasional insights, which has led me to wish to understand this process more deeply.

In myths and legends, time spent wandering across vast plains, deserts, or oceans, through barren wildernesses, or down into deep, forbidding valleys is a recurring theme. These images depict a period of desolate struggle when the traveler, having journeyed far from a familiar homeland, enters a state of terrible psychological desolation, barrenness, and flatness. He or she is lost, wandering in territory that is wild, desolate, perhaps hostile, and almost certainly empty and melancholic. In many stories the hero struggles across wild seas or hostile mountains where brigands, thieves, and outlaws dwell. These are the doubts, fears and, delusions that haunt us on the journey. In the guidebooks to the magical kingdom of Shambhala[22] the traveler passes though hot, windy deserts where "showers of diamond hail" and shrieking eagles descend to tear at the flesh. Here, nameless fears manifest as fiery-eyed demons to invoke terror.

These images depict a time of descent into the depths of our being to confront the Shadow, our fundamental aloneness, our mortality, and the nature of the ego. At these times, the traveler is challenged by feelings of depression and melancholy, of pointlessness and futility. He or she may feel lost, without refuge, and beyond hope, with little to do other than trust that this is what must come to pass. These periods must be passed through without knowledge of how things will turn out. The depression that accompanies this dark night involves a loss of vitality, enthusiasm, and meaning, a loss of what was secure and familiar, and a loss of our ability to control what is happening. In my experience, such a crisis will also challenge our relationship to the Buddha Dharma and our depth of understanding. We will discover whether we have the capacity to go beyond knowledge and open to true refuge.

The brigands and bandits on this journey are our own inner thieves that lurk in the shadows waiting to pounce. They are our insecurities, fears, and doubts; our aggression, self-denigration, and self-destruction. They are the emotional habits that can steal away our ability to remain centered and clear. As we wander in this wilderness of pain and desolation, we see the roots of our emotional wounds.

In crossing the wasteland, we encounter the darkness of our Shadow in a rite of passage, a journey of death and transformation. We enter into the dark valley and pass through a period of self-searching. We may repeat this journey at significant times in our lives; it is not necessarily a one-time experience. In our culture, however, we are never taught how to appropriately deal with depression and periods of crisis and descent. We are often afraid of them, both in ourselves and in others, and prefer to shut them away and deny or cover them up. Seldom are we willing to live with the pain of depression, recognizing its significance in our lives. We see depression as a curse that will disturb us if we allow it to get the better of us. We fight it and try to anesthetize ourselves against it by taking refuge in drugs, food, the television, or even work. Seldom do we want to see others in depression and so make remarks like "Pull yourself out of it" or "Pull yourself together." Pulling ourselves together, however, is the last thing we need to do at this time.

The journey into the wasteland has a profound psychological significance if we are willing and able to acknowledge it. The descent, introversion, and withdrawal of energy characteristic of depression are often the psyche's means of healing, if we allow the process to unfold. Depression can take various forms and be of varying depths, but there is usually a significant process taking place. It will occur when we have suffered some severe blow or shock that needs to be integrated and digested. We may have suffered the loss of a loved one, requiring time to grieve and heal. There may have been some crisis around work or financial matters that needs to be digested in order for us to discover how to move forward. We may have experienced some major disaster or accident or illness that is asking us to look at our life and see what needs to change both inwardly and outwardly.

There are times in our lives when we become stuck in ways of being in the world that cease to serve us. We may have developed ego structures and emotional habits and strategies that have, in the past, enabled us to cope with difficult or intolerable circumstances such as emotional trauma. These patterns may have been necessary natural responses that protected us at the time, as Peter Levine explains so clearly in his work *Waking the Tiger*[23] on shock and trauma. Later in life, however, these same patterns become a problem; they prevent us from moving forward. They freeze our natural capacity to respond to the world in fresh and creative ways. If we are to grow and move forward, the feelings and emotions that gave rise to our coping strategies may need to be brought back to the surface to be healed. There may be a need to change some fundamental beliefs about ourselves—the view we have of our lives and relationships. Such a crisis, requiring change and deep self-assessment, is often precipitated by external events.

BREAKING DOWN

When our personality structure and emotional patterns have become too rigid and unhealthy, the process of change that begins to unfold is often experienced as what might be called a breakdown. In the journey of individuation our ego-identity may need to die to go beyond its limitations and free our natural capacities. This death will be important in enabling us to experience a deeper, more whole relationship to the psyche. The process of breakdown demands the death, disintegration, and eventual reemergence of our sense of identity. The consequent depression that occurs at these times can be both painful and terrifying, and how we deal with it can determine greatly whether we grow from it or not. Denial, avoidance, and anesthetizing the pain can prevent us from facing the journey we are on.

The early stages of this journey are often marked by an acute sense of fear and foreboding as we progressively lose what was safe and familiar and are drawn relentlessly into the unknown. We may feel we are losing our grip, falling apart, and are no longer able to maintain things as they were. Our familiar sense of self may be gradually eroded by events we could not avoid. We may feel lost and bewildered, as though everything is disintegrating. This breaking up is very frightening, and we may be tempted to try to consolidate and pull back from the brink of the descent. Some people are tempted at this time to cement up the cracks in their world and pretend that all is well. Personally, I have found that the more I have resisted falling apart, the more painful and frightening the experience actually was. Holding on at these times is not the answer, nor is taking some form of anesthetic to cover up the reality of what we are experiencing. The step we must take is to courageously begin to open and release the tendency to contract and tighten through fear. If we feel we are slipping relentlessly down and are desperately trying to claw our way out of a pit, it may be time to let go and trust. Trying to hold on will become even more painful.

The solid structures we have carefully constructed around our ego-identity can become an edifice that needs to crumble, as is depicted in the "Tower" card in the Rider-Waite Tarot, which shows a stone tower being split in half by a lightning bolt. The ego experiences this fracturing and fragmentation as a very frightening process. But as in the case of the chrysalis of a butterfly, only when the solidity is cracked open do we discover the energy and richness trapped within. While we tend to fear breakdown, and it is certainly stigmatized in our society, it may herald the beginning of healing.[24] Breaking down frees us from the past and the solid, stuck history we have become imprisoned within.

Once the process is initiated, we may feel intense grief and sadness as we mourn the loss of the past security and dreams of a life we thought was stable. We may feel great loneliness and despair as we make the descent alone and without allies. Our world feels drab, lifeless, and pointless. Our vitality goes and we may have almost no interest in doing anything about it; we are uninspired and incapable of responding to life with anything other than an acute, painful pessimism.

Self-reproach, despair, and hopelessness are the demons that tear at us in this state. Depression will often bring out patterns of self-destruction such as being a victim or becoming chronically self-indulgent. These habits may be deeply entrenched and need to be challenged to enable healing to take place. When we get caught in them we are unconsciously blocking the evolution of depression. Even so, these tendencies may be part of the process of depression that must be recognized and faced.

This is when some form of anesthetic will seem almost irresistible in our desperation to alleviate the pain. If we visit conventional doctors at this time, they are likely to respond to our cries for relief with prescriptions for antidepressants. Sadly, this solution is only an anesthetic, a means to alleviate the distress by suppressing a process that is unfolding. For some with more severely entrenched and debilitating depression, however, this may be the only solution.

Ultimately we have to travel this journey alone, for it is in our inward solitude that we learn the lessons depression brings. This does not mean we should not seek support and the help of those who have an under-standing of the process we are going through, such as counselors or therapists. What we do not need are those who desperately try to make it all better because they fear where we are going. We need people who are willing to be there as we struggle, to hear our fears and distress and allow them to be. One of the most familiar images of depression is of a black pit of despair and loneliness. As we slip into this pit, our sense of hopelessness will often bring out in others the compulsion to be positive and compensate for our blackness and negativity. To be con-fronted with someone who compulsively has to make things positive in order to cope with our pain is not what we need. When we are in the depth of our despair and hopelessness, the last thing that actually helps is someone trying to make us "look on the bright side."

I recall a period some years back when my life had turned a fairly dramatic corner and I was feeling desperately negative, cynical, and bitter about everything in my life, including my spirituality. One evening I was talking with a friend, and the more negativity I expressed, the more he tried to be positive. I ended up feeling extremely angry that he had failed to simply allow me to be really negative. It was as though my negativity was intolerable to him and had to be neutralized by his being positive. What my negativity needed was simply the space to be acknowledged for what it was. I needed a compassionate presence that accepted where I was and did not fear it, judge it, or try to make it something else.

FACING OUR TRUTH

Once we have slipped irresistibly into the descent, we will settle into the heavy grayness that characterizes the bottom of the pit. The *nigredo,* as the alchemists would call this phase, is typified by a leaden, deathly melancholia that can feel intractable. [25] In this place we may need to face something in ourselves that has been left unaddressed. We must face it willingly and openly and surrender to its reality. We can no longer fight it and deny its power over us. It may be a deep childhood wound;

it may be facing our mortality, our aloneness. It may be recognizing the emptiness of the ego we have held as fundamental to our existence. We may find something we have been holding on to that needs to finally die and be buried.[26] A lost loved one, a dream, an ideal: our past may all still be with us as corpses we lug around. It may be our self-identity that needs to die, or our youth that needs to be mourned as we pass into middle age. Most often, we find in this underworld the negative self-beliefs that have evolved from childhood. Painful though they are, becoming more conscious of them enables us to face them and see how destructive and limiting they have been.

While in the depth of the wasteland we discover the source of our wounds, we may also for the first time find the aspect of ourselves we have always needed to empower our lives and give them meaning. Often we bury important qualities to protect ourselves in potentially hostile environments. For some, this buried treasure may be the capacity to actually be powerful and effective; the capacity to engage in life fully and fearlessly. For others, it may be the capacity to open and love or trust for the first time. We may discover in the depths our buried rage and anger that hold our capacity to be assertive and true to ourselves. We may even find our real sense of self. Whatever we uncover, we have probably been aware of its absence and how this has affected our lives. Whenever important resources are buried, repressed, and inaccessible to us, we will often feel a sense of limitation, ineffectiveness, or lack of vitality that blocks us.

In Greek mythology, Pluto is the god of this underworld. He is the one who draws us into the depth of pain and death to prepare us for transformation. He is also, however, "the bringer of riches." Lucifer, the Christian fallen angel, is also, as his name denotes, the bringer of light. However we understand the meaning of this dark god, we are living in his domain during the journey of descent. We may see him as terrifying and destructive and fear his power, but such is the power of death and transformation in the journey of the psyche. It will never be a time of light and laughter, but in the depths we will discover a potential source of renewal.

In the wasteland we may discover the "treasure hard to attain"[27] that must be brought back to the light of day. It may be our creativity, our sexuality, our strength and confidence. It may also be a renewal of our relationship to our spirituality and a sense of meaning.

Anyone involved in a spiritual quest will be tested beyond the limits of faith and trust while crossing the wasteland. A dark night of the soul is almost inevitable at some point in the journey and represents a significant time because the roots of our faith are challenged. In Buddhist language, this can be seen as a "crisis of refuge" when we are truly confronted with the depth of our understanding and insight. If we are clinging to beliefs with blind faith, these may be utterly shattered. If we have intellectual knowledge but no depth of experience, this will become apparent. Conversely, if we have had no sense of meaning, this may be the time when we actually discover it. We may begin to recognize that there are forces at work in our lives that are greater than the ego, and that we must learn to trust and open to them. We may be forced to surrender the power of an over-controlling ego. To use Jung's language, we are being confronted with the power of the Self, rather than the limited values of the ego, as the root of meaning in our lives.[28] In times of death and transformation, however, the Self does not manifest its light, bright, positive side; instead, we encounter its destructive side that tears us apart and leaves us to gradually heal.

The experience of the dark night will challenge us to discover whether our spirituality is based upon genuine truth and wisdom or simply superficial faith or knowledge of doctrine. During a particular period of retreat in India, I descended into periods of intense doubt. I found myself railing at God, the Buddha, the universe, whatever name one gives it, for not taking care of me and giving me some sense of "grace," a sign that would support my faith in practice. I felt totally abandoned and would scream with both grief and anger, "Why?" and, "What have I done?" I felt as though I was being punished for something. The feeling of alienation and isolation was intense. I recall on one occasion throwing all my ritual instruments around my meditation room in anger and desperation. I suppose I began to understand what Christ may have felt in that last moment of doubt when he said, "Why hast thou forsaken me," or, as Coleridge put it in "The Rime of the Ancient Mariner":

> Alone, alone, all, all alone,
> Alone on a wide, wide sea!
> And never a saint took pity on
> My soul in agony.

This time of letting go of expectation and hope is not easy. The ego wants something to hold on to to survive intact. If we are at a time in the journey when we must die and be transformed, then there is nothing to hold on to, not even hope. In the words of T. S. Eliot in "Four Quartets":

> I said to my soul, be still, and wait without hope
> For hope would be for the wrong thing; wait without love
> For love would be love of the wrong thing; there is yet faith
> But the faith and the love and the hope are all in the waiting.

THE EGO'S SURRENDER

In the wasteland we may feel the presence of forces at work which may be both awesome and terrifying. This terror is in part the recognition of the frailty and relative insignificance of the ego. Ego-grasping is a kind of inflation or omnipotence that holds the ego as the center of our reality. Whether it is the sense of being self-satisfied or a self-pitying victim, both are a kind of narcissistic inflation. This inflation alienates us from our Buddha nature, and in the time of the dark night, we may feel totally blind, lost, and out of relationship to our true nature. We are, however, being asked to let go of this inflated ego-center and finally surrender to the greater power of our Buddha nature. If we are able to truly open at this moment we may discover a

THE WISDOM OF IMPERFECTION

depth of wisdom we have not previously understood or experienced.

During the retreat mentioned earlier, I suffered a terrifying sense that I was gradually being torn open and dismembered. I found myself on a number of occasions visiting a huge, flat rock surrounded by enormous rhododendrons high on the mountainside where I was living. I would lie down upon this rock and cry out for help only to find that as I did so, I would burst open and let go. It was as though something in me knew I had to die. This gradually enabled me to open to a space that seemed utterly free of any sense of who I was. I felt as though I *had* died and the pain of holding on to myself had been purged away.

During this period I walked down the mountain and visited my retreat guide, Gen Jhampa Wangdu, who had lived most of his life as a hermit in retreat. When he saw me in my forlorn state he just laughed and said, "You are so fortunate. Tibetans pray for this kind of experience; get back up the mountain and get on with it." I was relieved by his confidence that dying was part of the journey, but also a little put out that he was not in the least sorry for me. A while later, when I met Lama Yeshe to discuss my retreat experience, he simply said, "Sometimes something has to die."

In Coleridge's epic poem the ancient mariner wishes to die so that his torment can finally end. Suddenly the moon rises over the horizon and blesses the situation. He eventually relaxes and falls into a deep sleep. Coleridge writes,

> An orphan's curse would drag to hell
> A spirit from on high;
> But oh! more horrible than that
> Is the curse in a dead man's eye!
> Seven days, seven nights, I saw that curse,
> And yet I could not die.

Jung recognized that the Self is not just light and positive but also terrifying, dark, and awesome. Even so, in both its light and dark aspects, the Self is solely oriented towards wholeness. In the tantric tradition the wrathful deity represents this dark, awesome face of the Self, our Buddha nature. This demonic, terrifying personification reminds us that the sole issue at stake is the death and transformation of the ego. The wrathful deities depicted in Tibetan icons are covered in skulls and bone ornaments to symbolize this death.

When the ego's solid structures and limitations become a hindrance to wholeness, the Self can become ruthless in its power to effect change and break these obstacles down. In the process of death and transformation the Self becomes the dark angel, like Pluto, lord of the underworld, who demands that we give way. This inner archetypal intent can be felt as an awful and awesome relentless force that will tear us to pieces and dismantle our world so that we are transformed, even though change may be excruciating and terrifying. The fear that arises, however, does so only because of the ego's disposition to cling to existence.

From a Buddhist point of view, when we have no understanding of our true nature, we may feel we are staring into the abyss of annihilation. If we understand our true nature, there can be a greater trust in the process of opening. Our essential nature is clear, spacious, and luminous, free of the dualities of good and bad, light and dark. While we cling to relative concepts about our self and our reality, we suffer and become torn apart. As we empty and release, we come to a place of ease and spaciousness that is beyond the ego's limiting fears and identity. In Tibetan Buddhism this is known as the nondual ground of being, a quality of awareness where there is no person, no form, no struggle, and no suffering because there is no one to suffer.

The point of letting go is a special moment. It is the still, quiet pause of death. There is no movement, no sound to stir the quiet tranquility, like a silent morning on a lake when nothing stirs and there is not a breath of breeze. At this moment there is no horror because there is no one to be horrified. There is no despair because the worst has already passed and we have given up. In this moment there is only quiet presence and rest. It is a powerful moment to meditate upon the clarity of our innate nature. We can taste our essential totality—the complete absence of self in the experience of clear, present awareness.

Renewal

As we pass through this dark passage, one quality of being is immensely valuable but often lacking—namely, compassion. In our darkest moments, it is almost impossible to see ourselves with compassion; it needs, rather, to be reflected from outside. This can be an important ingredient of any support we may get from those around us. In the myth of the descent of Innana to the underworld to meet her sister Eriskegal, Innana lies dismembered and waiting, having gone through a gradual stripping away of her upperworld identity. Eriskegal, the dark goddess, is pregnant, wailing and moaning in the pain of labor. At that moment Enki, the upperworld god, sends two little creatures whose task is to show a simple reflection of compassion. They respond to Eriskegal's pain by saying, "Woe to your pain." Their act of sympathetic reflection does not interfere or change the pain; it merely honors the pain so that it is possible for Eriskegal to surrender.[29]

As we begin to emerge from our descent and death, a glimmer of compassion and forgiveness for ourselves may also grow. Prior to this, we have probably been unable to see our pain objectively and recognize what we are going through. When we have the space to see our suffering a little more objectively, we can begin to respond to our situation with love and compassion.

Gradually something in our psyche changes and we become conscious that the dark foreboding has begun to lift. During these periods in my own life, I have suddenly become aware that the deep fear and hopelessness has gone and there is a seed of hope germinating. I begin to notice things again, as if I had returned from a land disconnected from my surroundings. I see plants and flowers again and start to notice their beauty and color with renewed enjoyment. It is the time when spring returns following a hard winter, as symbolized, for example, by the release of Persephone from the underworld, where she had been taken against her will by Pluto. At this stage, I have felt like someone walking on legs that had not been used for a while. I am not sure who I am and how to relate to the world from this new sense of myself. A rebirth is taking place, one that needs to be protected as we would protect fragile new shoots emerging after winter.

To protect this process, we will need others around us who understand and respect the fact that we are vulnerable and learning to relate again. We should give this reemergence time and not expect too much of ourselves. We will often need to restore some of our persona and protection before we return to the world, so that our sensitivity is not violated. We may need to choose carefully those people to whom we relate our experiences. If we are unskillful, we may disclose things to those who do not understand or respect what has happened. This can be very wounding when what we need is to be acknowledged and accepted. This care is equally necessary when we finish a meditation retreat, for very similar reasons. We may not have experienced the same depth of pain or disintegration, but the sense of returning from a deep place back into the world can be just as disorientating at first.

As we reemerge from the wasteland, we have been deeply and subtly changed. We may not fully understand the nature of that change, but we will have a deeper insight into our fears, wounds, and Shadow. Once we have faced these sides of ourselves, we will grow through the experience. As our vitality and creativity returns, time is required to rebuild confidence in ourselves again. One of the gifts that can come with this descent journey is a greater relationship to our inner resources and ability to accomplish what we need for ourselves in life. If we have been able to touch the "baseline" of our true nature, we can have a deeper trust and confidence in this reality. This may particularly enable us to start to live from a different center, in our true nature, free of the ego-centered habits and fears that limited us before.

In the dark night, our alienation is felt as a loss of or separation from our true nature—from the Self or God. The journey we have been through happens because, to use Jung's language, the Self is trying to restore our relationship to its presence as the source of wholeness and healing. We may need to undergo this process more than once in our lives, particularly when we lose our way. Far from being a sign that something is wrong with us, this experience of descent or crisis is the natural mechanism used by the psyche to make us whole. In this respect, the journey of descent is not something to fear; rather, it is a natural process of healing.

I have learned to respect this journey of descent as sacred, rather than seeing it as something that should be hurried or perceived as an obstacle. Sadly, in our culture, we generally do not respect or appreciate the significance of times of transition, death, and transformation. Our working environment and the demands of Western life are such that we can seldom drop what we are doing and have the luxury of going into retreat or taking time to heal. Occasionally our body will demand that we do so, however, by becoming sick or incapacitated. We need to respect that this period of transition will require time and understanding. We need friends and relatives who will at the very least respect what we are going through and not criticize us and demand that we stop being indulgent. We will most likely be antisocial and wish to be alone, yet at the same time need the support of those who can genuinely help. If these wishes are not respected, we may feel others' expectations to be an unbearable burden. Time, sympathetic understanding, and a healing, non-judgmental environment of acceptance and compassion are very supportive to the healing process. The last thing we need is someone trying to make it better or to get us to snap out of it.

Those who are used to being in control and having methods and techniques to deal with their problems will find periods of depression a major test. There are, however, few things that can make the process comfortable or manageable. What may help is some form of expression through writing or painting. It can be particularly helpful to use meditation as a means to stay with painful feelings and allow them to take their course. During times of descent and transformation, the two most important aspects of being with the process are to try to maintain a conscious awareness and to give the unconscious a means to dia-

logue. Meditation can provide a powerful basis for the former; the latter may need a means of support such as therapy.

In the journey of individuation, it is almost inevitable that at some
point we will pass through a period of spiritual crisis. This may well
bring us to the journey of descent, death, and transformation. If we are
to grow on this journey, we need to understand the significance of
what is taking place. When we respond to the psyche skillfully and discover the meaning and insight gained from crossing the wasteland,
healing and transformation can take place. There are those who believe
the spiritual journey should be one that brings only experiences of
transcendence, light, love, and joy. For many of us, however, the journey involves a descent into the underworld where there is a depth of
wisdom to be found that is not so idealistic and naïve. Liberation
comes when we are able to touch the depth of our pain, allow ourselves to surrender, and reemerge transformed. This is not a journey
for the fainthearted, but then, there is often little choice. In my spiritual path I have offered many prayers to be able to transform and grow
to overcome my limitations and fears. I suspect that I often had a sub-
text, however, that was saying, "but please don't make it be too
painful." It has only been with time that I have grown to genuinely
accept the growth that comes through pain and turmoil.

O N MYTHICAL JOURNEYS there are often places where in order to cross a particular threshold, it is necessary to make an offering to the guardians of the gateway. In Greek mythology, before the souls of the dead may cross the river Styx on their journey to the underworld, they must pay a fee to Charon, the ferryman. In the myth of Amor and Psyche, Psyche descends into the underworld in search of the salve of beauty, which Aphrodite had demanded. To cross the Styx, she needs a payment for Charon as well as some scraps of food to give to the dog Cerberus. This payment or gift is known as a *talent,* without which it would be impossible to cross over.

There are many other examples in fairy tales and myths in which in order to cross a threshold, it is necessary to have the right talent. The word *talent* has a number of meanings, the most obvious being the possession of a quality or skill. A talent also refers to a coin or currency that is needed in an exchange of goods or services. In this sense, a talent is connected with the power of money to enable us to accomplish or gain something. The talent is an enabling capacity that gives us the power and right to pass, to cross a threshold. From a psychological perspective it may be said that in order to cross a threshold, we must have the quality or ability needed to go on. The talent is an inner resource, an inner personal power or vitality that helps one to proceed on the psychological or spiritual journey and gain deeper insights.

An example of this need for personal vitality occurs in the process of guided imagery that I use in workshops. If we are intending to cross the threshold into the unconscious, whether in the context of therapy or guided imagery, we need vitality in the mind to do so. Anyone who has been involved in imagery work will recognize how much energy is used in the process. It can be very tiring and requires that we do not use the process for too long a time.

While it is true that much deep psychological work can release energy untapped in the unconscious, at the same time, rest is vital. When we are engaging in deep emotional work, we experience how draining it can be. If we wish to go deeper on our own growth path, we will be able to do so only when our psyche is ready and we have the vitality for it. It is as though there is a natural protective mechanism at work to prevent us from pushing our process, even though we may try. Often, after long periods of emotional stress or turmoil, we will need to stop and rest. If we don't, our body may tell us to do so by getting sick. Basically, we will have run out of talent.

The talent, therefore, is the symbol of the inner power, energy, or vitality we require to make transitions on our journey. One could see this more literally in the way that we may require certain knowledge or understanding to be able to take the next step. We may need to reach a certain strength or stability in ourselves before we are able to make the descent required to heal some very painful wound. This descent can often only be undertaken when we are ready and strong enough to face it.

In a similar way, often there are things we may want to do or achieve, but everything seems to block us. We may be struggling to earn money or get our work to develop, or we may try to set up some project, only to find we are blocked. Again, we may not yet have gained the energy or talent to carry it through. We may need to be patient and wait to build our resources; we may need to tap a deeper source of vitality in order to go on.

I have seen many examples of this experience in therapy, but one person stands out in particular—someone who had been unable to change, both psychologically and externally in her life, because there was a profound sense of a lack of personal capacity, vitality, and will. She was like someone with no bones trying to push her way out of a thick cocoon. No matter what we attempted to explore in the therapy situation, it was apparent that it was always coming to nothing. She needed to tap into an inner resource of vitality that could begin to engage her in her life, but this source seemed inaccessible. Gradually, a depth of frustration grew that released some of her hidden anger. This release caused a shift, and she began to focus her attention on small tasks that could be achieved. She succeeded in accomplishing these tasks, and it released in her the energy to move towards other things that she began to feel were possible. This in turn generated more vitality to engage further, and slowly she was able to gain a sense of her capacity to do things she could never have done previously.

If we need a resource of vitality to accomplish things in our normal daily life, in a more subtle way we need this resource to cross certain thresholds on our spiritual journey. From a Buddhist perspective, we might consider what the Tibetans call "merit" (Tib. *sonam*). The "accumulation of merit" emphasized in the Tibetan traditions can sound like a materialistic, acquisitive attitude, as if one is collecting credits or good deeds. Even so, the concept of merit and its accumulation has an important significance once we understand it.

In a story that comes from the guidebook to Shambhala, one of the few examples of a mythical journey within the Tibetan tradition, there is an interesting reference that links the mythical talent with the need for merit.[30] A specific instruction is given pertaining to the accumulation of merit required to make a boat manifest to cross a huge lake and then create a fair wind to sail it by. In this journey, which could be seen as part mythical, part literal, whenever specific places of transition are encountered, an accumulation of merit is necessary to cross them. With merit the traveler can move forward, but without it, many hindrances will occur.

Within Buddhist Sutra teachings the idea of merit is an aspect of the understanding of karma. *Karma* is usually translated as an action which gives rise to specific results, either positive or negative. Unwholesome actions give rise to negative and unpleasant results, and wholesome actions to positive results and happiness. Merit is considered to be a particular kind of karma that is generated as the cause for a specific effect, namely enlightenment or liberation. While ordinary karma ripens within the context of samsara, the cycle of death and rebirth, merit is karma that ripens specifically to enable the mind to awaken and go beyond samsara. It is sometimes called non-samsaric karma. Merit is therefore considered to be the potential in the mind that is cultivated to enable so-called realizations and experiences of practice to ripen. Many Tibetan Buddhist teachers in particular will emphasize that without an accumulation of merit, there is no possibility of realizations ripening in the mind. One of the major factors that generate this kind of karma is the quality of intention, the motivation. In the Mahayana tradition, the bodhisattva generates the intention of bodhichitta, which is said to be like the trajectory of a rocket that propels the karmic result towards a specific goal of awakening, or enlightenment.

An important and subtly different understanding of merit comes within the Tantras. The accumulation of merit is viewed as the development of a kind of energy or vitality that is associated with a subtle energy-wind body.[31] From the tantric point of view the mind has two characteristics. One is the quality of awareness and knowing, and the other is the quality of movement and luminosity. This second attribute is considered to be a subtle energy-wind body that is enhanced through the accumulation of merit. This in turn generates the power of the mind to be able to accomplish certain effects. Only when we have gained a sufficient degree of vitality will we be able to develop the power of the mind to experience qualities in meditation such as tranquil abiding, or the power to visualize a deity clearly. Only a mind with vitality will have the power to step across certain thresholds of awareness. To gain the power to understand emptiness, or opening to our higher nature, energy is required. In the tantric tradition, the ability to awaken the inspiration and qualities of a deity requires a great deal of vitality.

The attribute of the mind that gives rise to inner vision requires the cultivation of vitality that gives it luminosity, inspiration, and creative energy. The unconscious reveals its innate wisdom through symbol and archetypal image. In Buddhist Tantra this is the deity, which gradually manifests in meditation through the cultivation of merit, that gives the mind the power to open.

If this energy is lacking, we cannot force a process to occur. Some people when in retreat try to push and squeeze "realizations" out of their practices of meditation. This usually results in exhaustion, disappointment, and sometimes mental or physical sickness. I experienced this myself when in India attempting to do a nine-month tranquil abiding (Tib. *shi né*) retreat. I pushed and pushed, attempting to develop a capacity of concentration, as if squeezing dozens of oranges into a small container. The net result was a disruption to my energy-winds that for a time seriously affected my eyesight. I have had friends who have also pushed themselves in retreat and suffered similar energy-wind disorders that caused terrible pains in the heart or the head.

It is important to recognize our limitations and not to try to force the ferryman to take us across when we don't have the fare. To do otherwise is foolish and dangerous. When we encounter obstacles, sometimes we need to allow that to be so for a while until we are ready.

At these times we may experience something akin to depression. Our energy and vitality have been drawn down into the unconscious. We may feel incapable of moving on and will need to just wait. Deep within our unconscious a process is taking place, one that is demanding that our normal energy be elsewhere. This, too, is like a protection that stops us from being able to participate at a time when we need to replenish our energy. At these times the energy of the psyche has withdrawn to be used to effect transformation deeper in the unconscious. When the process is finished, our energy will return and we will probably feel a sense of renewal.

In the Tibetan Buddhist tradition there are specific ways of preparing ourselves for the path. These take the form of "preliminary practices," or *ngöndro,* specifically designed to perform two functions. Firstly, there are ways of clearing any potential inner obstructions that might prevent us from going forward. Secondly, there are practices intended to cultivate the necessary merit or vitality to enable insights to be gained in the journey. Thus, particularly in the tantric path, the processes of purification and accumulation are given great emphasis, for without them we will not be prepared.

One of the most important practices for the generation of vitality is that of generosity, whether this is seen as the way one lives one's life or, more specifically, as ritual offering. Among the many practices involving offering, one in particular, the mandala offering, is very interesting. This involves generating a visualization of the wealth and riches throughout the universe and offering them to the Buddhas. In the traditional teachings this is described in a particular way that builds up a symbolic picture of the universe based around a central mountain called Mount Sumeru. This visualization is accompanied through an actual construction of a symbolic mandala.

The psychology behind this practice is very important, as it symbolizes the universe that each of us inhabits. The mandala is a symbol of our totality in the form of an archetypal universe. This universe is made up of different aspects of ourselves—our material and emotional lives and our relationships. These we offer to the Buddhas as a gesture of surrender of every facet of ourselves, our potential wholeness or totality. In this process we are learning to open and let go, and as we open we free our innate capacity. In the process of releasing we are able to receive the capacity to awaken.

Other practices for accumulating vitality, such as prostrations and certain deity practices, are also connected to the purification, cleansing, and healing of what blocks our vitality. Such a block can be seen as the toxicity that accumulates in our life and acts as an obstruction. Once this obstruction is cleared, our innate vitality is freed. We may understand this on a purely energetic level; we may see it as an aspect of our emotional health; we might recognize this within our bodies, or we could see it reflected in the environment we inhabit. Essentially, the effect will be the same: our energy will be released and become available to us in a more creative way.

In the tantric path, the energy and inspiration we experience come from a deep connection to a deity. As an image of the Self, to use

Jung's term, a deity is the source of true inner power and vitality. When we touch this source it will enable leaps of awareness and insight that can have a profound effect on our lives.

When we come to certain points in our path, we must, from a Tibetan Buddhist perspective, make the necessary preparations in order to go forward. If we do so it is like preparing the soil for planting. When the soil is cleared of stones and rubbish and well-fertilized with good compost, plants will flourish. If the soil is tired and all the goodness leached out, little will grow and what does will often be stunted and weak. So too with our spiritual journey: when the mind and its vitality are prepared, the next step will be a relatively natural one. We will be able to cross the threshold into the sacred ground of profound insight.

Palden Lhamo

W HEN WE ARE CLOSE to the threshold of the sacred, we may encounter guardians at the gate. They will ask of us that we relinquish our dearly cherished identity before we can step through. Only those prepared can enter the sacred ground, and to do so without preparation can be psychologically hazardous. It is with good reason that fierce creatures usually guard temples and sacred places. These are not inviting figures. They are there to make us stop and reflect. Do we truly wish to cross this threshold? Are we doing so consciously? Are we ready for the consequences of our rite of passage? As Joseph Campbell writes, "The adventure is always and everywhere a passage beyond the veil of the known into the unknown; the powers that watch at the boundary are dangerous; to deal with them is risky; yet for anyone with competence and courage the danger fades."[32]

In my travels to the Far East, India, and Nepal, I have seen these guardians time and again at the entrances to temples and holy places. Often they are demonic-looking mythical creatures. Sometimes they are powerful warrior-like figures who look down at us with terrifying ferocity. They may cause the fainthearted to pause and turn back, and may repel those with malicious intent by reflecting back that malice. They are a call to wake up and have integrity so that we do not act with ignorance and frivolousness as we enter the sacred ground. They mark a threshold and seem to say that what lies within or beyond is not for everyone.

In 1973 I visited the island of Bali in Indonesia and stayed for a while in a village called Ubud. Close to the village, a river had carved a deep ravine filled with lush vegetation. In the forest that surrounded this ravine was a Hindu temple that I often passed on my way down to the river, where there was another, smaller temple. I passed this forest temple and never went inside, so I have no idea what it was like within the high, elaborately carved walls. This was partly because a group of aggressive monkeys lived around the temple and I did not like getting too close to them. More significantly, however, I did not enter because standing to either side of the entrance were two imposing statues of a Hindu goddess the Balinese call Rangda. She stands with fierce, bulging eyes and a long tongue extending to the ground. In her mouth and hands she holds babies that she devours with huge fangs. This is a temple to the dark, devouring mother goddess, a powerful and very frightening figure that I felt extremely reluctant to offend. I felt instinctively that I should keep out.

In myths and folk tales there are often such figures that stand at crucial thresholds. They stand at the entrances of sacred places such as churches and temples. They may take the form of sphinxes, lions, dragons, monstrous demons, giants, and other creatures. Their function is to guard a point of transition from those who are not ready to cross. They often protect a sacred object or treasure, and only those who have the right qualifications may pass. This may require answering a specific riddle, as with the sphinx. Placating them may mean having a certain gift to offer, or that we are willing to give up some aspect of ourselves and surrender. They may require that we have a particular knowledge or attitude of mind such as fearlessness or loving kindness. Occasionally, the guardian may need to be slain or overcome by force.

In the Buddhist world these guardians are also present, and an understanding of their meaning comes particularly from the practice of Tantra. One may ask, however, where does this archetypal expression of guardians arise from, and what is their relevance to us? A psychological understanding of such figures may be important. What is the point of this threshold that is so closely guarded? To make sense of these questions, it may be useful to consider the psychological significance of the threshold within the psyche between consciousness and the unconscious.

Our early years as children were full of imaginative fantasy that did not separate the outer world from the inner life. We may have talked to the trees and flowers and had invisible friends around who formed part of the magic of childhood reality. Adults may not have been able to enter this realm, but it felt very real to us. There seemed to be no delineation between the inner world of imagination and the outer world of material objects. Rather, we experienced the inner world as if it existed out there. There was no need to consider it as a projection because inner and outer had not yet become differentiated.

With time, we learned to differentiate our inner life from outer reality. Many aspects of our inner life, including much of the imaginal fantasy aspect of childhood, gradually sank into the unconscious. According to Barbara Somers, at a point in childhood, often around seven or eight years of age, a threshold will develop that separates the inner life from the outer. There may be a marked increase in fearful dreams and in thoughts about creatures of the night that frighten us. The psyche is beginning to close off aspects of the inner world and create a domain that is increasingly shadowy and contains mystery and unknown, dark contents. There is a growing threshold between consciousness and the unconscious. This mechanism gradually becomes a necessary protection so that consciousness and a stable ego-identity is able to form and emerge from the amorphous world of the unconscious with its magic, gods, demons, monsters, and fairies.

Were we not to develop this threshold it could eventually lead to psychosis, a state in which consciousness becomes flooded with unconscious life and we potentially lose all sense of conscious reality and self-identity. As the threshold develops and strengthens, so too does our sense of self. When the threshold is poorly formed or very permeable, as in those who do not have a strong sense of self, there may often be fears of the loss of self or feelings of disappearing or drowning, as if one is being sucked into a sea of annihilation. For others, the lack of threshold may provide a welcome retreat into a dreamy fantasy world that feels safe, out of touch as it is with the real pains of life.

The consequences of abusing or ignoring threshold warnings can be psychological problems, including psychosis. However, there is in the psyche a natural mechanism, of which guardians and protectors are a symbolic expression, that protects us from the dangers of having no defined threshold between different states of awareness. I recall an occasion in retreat when I was paying a lot of attention to my dreams, always noting them down and becoming fascinated by their content almost to the point of obsession. This was having an increasingly disorienting effect on my relationship to the normal, daily world. My dreams were becoming almost too powerful for me to cope with. One night I had a dream of a huge bear standing in the window of my retreat hut and then trying to get through the door. On another night I dreamed that the face of a black witch appeared at my window saying, "If you are not careful, I will destroy you." It was a tremendous jolt to my psyche, and I suddenly realized I had to close down the threshold for a while or be flooded by the unconscious. I stopped my obsessive dream watching and began to feel more stable again.

These guardians at the threshold, therefore, function in three different ways. Firstly, they enable a differentiation of what is inner and outer in our own psyche. They symbolize the creation of a necessary threshold between consciousness and the unconscious—between one state of awareness and another. This distinction is necessary for the cultivation of a sense of identity and the capacity for conscious focus. Without it, we would have serious psychological problems.

Secondly, the guardian marks a point of transition in the journey where we may encounter a rite of passage necessary to go forward. There are various times in life when we pass through periods of transition. Puberty, the "Saturn return" at around thirty, mid-life, and so on are all times of transition. To pass through them and go forward, we may find we must let go of some aspect of the past and change our view of ourselves.

Thirdly, the guardian is there to protect the threshold to what is ultimately a sacred truth or insight that has great significance and power. This is often symbolized by some sacred object, which in the wrong hands becomes a source of destruction and "evil." Symbolically, this sacred object may be held in a sacred place protected by guardians. The guardian is there to ensure that nothing crosses the threshold that will violate the inner sanctuary or the world beyond.

In Tibetan Buddhism particularly, the principle of the guardian has been developed to an extraordinary degree. The protectors of the Dharma are evoked and propitiated to maintain, preserve, and guard the sacred. On a psychological level, they can be understood as protecting the psyche from what is without or within. The Dharma protector may protect the practitioner from outer negative and chaotic forces he or she may encounter which might invade or violate. This could be understood as the literal invasion of the psyche by interfering entities. Equally, it could be understood as the potential invasion of particularly powerful negative collective energy, the kind of energy that can be generated in parts of cities. In some tantric practices, guardians can be used as an aid to protect from the potentially destructive polluting energy that is in our environment.

Dharma protectors can also be understood as a means to protect us from inner interferences. These are aspects of our own unconscious lives that may erupt from time to time and hinder our state of mind, and may include harmful doubts, depression, and negativity that prevent us from being able to remain with clarity and awareness. Inner hindrances may also be mental instability, or disturbed and unhealthy energy within our psychophysical nervous system. They may additionally be understood to be karmic obstacles that would make Buddhist practice difficult. Perhaps the most damaging inner hindrance, therefore, is the fundamental veil of ignorance that obscures our minds.

Dharma protectors ensure that only those who are prepared for particular spiritual experiences are able to go beyond the veil of ignorance and to step into an utterly radical view of reality. The realization of emptiness, or *shunyata,* shakes our reality. It will take us to a way of being from which we cannot return, like Adam after he has eaten of the fruit of knowledge, and we must be prepared to accept the consequences. When our wisdom eye is opened we cannot blind ourselves to the truth. As is indicated in the bodhisattva precepts, one should not teach the profound view of emptiness to those who are not ready.

In Tantra, to enter the sacred space of the deity also requires that we be prepared psychologically. At the threshold of this experience stand the guardians of protection. Many of the guardian forms that are used in the Buddhist traditions have a semi-mythical/historical origin. They may have been harmful demons that have been subdued and transformed into what are called "oath-bound protectors" sworn to guard sacred places, practitioners, or the teachings. Others are direct manifestations of enlightened activity as deities specifically intended to protect practitioners from harmful interferences, to guard the inner sanctity of the mandala in tantric practice, or to protect external sacred places.

Guardians and protectors may reflect to us the way we deal with boundaries. Sometimes we are very bad at creating or defining our boundaries. Some of us are too afraid to say no. We may have a tendency to be over-influenced and infected by the energy of others around us. We may simply have no ability to protect ourselves from the demands of others. Because we are in a spiritual tradition, we may develop the attitude that to be selfless means to be formless and without boundaries, always giving up our own self for others. This kind of posture is very dangerous, and we can confuse living with an open, giving attitude with a complete inability to clearly define our boundaries and thereby maintain a sense of self-identity. In practice, however, we cannot go beyond boundaries until we are clear about them. We cannot go beyond self until we have a clearer sense of self.

The principle of the protector in this case really represents a very practical willingness to stand firm in defining our boundaries. The quality of the protector or guardian is to define the point beyond which others may not pass and infringe upon our personal space. We may need to become much clearer with others about what we will allow, before our sense of self is violated. Many of us find asserting our needs very difficult and thus do not create clear boundaries. It is most often this lack of assertiveness and the resentment that builds up as a result that is a cause of so much anger. This in turn causes us to develop rigid defensive strategies that shield us from hurt in a totally unhealthy and unbalanced way. If we can be clearer about and protect our boundaries, this need not happen. There is a vast difference between defensiveness and having clear boundaries.

A further area of protection that we need to consider is in the area of our life that is most sacred to us. At times in our journey, some new experience may grow that is both fragile and vulnerable. It may then be vital to protect ourselves from the opinions, judgments, or criticisms of others, even those closest to us. They may ridicule or denigrate our deepening inner life in a way that can be extremely damaging. We may need to create a sense of protected space, which can require some degree of secrecy. I have observed the need for such protected space in workshops I lead where participants have taken part in deep guided imagery exercises. These exercises may bring to the surface things that are extremely vulnerable and sensitive. Sometimes this material needs to be kept relatively private so that it is not violated. Occasionally participants have gone home and discussed this material with someone like a partner only to find it misunderstood, dismissed, or devalued. The resulting sense of violation can be hard to heal. This might not have occurred if there had been greater awareness and sensitivity to the need for our inner life to be held sacred and protected.

The sacred space in which we meditate can be another place that needs to be kept safe from inappropriate eyes and intrusion. When we are stronger it may be less necessary to protect ourselves in this way, but the early sprouts of inner awakening may require careful protection. The culture in which we live has little respect for or understanding of the sacred. What we may do in our sacred space can be easily misinterpreted or misunderstood.

Secrecy and an understanding of the need to value and respect the sacred are supported by the presence of guardians. In this respect, the

Buddhist Dharma protectors such as Palden Lhamo a wrathful ema-nation of Tara, and Mahakala, a wrathful aspect of Chenrezig, act as a vital means to protect our inner experience of the sacred in our lives, particularly when there are people and circumstances in the world who will disregard or demean it. They are also there to remind us that the path is not to be taken frivolously but requires that we prepare ourselves skillfully. Once we learn to respect the nature of the guardian's intention in protecting our own evolution from the hazards present in the path, we can face them with honesty and con-fidence. When we prepare ourselves for the step across the threshold, we will have nothing to fear, and the guardians will be no obstacle. What they will ask of us as we cross over, however, is that we let go and surrender those aspects of ourselves that prevent awakening.

A PLACE IS INEVITABLY REACHED in the Buddhist path where we are challenged to go beyond the limitations of our normal ego-identity. We arrive at a threshold that requires that we relinquish our grasping at self and surrender its domination. Prior to this moment we may have had some intellectual knowledge of what it means to let go of the ego and realize emptiness. To be challenged to completely surrender and open is a transition to another level of experience, however, and it is best that we be well prepared. The guardians of this threshold demand a heavy price for us to cross over. Once we are ready, however, we can enter what could be seen as the most profound stage of our journey. We clear the veil that obscures our true nature.

There is a veil of ignorance that clouds our capacity to see things as they truly are. It separates our normal, narrow, limited, daily mind from an awareness that is clear of conceptual clutter, more spacious and open. While the veil is present, our world is bound by our hopes and fears, our expectations and dissatisfaction. We suffer getting what we don't want and not getting what we do want. We see a world where appearances are held to be what they seem to be: solid, substantial, and self-existent. We are caught in an illusion. If we were to penetrate this veil of illusion, we would suddenly recognize the folly of this deception. We would see that the way things appear is not how they actually exist. What seems permanent and independent softens into a fluidity of interdependence and fleeting presence.

On one side of the veil, the world is caught in time and set into forms that crash against each other in an endless collision. This colli-

Mahakala

sion of cause and effect is the source of much suffering and gives rise to the constant sense that our world is deteriorating, wearing out. We inhabit a contracted, restricted sense of space and time that becomes ever more stressful and demanding. This is what we might understand as relative truth. As I pointed out in Chapter 3, the degree to which we suffer is relative to the degree of our tendency to contract. One could equally say that the degree of our suffering is relative to the discrepancy between our view of reality and the nature of reality itself. Our blindness to the true nature of reality leads us to endlessly struggle to make secure what is fundamentally untrustworthy. When we see through the illusion in which we are caught, we awaken to an insight that transforms our experience entirely. We can begin to rest in an entirely different way of seeing.

In the Tibetan tradition much emphasis is placed upon the distinction between relative and ultimate truth. While we are caught in relative truth, we are blind to the nature of ultimate truth. Our blindness to, or ignorance of, the nature of reality is called *ma rig pa,* literally "not seeing," in contrast to the state of insight or *rig pa,* literally "seeing." When we are in a state of ignorance, we hold relative appearances to be absolutes and are blind as to how they actually exist. We see impermanent things as permanent. We attribute qualities to objects and are blind to the fact that our exaggerated view of objects arises through our projections, not from the objects themselves. We attribute solidity and self-existence to a world that is fundamentally insubstantial and fabricated. Our blindness wants to see a world that is reliable, predictable, and secure, when no such reliability can be found. We live with an illusion about our reality that sets us up for suffering. When the world fails to live up to our false expectations, when the illusion crumbles, we feel disappointed, betrayed, insecure, or even angry.

In Buddhism the fundamental dichotomy is between ignorance and insight, as opposed to the struggle between good and evil found in most theistic religions. Blindness and ignorance may indeed lead to "evil" actions, but this is not to imply possession by some form of absolute evil. Insight into the nature of reality will change the very root of all of our actions. We may call this insight an "enlightenment," but this term can be misleading.

The term *enlightenment* can be and often is used in ways that assume any number of possible meanings. Like the term *spiritual,* it can be applied in ways that offer no clarity as to the nature of "enlightened" experience. Enlightenment for a Buddhist, however, is very specific. It is not the sudden understanding of some obscure truth. It is not the sudden revelation or awareness of the presence of some divine entity or godhead. Rather than a presence *of* something, Buddhist enlightenment, paradoxically, could be seen as an absence. It is, however, an awakening to an innate inner wisdom, a state of mind, rather than some kind of divine presence.

The Tibetan term usually translated as "enlightenment" is *jang chub* (Skt. *bodhi*), which is derived from two syllables: *jang,* meaning "purified or cleansed of all defilements or obscurations" and *chub,* meaning "to have total or perfected comprehension of the nature of all phenomena." The Tibetan word for the Sanskrit *buddha,* which is *sanggye,* is also derived from two syllables: *sang,* meaning "cleansed or purified" and *gye,* meaning "possessing vast extensive knowledge."

These terms convey the sense of a state of being or a state of awareness that has two characteristics. One is the attribute of clearing or cleansing of all obstructions, and the other is the perfection of an expansive insight into the nature of reality. The enlightened state is one in which the veil of obscurations has been cleared of dualistic confusion and limiting conceptual clutter. Like the gradual clearing of disturbed or clouded water, this clarification leads to an expansion of awareness. The mind that was clouded and caught in the solidity of relative appearances and obsessive conceptual thinking expands and opens to the clear empty nature of all reality. This state of awareness is sometimes named the "ground of being" or the wisdom of dharmakaya and is often symbolized by the ocean and a deep blue color.

While this wisdom of ultimate truth is experienced continually by a Buddha, it exists for the rest of us as an innate potential we may glimpse on occasions when our minds open. While we are unable to penetrate the veil, this underlying wisdom remains an unconscious dimension of the psyche we may know only through its symbolic metaphors. It is perhaps more than just coincidence that we say things come out of the blue.

When our mind is prepared we may begin to penetrate the veil. The mist of our mind begins to clear and the solidity of our reality begins to soften. Through the cultivation of meditation and a process of purification and clearing of the mind, we may suddenly see through the illusion of reality. Like a thin film of tissue paper punctured with a glowing piece of incense, our mind can experience a "penetrative insight" (Tib. *lhak tong*, Skt. *vipashyana*). We have penetrated the veil and gained an insight that radically changes our understanding. Light shines through this opening and begins to illuminate our darkness.

It is important to recognize the difference between an enlightened experience and the state of enlightenment. To penetrate the veil is to see the nature of reality for the first time. This enlightened experience in the Zen tradition might be called a *satori*. This is a powerful shift of insight that shakes our reality. No longer can we live with the delusion we may have once held. Our solidly held concepts about reality begin to crumble. Samsara shakes, as Lama Yeshe once put it. This experience may not be comfortable. To come so close to this existential threshold challenges our secure sense of identity and can be frightening. Indeed, as a Tibetan lama once said, this fear is a sign that we are close to the edge. We are beginning to recognize the lack of substance of our ego-identity. Our "wisdom eye" has opened to a new truth— an ultimate truth, as opposed to relative truth.

When we penetrate the veil, however, the work is not yet done. We may have had an enlightened experience, but there is further to travel. As Gen Jhampa Wangdu once said while I was in retreat, it is not difficult to experience emptiness; the problem is holding it. For this insight to have its full effect, the mind needs to be able to sustain awareness for prolonged periods of time. Tibetan teachers will some-times say we may hit the nail, but only with a quality of focused attention can we repeatedly do so. With the development of tranquil abiding, the veil can be cleared completely in the way the red ring of fire created by the incense burn slowly expands and consumes the entire film of tissue paper. The mind is gradually cleansed of the emotional turmoil and confusion that is generated by the misconceptions we have about reality.

As the illusion falls from our eyes, we see through the "hallucination," as Lama Thubten Yeshe called it, we have believed for so long. The example that is often quoted in Buddhist texts is that of a person who, walking through a dark street, suddenly sees a coiled rope and thinks it is a snake. In a state of misapprehension, we will react with all the emotions that relate to the snake, until the true nature of the rope is perceived. This is true of our life as a whole. While caught in the illusion of reality, we react as though things are as they appear: solid, true, and self-existent. Once we recognize the illusion, our reactive mind is slowly pacified. There is nothing to react to; there is also no one to react.

This illusion can be just as strong in relation to our spiritual and psychological beliefs. While we cannot or do not distinguish between relative and ultimate truths, we may hold on to our relative doctrines and concepts about our spiritual life as though they were absolute, ultimate truths. When through ignorance, fear, and insecurity we turn relative doctrines into absolute truths, we create dogma and suffer the consequences. Clinging to spiritual beliefs rather than living with uncertainty or spaciousness is a fragile security. When threatened it can lead to the kind of violent defensiveness seen all too often in religious fundamentalism.

Our spiritual beliefs, therefore, can also be part of the veil. Like maps, they are not the territory. They are relative worldviews that help us to map reality on different levels. They enable us to have some way of conceptualizing and making sense of experiences that are often, in essence, beyond conception. The term "God" and all the concepts we may have about God are an obvious example. They are, however, still relative conceptual conventions that are not an ultimate insight into reality. Holding on to beliefs and doctrine, even within Buddhism, as Stephen Batchelor points out, is just as much a subtle level of blindness.[33]

When we are able to let go of holding any relative view as ultimately true, there is a greater freedom in the mind and our beliefs will not become part of the veil that blinds us. An important Indian Buddhist philosopher named Nagarjuna was the propagator of a philosophical view that became known as the Prasangika Madhyamaka. The term *prasangika* could be translated as "consequentialist" to imply that rather than proposing a particular view as correct, these practitioners would simply look at the consequences of holding on to any particular view. They would show that whatever views someone held would have a tendency to limit, polarize, or rigidify the mind. What they attempted to find was a "middle way" (*madhyamaka*) where dualistic polarities are resolved in a paradoxical middle ground that is neither one nor the other. Nagarjuna asserted that a bodhisattva should learn to tread a path that ceases to cling to any belief, view, or ideal as an absolute. If he or she can allow the mind to rest without grasping at extremes, there will be no reason to become caught in contention.

Living with these different levels of blindness brings endless confusion and conflict. Only when we lift this veil of illusion will we begin to face reality. But the illusion is deeply ingrained and is cleared only gradually. It is not so difficult to recognize that things are impermanent. We can see through much of our exaggerated projections upon objects that attract or repel us. It is less easy to see through the veil created by our beliefs and our sense of self-identity. It is even more difficult to shift the view of appearances as solid entities existing "out there" as separate, self-existent things.

THE PRACTICE OF EMPTINESS

The veil that separates us from an understanding of the true nature of reality is penetrated only by a particular quality of mind. Thinking endlessly about it and cultivating sophisticated philosophical and theolog-

ical systems does not do the job. Indeed, it may even strengthen the
veil. Insight (Tib. *lhak tong*; Skt. *vipashyana)* comes with the cultivation
of a quality of awareness that is largely the result of meditation.

Our usual daily mind is busy and preoccupied with discursive chatter the Tibetans call *namtok*. We are constantly caught in thinking
processes that actually obscure our capacity for insight. The concepts
and beliefs we construct are also not easy to transcend. There may be
flashes of insight that arise at certain times in our life, like Maslow's
peak experiences. Our reality may crack and open at certain critical
times of crisis. A sustained state of being that is open to this insight,
free of discursive thinking, is, however, gained principally through
meditation. There are many different styles of meditation, but the one
I wish to refer to, called *Mahamudra*, is practiced particularly within the
Tibetan tradition.

Mahamudra emphasizes the nature of the mind, as opposed to the
breath, feelings, or visualizations, as the primary object of meditation.
The intention of meditation is to gradually cultivate a quality of presence that is clear and open. As awareness becomes increasingly quiet,
clear, and free of discursive chatter, we will be able to remain present
with the arising and passing of our experiences, whether they are feelings, sensations, thoughts, images, sounds, sights, and so on, watching
their passing without interfering with them. With experience, the mind
becomes gradually more relaxed yet alert and able to remain in a state
of clarity and presence that is no longer disturbed by the arising of
appearances, thoughts, or feelings. As this "bare awareness" stabilizes,
we begin to see that the relative appearances that normally affect our
mind are fleeting and insubstantial. They are an illusory play, like a
dream or a mirage, lacking inherent solidity. In the language of Mahamudra, they are recognized as the play of emptiness.

Through remaining present within our inner processes we will also
begin to see the subtle pull of our emotional and feeling life. We will
perhaps for the first time be able to watch the process of our emotions
and the activity that arises from them without becoming caught in their
compulsion. As we are freed from their power and influence, we may

then also start to recognize that the ego that is held so strongly as a focus of being is also an illusion.

As awareness settles and opens to a more spacious presence in whatever arises within the body, feelings, and mind, it becomes apparent that there is no central, solid, permanent axis of awareness. Our sense of a self is insubstantial and momentary. It is a focus of attention that is created in each moment as a subjective self in relationship to objects of awareness. It has no continuity as a substantial entity. As meditation deepens and awareness opens, our sense of self becomes increasingly permeable, fluid, and spacious. Eventually, it becomes natural to experience a state of being that does not hold to a contracted identity at all.

This experience will contrast with that of the contracted, emotionally charged sense of self that can be felt to be a solid entity. As we have seen in Chapter 3, the "ego-grasping" that contracts around a "vividly appearing I" is the wounded sense of self we have developed from infancy. It will often carry fundamental emotional beliefs about ourselves—for instance, that we are worthless or unlovable—that are held as absolutes. At the core of all these emotional wounds we will also discover an underlying existential anxiety that is the essential emotional tone of ego-grasping. With clear, present awareness we will begin to feel the fleeting, insubstantial nature of this vivid "I" which, like writing on water, cannot ultimately be found. This may at first accentuate the sense of anxiety, as the sense of self we have held for so long begins to unravel. This is an important moment because we are on the edge of a profound shift in our inner landscape. If we stay with the process of opening, we can step finally into a space of no-self where the contraction and anxiety that has held on for so long begins to evaporate. We will be left with a deep sense of ease and spaciousness. There is no anxiety because there is no one to be anxious.

This is not to say that the "I" or ego does not exist or has no relative value. Although many people receiving teachings on Buddhism fall into a notion that the ego must be gotten rid of, this is a very misleading idea. Without a relative sense of ego-identity we could not function in the relative world. We are able to say "I sit," "I eat," and so on. This "I" is a perfectly valid expression of a focus of self-identity. It is, however, merely a label placed upon the whole of the person. To lose this label is to actually endanger our sanity. When we negate the relative "I," we end up losing the thing that enables us to function and remain functional. Without it, there is the probability of psychosis. Essentially, we must have an ego before we can go beyond it.

Once we have established the nature of the functional ego or "I," we can safely recognize its illusory nature without insanity. The Dalai Lama has said that a bodhisattva requires a strong ego to follow the path he or she is on. This does not imply that the bodhisattva is blind to the true nature of that ego. Instead, it is still possible to live with a strong, stable "relative I" while recognizing its ultimately empty nature.

The recognition of the empty nature of the ego will loosen the contraction around "I," the ego-grasping that holds the "I" as something ultimately solid or true. This loosens the relationship to the core of our emotional life, as there will be less and less disposition to contract around emotions and create dramas out of nothing. Fear may arise but can pass through without anyone being caught in identification with its energy. Anger may come, but its energy can be allowed to pass through and be freed into its essential nature. This may bring a capacity to be strong and assertive without getting caught in egotism.

Penetrating the veil is the beginning of a process that cleanses the mind of all tendencies to be caught in dualistic thinking. Returning again and again in meditation to the spacious clarity of the original insight gradually clears the veil. As a result, the mind increasingly settles in a quality of tranquil abiding (Tib. s*hi né*; Skt. *shamata*). While the term s*hi né* is sometimes translated as "concentration," this can be profoundly misleading. The experience is not of the mind concentrated like oranges in a bottle. Rather, it is a quality of mind that is naturally settling in a state of awareness that is neither too loose nor too tight. In the "Song of Mahamudra," Tilopa describes how one should remain loose and natural, resting at ease so that the mind gradually settles into its pristine clarity.[34]

As the mind's pristine nature shines through, luminous and free of duality, our normal, dualistic mind evaporates like clouds dissolving back into the blue sky. The veil clears and we open to nonduality, the ground of being. Once stabilized, this enlightened wisdom is known as *dharmakaya*, the "truth body" of a Buddha. The meditator's mind has opened to the vast, expansive, empty nature of reality, within which appearances arise as the play of emptiness.

PRESENCE

As we settle in meditation, we encounter a paradox at the heart of Buddhist understanding. We may practice a path that unfolds through life, and yet the primary ingredient of transformation rests in being utterly present. As a psychotherapist and Buddhist practitioner, I have often been torn between what at first seem to be two very different views of psychological healing. One view sees the unfolding of a process as the natural progression of change and transformation. The other sees that psychological healing occurs when we are able to remain present, open, and accepting, whatever is happening.

Our paradox remains: there is a path, a process that unfolds, and yet the truth that dawns is about presence. The Buddha's most profound recognition, as a consequence of his own personal journey, was that there was really nowhere to go. He gained a state of awareness that was no longer endlessly drawn into the cycle of change and movement. In striving towards awakening he came to a place of sublime stillness and presence. He saw that the process of going somewhere was an illusion based on the premise of there being an inherent self or "I" that was going. The dawning of this realization brought him to the notion expressed in the *Heart Sutra:* "In emptiness there is no suffering, no cause of suffering, no cessation of suffering and no path".[35]

The Buddha saw that so long as we are caught in relative conceptions about our life we live in an apparent linearity of a process unfolding and are blind to the truth. We may travel a path in search of the truth, we may strive for self-improvement and realization; but when insight comes, the truth seems somewhat ironic. To paraphrase Chögyam

Trungpa, we go around and around, trying to improve ourselves through struggle, until we realize that the ambition to improve ourselves is itself the problem.[36] Why could we not see it? In the present moment all is essentially empty, fleeting, and like a mirage. If we can rest in the present and let go of the self that is trying to understand and get somewhere, all is completely as it is. In the moment there is no separate, substantial person and no solid, inherently existent world of appearances: there is no split, no duality. Both subjective self and objective world are a fleeting play of appearances that are momentarily arising and passing away.

When we settle into this quality of presence we find a state of openness and acceptance of what is. Nothing needs to be different, as it is experienced with clarity and openness. In the Mahamudra teaching, the fruit of practice awakens as the realization that our essential nature is pristine, pure awareness, free of defilements. This has been there in the beginning as our essential nature; we have simply failed to recognize it in our busy, chaotic state. When we awaken this experience, there is nowhere to go as we remain in the unfolding of the present moment.

The shift of view from the unfolding process of our journey to a quality of presence can occur at any point (see Appendix). One could say that clear presence is the most profound way to relate to any experience in the path. We could be standing at a painful threshold in our life and shift the focus of our attention to exactly what is in the present moment and simply witness the fears, anxieties, or the excitement and anticipation of the journey. We could be in the wasteland in a state of utter despair and, in that instant, simply open our awareness to the clarity and spaciousness of the moment. This shift is simply our capacity to remain open and fully accepting of exactly what is in that moment. When we are able to make this shift of awareness, our emotional or felt relationship to what is happening is subtly transformed. Rather than being pulled along by fears and worries, we can open to the spaciousness that is there in clarity and presence.

In the experience of presence, the ego lets go of the tendency to interfere with the world and struggle to make it different. This letting go is a fundamental acceptance that all is as it is: no fighting who we are, no judging ourselves to be this or that, no clinging to beliefs about ourselves, no struggling to be different. Such thoughts and feelings simply solidify and close us to reality. We contract around that sense of self and get caught in the entire process of the need for things to be different. In present awareness we unfreeze our reality and enable it to unfold as it is. The mahasiddha Saraha likened our ignorance to a freezing wind that solidifies the waves of the ocean into solid, static entities.[37] The wisdom of present, open awareness found in Mahamudra unfreezes these waves and allows the natural, unfolding play of reality.

As we have seen, psychological wounding comes from contracting around a sense of "I" that is actually an illusion. This emotionally charged, vividly appearing "I" has at its root a profound, existential anxiety that never subsides while we still remain holding on. The antidote to this anxiety is to cultivate a quality of presence that ceases grasping at entities. As if diving into space and remaining in free fall, the mind becomes accustomed to having no reference point. In that experience, anxiety may reach its peak and then evaporate as the mind lets go.

This experience became horribly familiar to me during periods of retreat in the high mountains in India at the time of the monsoon. For months at a time the place would be so entirely enveloped in cloud that there was no visibility whatsoever. This had a curious effect. I had nothing to visually hold on to, to distract myself. My anxiety levels would keep rising. The vivid sense of the fragility of my ego-grasping became so acute that I was forced to face a letting go I could hardly bear. Eventually, something did let go and the sense of spaciousness became a friend rather than an enemy. I was reminded of this again when, years later, I was attending group therapy training. Each week, the thirty or so students would sit in a huge circle for group therapy. The first ten or fifteen minutes of this meeting were silent, as seldom was anyone willing to be the first to speak. This silence was like once again staring into that gaping space. It would be either a terrifying, anxious black hole, or if I let go, just spacious and clear. I would just sit and meditate in the space, which I am sure was completely the wrong thing to do from the facilitator's perspective.

As the mind opens to nondual presence, it rests in the place of the constant stream of creative manifestation. To use Saraha's analogy, this is the moment waves come into being and then dissolve again. On this threshold, the reality we experience in our normal, relative world arises as a creative expression of emptiness. On this threshold between form and emptiness we will experience what in Tantra is called the *sambhog-akaya,* the vitality of manifestation. This threshold is where a powerful meditator can engage in reality in possibly the most creative and dynamic way. Without separating from the experience of emptiness and spaciousness, it is possible to engage in the constant movement of reality as it manifests spontaneously moment to moment.

In the natural experience of presence we will also discover our innate capacity for love and compassion. Like moisture in the atmosphere that forms droplets only when there is a leaf to settle upon, this moisture of unconditional compassion will respond when we come into relationship. It is this love and compassion that make us realize the importance of remaining in the world of relative appearances for the welfare of others—others who are genuinely trying to live their lives the best they can yet who are entangled in the illusions they are creating. Out of love and compassion, a bodhisattva returns from a place of profound inner peace and openness to enter the world of duality and conflict so as to bring a different message.

✦✦ ————————————————————————————

IN THE OX-HERDING PICTURES of the Zen tradition, the ninth image is known as "return to the source." The yogi or meditator has tamed the ox of the mind and has settled in a state of nonduality. The mind's quality of quiescent equilibrium merges inseparably with the spaciousness of nonduality like a drop of water dissolving into the ocean. In the ox-herding pictures, this experience of nonduality is often depicted by the eighth image of a circle encompassing space. Following this image, "return to the source" depicts a waterfall descending from a natural spring deep in the mountains.[38] This evocative image of the source gives the sense of a place that is remote and sacred, natural and uncontaminated. The meditator has gone deeply into his or her nature to reveal its innate primordial source of extraordinary potential, its Buddha nature.

In myths and fairy tales a frequent motif occurs which Jung and Campbell called "the treasure hard to attain."[39] This is sometimes described as a sacred object like a spring, fountain or well as the source of the elixir of life. It may also be seen as a sacred place, such as a temple or grotto, within which the source may be found. These images point to an aspect of our psyche that, once touched or tapped, will bring healing and restoration to our fundamental malaise, whether it manifests psychologically or physically. There may be some value in leaving the notion of the source on a poetic, metaphorical level. Its mystery and numinosity then remain something that draws us deeper and invites and inspires the imagination. This in itself can be profoundly moving and will inevitably evoke a creative expression that enriches our life. A loss of relationship to this source brings aridity, barrenness, and creative impotency.

In a more direct way, our loss of relationship to this source of vitality and health brings suffering and confusion. When we return to the source, we restore our relationship to its innate quality of intrinsic health. In the alternative medicine world there are those who see the route towards health as a fundamental reconnection to this source. Once our relationship to the source is restored, the natural capacity within our body and psyche to move towards a state of health can unfold. In this view, it is the loss of connection to this natural capacity that ultimately leads to ill health and suffering.

The notion of an essential source is particularly significant within the Buddhist tantric tradition. In the Tantras it is understood that since beginningless time the essential nature of mind has existed as "primordial mind" in the nature of bliss and voidness.[40] This primordial mind has always been free of defilements yet is obscured by the veil of ignorance and delusion. Although obscured, the primordial mind has never been contaminated or mixed with ignorance and delusion. The veil is temporary and once it is cleared, our innate primordial mind will shine through like the sun through clouds.

Primordial mind could be understood as comprising particular qualities or characteristics that reflect its intrinsic nature. It is the union of energy-wind (Tib. *lung*) and mind (Tib. *sem*), where energy-wind refers to the characteristics of luminosity and movement and mind refers to the attribute of clarity and awareness. Primordial mind is the union of lucid clarity and movement, of awareness and luminosity, of emptiness and bliss. Hence, primordial mind is known as the mind of clear light (Tib. *ösel*), and its nature is bliss and emptiness.

According to the tantric view, we naturally access primordial mind, or clear light, at the time of deep sleep and again at the time of our death. This clear light mind exists within what is called the indestructible drop within the heart chakra. This combination of extremely subtle mind and the energy-wind known as the life supporting wind enters this drop at the moment of conception. The drop itself consists of a union of two subtle elements, one gained from the mother and one from the father. In the tantras these are known as red and white bodhi-chitta and are considered to be a subtle element of blood and sperm.

From a tantric point of view, according to Je Tsongkhapa, we may realize emptiness and experience nonduality, but unless our mind is brought into this extremely subtle primordial nature, we are still experiencing emptiness with a relatively gross level of mind.[41] When through meditation the subtle energy-winds and mind are returned to the indestructible drop at the heart, primordial mind manifests in its natural purity as the mind of clear light. When this mind experiences nonduality, we return to the source. This mind is sometimes called causal mind since it is the source from which all phenomena arise.[42] It is the origin of both samsara and nirvana, depending upon whether we recognize its nature or not. Primordial clear light mind is the source of the mind that emerges and evolves through life, even though we lose a conscious relationship to its origins.

This primordial nature of mind is always present in our continuum but is for the most part veiled by confusion and karmic obstructions. As a result, it remains an unconscious "ground of being." So long as it remains unconscious, we may have no insight into its presence or, alternatively, it may remain a mysterious, numinous sense of our divine nature known indirectly through its countless poetic and symbolic expressions.

A debate that goes on within the Buddhist world is one that asks the question,

When we return to this depth of mind, does the individual continuum of mind become lost within or return to a universal mind or universal consciousness? Alternatively, does our individual primordial mind open to a quality of wisdom that is omniscient? This debate has continued for a long time within the Tibetan Buddhist world, even though when we experience it directly, the question may seem irrelevant. According to Lama Tsongkhapa, who was an exponent of the Prasangika Madhyamaka school of thought, to propose a universal consciousness is incorrect, as it implies a self-existent consciousness or *alaya*.[43] His view is that each individual's primordial mind is empty of inherent existence yet opens to an awareness of the nature of universal reality. This wisdom awareness is called *dharmakaya*.

When we restore our relationship to the source, the experience of primordial mind, we access a root of vitality within our continuum that radically changes our experience of reality. Our innate vitality is what Lama Yeshe once called our inner nuclear energy, which, despite the slightly dubious nature of the metaphor, nevertheless conveys the power of this quality. In the tantric tradition a primary intention is to create the conditions necessary to gradually release this potential. The ground is prepared skillfully so that its awakening does not overwhelm and potentially damage the practitioner. Once we tap into the source, we access forces in ourselves that are extremely powerful. If we are ill-prepared, the result of accessing such powerful vitality could be both psychological and physical problems.

Awakening this blissful wisdom energy within the central channel of the psychic nervous system brings awareness directly into relationship with the natural creative forces in our own body and also in the world around. Our mind and vitality wake up to an intimate connection to the blissful vitality that underlies the appearance of the material world. As one meditator in India described, it was as though he could feel the energy of every atom in his own body and the world around as one in a blissful union.

When we return to the source, we open to the inseparability of our innate clear wisdom and the creative vitality present in each moment. We restore our relationship to the natural expression of each moment to arise uncontrived and free of the obscuring veils of ignorance and emotional afflictions. The image of the spring and waterfall in the mountains gives the sense of a profound creative source that gives rise to the outflow of our lives. On the threshold between emptiness and appearance, there is a creative dynamic that we can experience only once we have stilled the mind and returned to its primordial nature. From this place of clear light, reality unfolds as a fleeting play of appearance.

Within the tantric tradition the source is therefore twofold: the primordially pure wisdom nature of our mind is known as *dharmakaya*, and the luminous subtle energy or psychic vitality is known as *sambhogakaya*. Dharmakaya, as the "ground of being," is the ultimate nature that underlies our reality. Dharmakaya is sometimes likened to an ocean as the underlying nature of nonduality that gives rise to the countless waves of relative appearance. Sambhogakaya is the experience of the underlying vitality in the movement and luminosity of the appearances of our relative world. For a Buddha, the union of dharmakaya and sambhogakaya is the source of an inexhaustible capacity to manifest for the benefit of sentient beings through visionary and creative expression seen in the richness and power of the tantric tradition.

Even though we may not have yet gained the supreme attainment of a Buddha, nevertheless we can engage consciously in a creative process that gives fluidity and spontaneity to everything we do. The more we are able to remain present on the creative threshold with clarity, the more we will feel the quality of our innate vitality. We can begin to live our life as a constant expression of our creative potential in whatever we do. What we do begins to do itself, so to speak, with a spontaneity that is free from limiting fears and inhibitions.

Once we have let go of the identification of the ego and the duality that arises from it, our creative life changes. We see that the person, the action, and the acted upon are empty of inherent separation. The creative process unfolds as a natural expression of the present, unselfconsciously and spontaneously. We hear musicians describe how they lose themselves to the music. We hear artists and poets describe how they feel they can just let go and open to the creative flow of the muse. Their experience echoes something encountered by the mahasiddhas of India whose spiritual path was often intimately connected to a creative process. Saraha was an arrowsmith whose arrows "made themselves." The musician Vinapa played as an expression of the nonduality of instrument and player and sound, achieving the state of Mahamudra. In the Zen tradition of Japan a similar relationship to the arts is expressed in the tea ceremony, the art of archery, and the gardener's art.

The meditator steps into a place where the creative process is unfolding without splitting into the duality of someone doing the art. The art-less art, as this is sometimes called, relies on the individual letting go of self and opening to the natural expression of the moment of creation.

In awakening primordial mind we open to the natural energy that flows through us as a reflection of our true nature, an energy that is blissful, clear, empty, and luminous. We have returned to the source and become a vehicle for its expression through whatever we do. This quality of presence brings together the two dimensions of reality as relative appearances arise as the natural play of emptiness. Emptiness and form are no longer contradictory dimensions of reality: they instead weave a beauty of manifestation that is fresh and spontaneous in each moment.

Returning to the Marketplace 26

THE TENTH OX-HERDING IMAGE depicts an old sage descending from the mountain with staff in hand, "returning to the marketplace." His work on the mountain has been completed. His mind, symbolized by the ox, has been gradually brought to a state of complete pacification. He has gone beyond the bounds of sorrow and freed himself from the obscurations that prevent full awakening to his true nature. Having reached such a place of opening to the nature of reality, he has one final task to perform: namely, to return to the world of people. But why? Why should he do so? Why would he not simply remain in the place of absorption in meditation upon the empty nature of reality and relinquish the need to become engaged again in the trials and tribulations of worldly life? Why return to this crazy life in a world that seems bent on its own destructive folly?

I am reminded of those who have been through near-death experiences. Often during these times people reach a point in the death process where they appear to be given an option to leave or return. Some report that at this moment they realize they have a reason to return to and engage in their life, perhaps in a way they previously had not considered. They may feel that they have unfinished business or that they must return to carry out some task. This task is often the recognition of some greater purpose, one that will benefit others.

It is rare to experience this near-death opportunity to evaluate our intention to incarnate. Even so, within the psychological process of our lives, there are times when we are called to embark upon a journey of transformation, enter the road of trials, and finally, to return to the world. This return is not always easy and may ask us to face the world in a new way.

In 1985 I was living India, continuing a series of long retreats in the Himalayas of Himachal Pradesh. I had my own isolated retreat hut way up in the mountains and had for the previous five years spent a major part of each year there in retreat. This was a beautiful and awesome place to live, on the edge of wilderness, and over the years I had grown to love my mountain life. My life was a rhythm of quiet practice with nothing to disturb my peace other than my inner machinations and the odd scorpion dropping from the roof.

I was not prepared, however, for the event that took place during that time which eventually launched me out of my quiet life-style. In 1984 Indira Gandhi was assassinated by one of her Sikh bodyguards. The resulting upsurge of reprisals was appalling. In New Delhi and other major cities, Sikhs were being beaten and burned to death. Homes were attacked and set alight, and for a short period the bloodshed and mayhem in the streets was terrible. At the time I was nowhere near these events, but their repercussions would eventually drastically affect my life.

Soon after this happened, British subjects were required for the first time to obtain visitor permits. After a year, however, the requirements became stricter so that eventually, the police department decided that every Western visitor was to leave the country within a set period of time. This was a chance for the Indian police to finally rid themselves of the countless Western hippies that were living in their country without any limitations. The local chief of police lectured a small group of us in a patronizing manner, saying that he was really doing us a favor by evicting us from India. He felt that it was time we grew up and took responsibility for our lives. He felt that we could not be genuinely looking for spiritual development because that was really the task of those in the third phase of life, from sixty years of age onwards.

The small group of Westerners living in Dharamsala close to the Dalai Lama's residence were finally forced to leave by the refusal of the police to renew visas. This made continuing retreat impossible, and eventually I returned to Delhi to make my way back to England. Before leaving, I recall speaking to my teacher Lama Zopa Rinpoche, who said that it was perhaps time to return and see how best I could begin to integrate my practice in the West. I did not feel too happy about this, as I still felt somewhat unprepared. I wanted to continue my retreats.

On my return to England the process that began was by no means easy. My return was not that of an enlightened sage. It was rather the return of someone who may have had some deep and insightful experiences, but who clearly had a lot of work to do. Integrating back into Western life after a five-year absence was going to be a challenge.

In my own experience the return was rather literal, but however it happens and at whatever level, we must nevertheless make the transition. It is a significant step and one that challenges us in many different ways. I personally felt a great resistance. For some, this challenge is too frightening to take up. I have known some who may still be found in India, wandering around getting stoned and having no particular direction in life. When I went back a few years later I met one or two such characters and saw how lost they seemed. As I observed earlier about the wanderer, sometimes there are those who are unable to stop.

While I have used a literal example of return, the psychological process of return is an important aspect of the journey. When Jung and Joseph Campbell speak of the return, they are not implying that the state of enlightenment or buddhahood has been reached. Rather, they are envisioning return as an aspect of the journey that may be needed many times in the course of our lives. As I said in Chapter 20, the return following a period of descent and depression can require particular conditions. If the journey we have followed is one of disintegration and depression, the return is a process of renewal that can require sensitivity to the delicate, vulnerable state of our sense of self. We may not know who we are. We may not be sure how to relate to the world. The world may not understand what we have been through.

I am reminded of watching dragonflies in our garden. I had not realized that our tiny pond had become a haven for dragonfly larvae. Suddenly one morning as I walked up the garden, emerging from a black, sinister-looking larvae skin was an extraordinary transformation. Gradually its wings unfurled and its long body arched its way out of the larvae shell. The dragonfly's eyes were covered over by a light skin and the wings were soft and delicate. I watched for a long time as the dragonfly waited for the sun to gradually dry and harden its wings, eyes, and exoskeleton. Many hours later, when all was ready, with a flash of its silvery wings it was gone.

As we reemerge with a new sense of self, it takes time for the skin to toughen. We will be somewhat vulnerable; we may be very open. This is a very familiar experience to anyone who has emerged from a period of retreat. If we step straight back into the outside world of city life or our normal work, we can feel somewhat disoriented. We may have touched insights and reached levels of absorption in meditation that were profound. In circumstances of retreat we had been held in a relatively insulated environment, which is the purpose of retreat. This insulation protected us from invasion from outside influences so that meditation could deepen. It also enabled us to become more subtle and sensitive in our awareness. As a consequence when we return to the world, our energy and sensitivity will be extremely vulnerable to the gross vibrations normally found there.

Having been through this experience many times, I have seen how difficult this process can be. The subtle, peaceful state resulting from meditation can be easily shattered by the chaos of a busy city. When I returned from India after long periods of retreat, the shock of being back in a city like London was hard to cope with. Adjusting took a long time. I would find myself exhausted on occasions because I was not used to the change in intensity of energy. Spending time with too many people would have a particularly draining effect. Shopping centers would be like energy sinks, sucking my energy out through my eyes. Even the effect of electricity and places with a large amount of florescent lighting could be draining. It was as though I was vulnerable to different forms of toxicity, and sometimes our environment is very toxic.

Returning from retreat requires time and a relatively controlled environment. Some of my Tibetan teachers would suggest that for every week of retreat, one should have a day of acclimatization, returning to the world gradually. For me, after five years of relatively continual retreat, it took around a year to readjust to living in the West and the need to find a way of working in the world. I have seen similar struggles while working in a Buddhist college in Devon. At Sharpham College we would have students resident for a period of a year, studying contemporary aspects of Buddhism. Many of these students were in a period of transition in their lives, and it would often take up to a year for them to begin to find a renewed sense of direction.

As a psychotherapist I have observed that the journey of therapy will often track the process from the time of the call through the path of trials to the eventual return. Psychotherapy offers a supportive environment in which this journey can be helped to unfold. The time of return during psychotherapy may happen many times as a person goes through cycles of descent and reemergence. The return in therapy is often associated with the rediscovery of a new way of being in the world. This may involve learning how to relate to people in a different way. It may involve the exploration of how to integrate new qualities into the person's life and relationships. Deep inner transformation slowly manifests in the world, and those in the vicinity of such a transformation may not always understand or be sympathetic. They may even be threatened by the changes.

I am reminded of a particular client whose childhood wounding caused her to remain in extremely limiting relationships in a codependency that was stifling yet also felt safe to her. During an extensive period of psychotherapy it had been possible to explore many of the childhood issues that had dogged her relationship and caused her to be caught in a childlike dependency. She had great difficulty not being overwhelmed by the emotional lives of others around her. She found it particularly hard to separate herself from what her partner experienced and to see whose feelings were whose. As she began to separate her own inner life from that of others, she became stronger and more independent. Her independence was enabling her to engage in her life more fully. It was not, however, making her relationship comfortable. Her changes were enabling her to begin to challenge some of the unwritten prescriptions that had held the relationship in a stuck dynamic. She was beginning to challenge her partner, much to his dislike. He was also being gradually forced to change in ways he was reluctant to face. One of the consequences of her journey into her own underworld was a depth of wisdom that precipitated the beginning of her partner's descent to look at his own emotional problems.

My client's return from a journey of deep inner change needed a great amount of support to enable her to stay true to her newfound sense of herself. This was made more difficult because her journey of self-discovery had brought out her acute sensitivity to others' emotional states. Where previously this had been a source of huge distress, she had healed much of her wounding, but her sensitivity remained. Her sensitivity gradually became something she could protect and use more consciously in her work and relationships. It became a gift rather than a problem. Eventually she was strong enough to move out into her life in a way that was self-supporting and very different from the way she had previously been. However, she had discovered a capacity for healing that did not easily fit into the ordinary world and needed careful guarding. She had to learn how to best look after herself in a world that would not readily understand her particular gifts. In this respect, the return to the world may not meet with support and understanding. Should this be the case, we need to be sure we have the capacity to protect ourselves in difficult or even hostile conditions.

There is something sacred about our return, whether we recognize it or not. Sacred can imply secret, in the sense that we may need to be able to contain our experience in relative secrecy. When people go home from weekend workshops or retreats during which they have gone through deep discoveries, I often suggest that containment may be necessary. They may need to keep quiet and not talk even to partners or friends about what has happened. This can sustain something of the quality of their experience without it becoming dissipated or tarnished by exposure.

The renewed sense of self or new sense of wholeness that is part of the return is often associated with or symbolized by the divine child. The divine child is a symbol of the birth of a new disposition in life, something fresh and to some degree vulnerable. The divine child embodies all the promise of life; it symbolizes hope and freedom from limitation. Archetypally, the divine child is part human and part divine. It represents a quality that is blessed by, or a vehicle of, the divine to emerge into embodiment and expression. The question that becomes vital as this quality emerges is, Can we embody and integrate what we have awakened in a practical and beneficial way?

The bodhisattva's return to the world is motivated by the power of his or her bodhichitta and compassion. The return to the world for one who has followed a path of deep meditation practice for many years can be of immense importance to those of us still blinded by ignorance and in need of guidance on the path. Were the bodhisattva to simply remain in a state of meditative absorption and not consider the welfare of others, we would be sadly at a loss, struggling to discover our own path of awakening.

When I lived in Dharamsala in India, there were a number of profoundly realized meditators who lived up in the mountains close to where I was in retreat. Some of them had been there for many years and would clearly have enjoyed remaining so until they died. Yet my teacher Lama Thubten Yeshe was asking some of these meditators to come down from retreat and begin to teach. He had many Western students around the world who were in need of guidance in their attempts to practice Tibetan Buddhism. With the support of H. H. the Dalai Lama, Lama Yeshe was gradually persuading some of the most experienced lamas he could find to embark upon something they would find incredibly challenging. He was asking them to come to the West and begin to make a transition from what had been a relatively isolated life to the demands of the Western world. One could not imagine a more challenging return to the marketplace.

In the West many of these lamas have been protected to some degree within the context of Buddhist centers. Nevertheless, is a difficult transition to be away from their peers, a familiar culture, and the peace of their retreat. Some do not stay long. Others have gradually settled in the West and form part of a very important resource for Westerners wishing to study Tibetan Buddhism. Without their kindness, self-sacrifice, and generosity of heart we would not have this gift.

However we make the return to the marketplace, the challenge is to genuinely integrate our experience and understanding in the world. For Westerners it requires a great deal of focus to be able to retain a quality of mindful attention to what is important and not be pulled back into old ways. As Lama Yeshe said many times, the power of the sensory world of samsara is so strong, we are being pulled out of ourselves all the time and need strong renunciation. Thus, it is not surprising that we lose our way from time to time. It requires a depth of compassion to accept that we will not always get it right; that we will make mistakes and will need to restore our clarity and presence. Slowly, this integration will enable us to become a genuine embodiment of our Buddha nature in the world in all that we do.

WHEN I RETURNED to the West following my time of retreat in India, it became important to find a way back into Western life. As I was a layperson, this inevitably meant working to earn a living. In many Eastern countries there is still a view that those whose intention is to live a life devoted to spiritual practice are offering something significant to society. As a result, the support of practitioners is considered a normal aspect of social life. In the West this view is largely absent, and as a consequence there are few opportunities to avoid the necessary practicalities of earning a living and engaging with the demands of Western life. There are a few Buddhist communities that will support practitioners, but these are rare.

To live in the West requires that practice be genuinely grounded in the world. In many ways one could consider the need for work to be psychologically healthy, particularly for those who have the Puer disposition mentioned previously. As we have seen, the Puer tendency to be absorbed in spiritual and creative visions and ideals often leads to the avoidance or denial of the need to be grounded in the material world. It is often feared that material demands will sully spiritual values, but the dangers of this kind of ungroundedness become apparent with time. To continue to live in an airy spiritual idealism is not a resolution to the journey, and the desire to do so suggests there are unresolved psychological issues that still need to be addressed.

Having been through a long period of retreat where I was supported by a number of particularly generous benefactors, I was challenged, on my return to the West, with the need to support myself. I discovered I was virtually unemployable and that my credentials as a meditator had little value. Beginning to engage in the process of finding a suitable livelihood was hard at first. I was returning to a society that was very different from the one I had left five years earlier. Once I had decided to train as a psychotherapist, I had to work on building sites to earn the money to pay for the course. In the end I actually found the capacity to be self-sustaining an extremely empowering process.

Once we accept our place back in the relative world of work and domestication after having journeyed far into the inner reaches of our minds, we can begin to manifest our potential to help others. I once received advice from a Tibetan teacher who said that having traveled and studied in the East for so long, I should stop in one place and stabilize my life and practice and then begin to serve others. If we have lived the life of a wanderer, it is often only when we stop that we can manifest the things in our life that will serve others. As a recently trained psychotherapist I found that this was certainly the case. The notion of right livelihood from the Buddha's eightfold path then becomes very significant.

As we learn to embody our spirituality we will also deepen our capacity to creatively manifest in the world. According to Joseph Campbell the capacity to manifest our spirituality in form is associated with the father archetype.[44] (By contrast, he saw the capacity to become embodied as associated with the mother archetype.) The archetype of Senex in particular is connected to the principle of crystallizing and materializing our visions and experiences in the concrete world so as to give them shape, order, and practical application. This inevitably moves us away from Puer spiritual idealism into the realm of what is practically possible in the "real world." In this spirit of pragmatism we must address the questions that arise when attempting to live in society. These include ethical questions relating to important issues in life such as the environment, birth control, abortion, health and welfare issues, and political values. Manifestation in this respect is engaging with the culture in which one lives rather than attempting to live in a vacuum.

In the Buddhist philosophy of three *kayas,* a Buddha's manifestation in the world is known as *nirmanakaya*. This is often translated as "emanation body" or "manifestation body." What motivates a Buddha's special ability is a decision to manifest constantly for the welfare of all sentient beings in an aspect that is appropriate and beneficial to them. There is an implicit pragmatism in this principle that recognizes the need to be in the "real world."

The compassionate heart of bodhichitta at the core of the bodhisattva's path leads to a commitment to remain embodied in order to bring benefit to others, particularly through the gift of the Dharma. A Buddha's capacity to manifest arises from the bodhisattva vow. It is the strength of intention of bodhichitta generated by a bodhisattva before becoming a Buddha that creates the eventual power to limitlessly manifest activities that will affect the lives and minds of others. This power is beyond our normal comprehension and can seem somewhat academic to describe. Maitreya nevertheless describes the extraordinary qualities of a Buddha in texts such as the *Uttaratantra*.

From one perspective, a Buddha can be said to be one who has mastered the capacity of creative manifestation. A Buddha's state of being rests in each moment of creation as our relative world comes into being. As ordinary human individuals, we can only begin to experience what this might mean with gradual practice. Through deepening awareness we can also experience the process of creative manifestation that is unfolding in each moment of our existence. We are, after all, an expression of it in each moment: the key is to recognize this process and wake up to it more fully.

When we cultivate a quality of clear present awareness, we begin to open to the vitality that is on the threshold between emptiness and appearance. We begin to recognize and feel more deeply the innate spontaneity of each moment of creation. If we are able to sustain awareness, our practical material life can then become a powerful and rich expression of that dynamic creative energy.

Manifestation is the capacity to be open to what can emerge from moment to moment as a natural expression of our Buddha nature. With clarity and presence we can gradually let go of the sense of self-conscious ego-identity that blocks our natural capacity to creatively engage with each moment.

This creative awareness is often represented in Buddhist Tantra by the daka or dakini, the archetypal male or female deity forms that symbolize the play of reality. The Sanskrit terms *daka* and *dakini* (Tib. *khadro* and *khadroma*) mean literally "space- or sky-goer," or more poetically, "sky dancer." The term *kha,* or space, signifies the space of emptiness from which the play of appearances arises. The dakas and dakinis represent a quality that is open in each moment to respond with fresh, uncontrived spontaneity. They express the fearless freedom from contraction that enables a dance with reality. It is like the freedom of the jazz musician who responds to each moment of music, moving in and out of the thread of the tune.

Our power of creative manifestation is often unrecognized, but when we awaken this capacity, we contact a vitality that is extremely potent, fluid, and dynamic. However, for some to experience their full potency as creative individuals can be both unfamiliar and frightening, particularly if we are afraid to be seen for who we are, afraid to express ourselves, afraid to be effective, or afraid to make mistakes. Learning to let go of fear and allow our creative vitality to be free is not always an easy process. It is, however, one that can bring unfathomable benefit to both others and ourselves. Once we tap into our innate vitality and open ourselves to its creative resource, extraordinary things are possible.

From a tantric perspective our vitality is a dynamic quality that has the power to flow through us in a healthy way, or it may become blocked and unhealthy. When it is freed from obstructions and cleansed of toxicity accumulated through life, its power is extraordinary. In the process of purification emphasized in the tantric tradition, we release a creative potential that is virtually limitless. My teacher Lama Thubten Yeshe demonstrated this in his own life by his capacity to teach and give out extraordinary energy to his students even though he had a serious heart condition. I have seen him look ashen and drained after a long, demanding period of teaching. By virtue of certain practices he was able to regenerate his vitality in a way that for most would be inconceivable. He would go to his room and spend an hour or so engaged in a particular practice and then return looking radiant and powerful, ready to yet again dedicate his energy to teaching.

Lama Yeshe's dynamism was something that inspired everyone who came in contact with him. His power to be constantly engaged in activities that would benefit those around him and the love, concern, and generosity with which he devoted himself to his students made him a source of constant inspiration. His example was one of constant manifestation of his bodhichitta intention to work for the welfare of others in practical ways.

The vitality of manifestation is a form of generosity, one of the six *paramitas* or perfections of a bodhisattva, and is an attribute of bodhichitta. When we are open to the richness within we can begin to enrich the lives of others. This generosity of heart is the willingness to dedicate our life and vitality to the welfare of others. This may be through material generosity, it may be through the gift of service in caring for others, or it may manifest through whatever work we devote ourselves to. For the bodhisattva there is no place for an inactivity that remains withholding and self-absorbed, when we have the capacity to do whatever we can.

Manifestation and embodiment take us away from self-absorption or self-preoccupation. Self-absorption can be an unfortunate symptom of the introspective nature of meditation practice. The emphasis in Buddhism is to tame one's own mind and be vigilant to inner intentions that could give rise to unwholesome actions of body, speech, and mind. Self-reflection is therefore an imperative. The habit some of us may have to be self-preoccupied does not automatically go away through the cultivation of mindfulness and meditative insights. A more conscious shift away from being so self-obsessed is required. When this happens it is important to begin to turn the attention outward towards those around us to recognize the nature of their suffering. In the teaching on the cultivation of bodhichitta we are constantly reminded that self-preoccupation is the root of suffering, while cherishing others is the source of all happiness.

The question will then be, How can we be of benefit to others in our life and practice? What do we have to offer? The bodhisattva's perfection of generosity is part of that gesture of concern for the welfare of others. It is an opening of the heart that takes us beyond narrow, impoverished closed-mindedness. As Shantideva says in the *Guide to the Bodhisattva's Way of Life*, generosity is not the action of giving to others; it is a quality of intention that is willing to be open and give whatever we can. We are able to naturally, spontaneously respond with compassion and wisdom when the moment arises and where we feel we are able.

While living in India I felt myself challenged by this experience whenever beggars in the streets confronted me. Part of me would recoil and want to shrink back into a safe inner cocoon unaffected by the horrors of seeing a leper's deformed hand thrust into my face. Another part of me would rationalize that it was not really helping to be giving a few paisas to a child begging on behalf of his parents. Yet another part of me wished I could really see what was useful to help someone in his suffering state. All I could do was to give some coins, knowing that when others saw this I would be surrounded by a fiercely demanding group of beggars.

This example brings into view the recognition that to manifest in the world requires both the compassion to move us towards suffering rather than away from it and also the wisdom to know how to respond. We may have a heartfelt desire to help, but the question will always be, What is the most skillful way to do so? Our perception of the consequences of our actions is inevitably limited. Perhaps once we have attained buddhahood our eyes will be open to the results of our actions. In the meantime, we can only learn to trust our own innate sense of what feels right from our experience. This invariably means we will get it wrong from time to time.

Manifestation is a creative process that requires that we understand deeply the nature of reality. If we have the quality of presence that can be aware of the natural creative process at work moment by moment, we can begin to participate in that dynamic process. To participate and engage in this dynamic is to live life fully and to begin to actualize the archetypal intent of bodhichitta, bringing together wisdom and compassion. As I indicated earlier, the bodhisattva learns to inhabit a space between two worlds. An insight into the true nature of reality opens the mind to an ultimate truth that must be embodied in the world. The bodhisattva chooses to live consciously in this place of creative tension between relative and ultimate truth. The intention of doing so is an act of selfless surrender that causes a bodhisattva to be a vehicle for the manifestation of Buddha activity in the world.

The bodhisattva is like a lightning conductor that is able to ground the wisdom, power, inspiration, and compassionate intent of Buddha nature within the world of sentient beings. This is no simple task and will often take its toll upon the vehicle that carries such archetypal intent. The fact that a bodhisattva is not yet a Buddha means he or she is still fallible, still bound by human limitation, and that there are still points of vulnerability. It is not uncommon for the weakest point to be found in the bodhisattva's physical body, resulting in sickness. One could see this as a symptomatic reflection of where there is still something to learn. It may equally be the point of greatest awakening. The image of the wounded healer is a familiar one to Western psychological understanding, and in many ways the bodhisattva's path embodies this paradigm. Whatever difficulties or failings may manifest become the source of deeper understanding, wisdom, and compassion. Often our times of pain and struggle are like cracks through which the light passes. This is the noble imperfection, the human fallibility or frailty that contains the potential for so much wisdom, beauty, love, and compassion, like the grit in the oyster that gradually forms the pearl.

Our capacity to manifest is found in our humanity, in our authenticity and our openness. It is to be found in our willingness to truly engage with what we do. This means to engage in the totality of life with love and care rather than hide away from it in a spiritual cocoon. When we are willing to accept ourselves fully and open to our true potential, it need not be something grand and outstanding that emerges. It may just be our capacity to be truly authentic with how we are with others, in our work, in our play, and in the creative expression of our true nature. Spirituality is then not a big deal; it is something very simple and uncontrived in the present, open and spontaneous.

When we are able to remain present, authentic, and open, we will be able to respond to each moment in a fresh and natural way. By remaining in this state we will be more prepared for those moments when, in meeting another, a genuine opening occurs to something deeper and more meaningful. This is like the sun that is always shining but waits for the clouds to open. Manifestation is a spontaneous and creative response to the moment, whether it is in helping another or in some creative process. As a psychotherapist I can see this potential in every session with clients. The challenge is to retain a sense of open presence that will enable me to remain spontaneous, authentic, and compassionate in relation to whatever is arising, rather than resorting to techniques and preconceived agendas.

What Dharma practice can bring is a depth of clarity that helps us to remain present and awake within daily life. Maintaining the mind's clarity will enable us to see through the illusions of our daily reality and recognize where we are going off-center. It will enable us to remain true to our innate sense of what is valuable and what is frivolous in our life, what is skillful and what is not. With clarity we can remain with integrity and honesty, not deceiving ourselves or others. Clarity leads us to a quality of authenticity so that we do not hide our fallibility or become grandiose. In particular, the maintenance of clarity will enable us to let go of the disposition to grasp at the sense of identity. Through remaining true to the empty, illusory nature of reality, such clarity enables us to be open and not caught in the ego's disposition to grasp at and limit what we do.

Our actions are most skillful and natural when there is less self-conscious ego identification involved. Whatever our creative expression may be, it will be cleaner and more beneficial when free of the ego's self-preoccupation and distorted intention. When we are clear, present, and free of ego-grasping there will be a fluidity in our actions not found at other times. Our capacity to manifest our innate nature will then be clear and spontaneous.

Manifestation does not have to arise through something exotic and magical. It is rather the simple, down-to-earth capacity to remain present, open, and creatively engaged in all that we do. We participate with love and clarity in the daily processes of our lives and give of ourselves fully and honestly. We are all fundamentally creative, not in grand ways like the great artists and composers, but rather, in all that we do. Every moment of the day we respond to the appearances of reality. We can do so from a place of unconscious, blind, habitual ignorance and create endless suffering, confusion, and misery, or we can awaken and participate in a creative process that is alive, vital, and beautiful in its sheer ordinariness, as the play of life itself.

◆ ◆ ————————————————————————————

WHILE I WAS LIVING IN INDIA there was a point in the Hima-
layan winter when I was unable to stay in my mountain retreat
because of snow. I was simply not equipped for such severe conditions. As a consequence, I used to descend into the plains and make my
way to Bodhgaya in Bihar, where the Buddha sat at the time of his
enlightenment. There in the magical gardens which surround the
Bodhi tree, I would continue my semi-retreat practices. I would make
endless prostration and candle offerings and join the visiting Tibetans
in performing *korwa*. *Korwa* means literally "to cycle," but in this context it means to circumambulate.

At certain times of the day, particularly evening, the Tibetan social
scene would appear and begin the ritual circling around the Mahabodhi
Stupa. There would be the muttering of prayers and mantras mixed
with the laughter of greetings as friends met and chatted in whispers.
Occasionally one or two would stop at a particular statue set into the
wall of the Stupa and, with palms held together at the heart and heads
bowed, offer prayers.

I too, on occasion, would join this rhythmical cycle of circumam-
bulations and make my prayers and mutter my mantras. When I did so,
I was often intrigued by the effect this circulation had upon me. There
was a definite feeling of being in relation to a centering of my being
that had a remarkably settling and ordering, even comforting, effect. It
was as though I was coming home, being brought back to a place of
wholeness that was a circulation around a central axis, an *axis mundi*.

More recently, I was reminded of this experience when I was preparing for a workshop I was leading. The theme of the weekend was the mandala. As I sat quietly trying to connect to the essential heart of what I wanted to explore over the weekend, I found myself impelled to stand up and begin slowly walking around in the room. This was not the frustrated pacing of a caged animal; it was more reflective and purposeful. I found myself gradually circling around the theme I was reflecting upon. My body was guiding me to a direct experience of something that is hard to experience any other way. I was entering into the very essence of what it means to circumambulate, to circle around a core of being.

I am reminded of the times that Jung speaks of psychological process as a gradual circulation around a centralizing axis. He often related to dreams as circulatory. They seldom present a sequence that is linear like the frames of a film. Rather, they spiral around a central theme, slowly deepening and expanding the understanding of meaning. The journey of individuation, far from being a linear evolution, is also more a gradual circumambulation around the Self as a deeper center of being.

In the therapeutic process I am constantly presented with the realization that the journey a client is on does not begin at a certain point and reach a particular goal. Rather, we repeatedly circle around one or more central themes. These themes are very often places of wounding, which bring us back time and again to the same issue met on deeper and deeper levels. Clients often express their feeling that I must be tired of hearing the same things again and again. They may equally feel they do not seem to be able to get rid of a particular issue even though they are changing in relationship to it.

In many ways it may be a fallacy to search for some definite point of cure at which the wound has gone. One could see this in another way. As is the case with the wounded healer, the wound is our place of awakening when we begin to circulate around it, going deeper and deeper into its nature. Does this wound ultimately heal and disappear, or is it like the grit in the oyster, the central theme that our process of awakening is fundamentally oriented around?

I know that, for myself, the central theme of my wounding does not go away; rather, as I understand and go more deeply into its nature I discover a quality that is, so to speak, the wisdom within the wound. I am reminded of the Leonard Cohen line, "There is a crack in everything, it's where the light gets in." In Tantra this principle is central to the way in which transformation occurs. The state of enlightened transformation emerges within or from the manure of the deluded base condition. When passion is transformed it becomes the "wisdom of discrimination." When anger and aggression are transformed they become the "mirror-like wisdom." When jealousy and self-doubt are transformed they become the "all-accomplishing wisdom." These qualities of insight arise as a reflection of the basic state of delusion once the emotion has been cracked and its innate energy released.

The same is true of our wounds. As we circle around them in therapy or on our spiritual journey, they gradually reveal the innate potential that is constellated through the particular nature of the wound. The pearl emerges as the grit aggravates the oyster. The pearl reflects the oyster's capacity to live with the aggravation and create something beautiful from it. Perhaps just as the oyster doesn't see it as beautiful, it is hard for us to recognize the beauty and quality that emerge as we gradually open to an experience of the Self, our potential wholeness. From a Buddhist point of view this means we gradually come to recognize that this circulation is bringing us to a deep experience of being utterly present in our true nature. As we come closer to the internal experience of the central axis around which we are circulating, we discover the quality of being that is centered as total clarity and openness in the present. It is in this moment that our life is emerging and unfolding.

As we circle around the central quality of our Buddha nature, at some point there is a subtle shift of awareness. In meditation I have been aware of this shift time and again. As I begin to sit I am conscious of the interrelationship I have with the flux of my life and all of its complexities. As my mind settles, I am less pulled by this complexity of forms and appearances. Suddenly I am aware of a shift. My awareness has settled in a space that is present, yet not bound by time and forms. I am reminded of the center of a cyclone, or the eye of a storm. The axis of my awareness has shifted from the relativity of forms to the nonduality of presence. Perhaps one could see this as the shift from a horizontal axis to a vertical one.

In this place of presence and emptiness there is no person, no "I" to experience an unfolding of the path. There is equally no path, nowhere to go. With nothing to hold on to as permanent and substantial, in the present we can experience simply the awareness of momentary unfolding.

IT SEEMS AN UNFORTUNATE TRUTH that whatever is achieved or created in this life comes to an end. A creative process eventually comes to a point of completion, one hopes, which is a crystallization of the original idea. The initial spark of inspiration or initiation is gradually formed into a shape that may or may not resemble the original vision. Creative artists experience this whenever they complete a work of art. Whether they are satisfied with the finished product is another matter.

Following the crystallization of an idea into reality there is usually a life span of the product. This is true for material objects as well as social institutions, business organizations, and psychological states. Any created phenomenon will have a life duration that leads to its eventual process of decay and death. We can see, looking at business organizations, that a company will flourish for a period and then reach a natural point of fulfillment after which it will go through decline and possible demise or reformation. Social institutions equally have a life span or life cycle that can be of varying lengths.

Jung speaks of how religious forms come into being, but if the energy that generated the form ceases to inspire through that form, it will die. When the fundamental principles of a religion cease to engage and transform the psyche of individuals, then it will naturally deteriorate.[45] We can see this with some of the ancient mystery religions of the past like Mithraism, Zoroastrianism, the Isis cults, and so on. There have been numerous religious forms that come to prominence and then die out. It is even said within the Buddhist tradition that the

308 THE WISDOM OF IMPERFECTION

Tantras, if they are not practiced, will gradually lose their power and effectiveness and die out.

The process of decay is partly connected to the Senex principle discussed earlier. When something has formed, shaped, and consolidated during the process of creation, this crystallization is often tied to the principle of Senex. Senex enables processes to mature and become consolidated. What it does not do is enable the process of renewal. Instead, it leads what has become consolidated towards a gradual ossification. Things become increasingly rigid, dogmatic, stuck, and lifeless; they stagnate and degenerate. This is true with outer processes as well as internal, psychological ones. Renewal, then, comes only after death has taken place.

In the journey of transformation there is a similar progression. Following the call, we emerge onto the path of trials, facing the challenges of transformation. As we reach a place of spiritual insight, we must return to the marketplace to rediscover our capacity to engage with the world from a different place in ourselves. This gradual consolidation and grounding of our spirituality leads to a time of greater maturity. What was once a tender new shoot of a state of being that has been cultivated from the manure of our past gradually becomes a mature plant. The person we are may be radically different from the one that answered the call ages back. We heard the call because we wished to grow and go deeper. Once we have passed through the path of trials and come to a point of return, nothing can be the same as it was.

The maturity that is gradually established as the path unfolds later in life can bring great fruitfulness and richness. I recognize this in some of my Buddhist contemporaries who in their forties and fifties are showing the signs of a spiritual maturity that has come from the grinding of experience. They are no longer so naïve and idealistic but have gained a practical maturity that can genuinely manifest in the world something that is beneficial for others. This has led me to believe optimistically that as Westerners, we are gradually learning to bring Buddhism to the West in an increasingly mature way. We are learning from our errors and there is a greater sense of inner authority and confidence that was never there before.

Working in therapy, I have seen this in some of my clients. Slowly there emerges a quality of strength and creativity that can enable a manifestation of talents and gifts that were previously just painful, unfulfilled dreams. I recall a woman in her forties who struggled with the painful consequences of her traumatic childhood, her father's destructiveness, a public school nightmare, and general lack of validation in any form. From being seen virtually as a hopeless waste of time, she embarked on the journey to unpack and free herself from this desecration of her creative soul. When she left the therapeutic process after several years she gave me a beautiful ceramic bowl she had made, which was a manifestation of her newly uncovered courage to be herself and create. It was a wonderful thing to see how someone's creative soul could be freed from the rubble of so much destruction.

If the process of maturation brings great fruit, it usually also leads to a further period of ossification, stagnation, and gradual decay that will need to be faced. Often this occurs at times in our lives when we have spent many years working or engaged in some task that has demanded great diligence, perseverance, and dedication. Even though this may have originated from a deep sense of calling, we will almost inevitably come to this point of stasis. The thing we have been engaged in may have become so familiar it no longer brings the inspiration it once did. We may have become so established in a way of being that this has once again begun to be unhealthy. Consolidation leads to rigidity and the dominance of a way of being that ceases to be able to change and respond. New ideas and ideals lead to gradual establishment, and establishment leads to decay.

In *The Psychology of Buddhist Tantra* I discuss the principle of the mandala as a symbol of our capacity to shape-shift and constantly adjust in order to remain whole.[46] To live in the mandala is to be able to constantly respond to our innate capacity for renewal and integration. On one level, we could see this as a process that occurs moment by moment. Equally, we could say that the entire process of individuation as I have described it here is a reflection of that same principle of homeostasis expressed in the mandala. The capacity for renewal is often sparked at a point of solidification and decay. Once again, the old way of being must die so that there can finally be an opportunity for renewal.

The time of ossification followed by a kind of psychological death will not be comfortable. We may have thought we had everything pretty much together when slowly this state of malaise creeps up on us. Loss of energy, loss of direction, loss of interest, and all the signs of disintegration and death arise. The cycle is moving towards a final death, which must occur before there is the potential for reemergence.

The natural cycle of individuation will lead to an eventual death, either literally or psychologically. This is part of the natural process of germination, growth, consolidation, and decay, which should not be seen as a problem and pathologized. In the teachings on the twelve links of interdependent origination (the Buddhist Wheel of Life) it is said that once we have been reborn, the last of the twelve links must inevitably follow, namely, aging and death.[47]

If we have a sense of some of the fundamental insights of Buddhist understanding throughout this process, we will have some valuable allies. Understanding emptiness and having the capacity to remain open and not contract around fears and insecurities will help. If we are not holding on to our sense of self-identity so rigidly because we recognize its inherent insubstantiality, it will make the letting go process far less uncomfortable. Our death, whether literal or metaphorical, does not have to frighten us if the capacity to let go and open is there. If we have a sense of compassion and self-value, understanding that what we are going through is yet another turning of the wheel, we can allow ourselves to fall apart and not be too disappointed with ourselves. It is natural and needs to be held with love and kindness.

The process of death and renewal is one we must encounter time and time again on our path. With every circulation we can go further into the depth of our nature. New insight grows and we meet new challenges. Within the tantric *sadhana,* or method of accomplishment, of certain deity practices, there is a constant theme of death and renewal. The meditator each day goes through a dissolution of appearances into a state of clear awareness, the clear light of death, which dissolves all the old self-conceptions into emptiness. The meditator reemerges from that death renewed, in the aspect of his or her true nature personified as the deity. This replication of the death process is performed in order to repeatedly familiarize the mind with the natural evolution of death and transformation. It is a rehearsal for our actual death, but it is also a reminder of the process of psychological renewal. This could be understood as occurring moment by moment. It occurs as part of the psychological recycling that takes place through our lives in the journey of individuation. It eventually occurs through actual death and re-incarnation.

In the Tibetan tradition great emphasis is placed upon the incarnate lama or *tulku* as an expression of the bodhisattva's capacity to incarnate for the benefit of others. The Dalai Lama, for example, is seen as the fourteenth incarnation in the line of Dalai Lamas, and there are many other incarnate lamas who have been recognized over a similar number of lifetimes. They are usually given the title *Rinpoche,* or "precious one." While this may be a contentious issue for some in the Buddhist world, in principle what these examples can demonstrate is the real possibility of reincarnating. In the journey of individuation, death does not have to be the final point. Instead we see the possibility that the journey goes on and that what we have cultivated in one life may bring fruit in the next. If one observes the way young reincarnate lamas grow up, it is apparent that they once again pass through the natural stages of growth and individuation we all pass through. The difference will be the depth of insight they bring to that process and the reemergence of experiences as they mature. We may well ask ourselves the question, What has emerged in our own life as it has unfolded that may well have its roots in previous lives? A sudden ripening of interest in and understanding of Buddhism, according to many Tibetan teachers, reflects previous life experience. My own experience as a thangka painter felt exactly like this.

In the case of the reincarnate lama, or tulku, I do not sense that this status automatically makes the process a lot easier. It has been noticeable that reincarnated lamas do not always deal with childhood and adolescence any better than the rest of us. Indeed, there are examples of young tulkus having relatively severe psychological problems as they struggle to reintegrate a stable personality into the world despite deep insights into the nature of reality. Having profound insights on one level does not automatically imply there is a stable conventional identity; this still needs to be cultivated through an individuation process. My own teacher, Lama Thubten Yeshe, in his current incarnation as the Spanish boy Lama Ösel Rinpoche, is no exception to this experience as he comes to terms with his adolescence.

The bodhisattva's pledge is to continue to incarnate to benefit sentient beings. The examples of this process found still today within the Tibetan tradition as incarnate tulkus demonstrate extraordinary capacities and realizations. I was among many Westerners living in India who were fortunate enough to meet and receive teachings and initiations from some extraordinary tulkus, such as Ling Rinpoche, Trijang Rinpoche, the Karmapa, Kalu Rinpoche, and others. Many of their reincarnations have, it would seem, been found and are now teenagers once again coming into active life as lamas. How they manifest their qualities is yet to be seen, but if one trusts or believes in the reality of reincarnation, they are a fascinating example of the possibility of the journey continuing.

It may or may not be useful to consider where this process eventually leads us. In Buddhist teachings there are descriptions of a bodhisattva's final stages of practice to become a Buddha, although these vary from one tradition to another. It is said in the Tantras that a bodhisattva in the final stages of the path cycles through a process of dissolution and regeneration time and again so as to clear any small obstructions to the unified experience of relative and ultimate nature of reality.[48] Eventually, a state of nonduality is reached whereby a Buddha experiences the manifestation of form and emptiness itself as simultaneously arising, without contradiction. This means that there is

no longer a cycle, as there is no distinction between form and emptiness. A Buddha remains awake to the spontaneous play of appearances within the vastness of emptiness. The Buddha is known as the
Tathagata, or one who has gone beyond the cycling of birth and death.

We may feel that the state of buddhahood is an ideal or aspiration
that seems unreachable or that it is somewhat academic to consider.
Even so, in our present day-to-day experience, the veil that separates
us from an experience of our innate enlightened nature is not so solid.
The key to that awakening is here in the present moment as we are
right now. This brings us back to an essential paradox I have spoken of
before. There may be a journey or path of awakening, yet the experience of awakening arises through a direct awareness of being utterly
present in each moment. As the Buddha conveyed in the *Heart Sutra,*
in emptiness there is "no suffering, no cause of suffering, no cessation
of suffering and no path. There is no wisdom, no attainment, no non-
attainment." There is nowhere to go and yet, paradoxically, there is a
path towards the full awakening of that experience. This paradox is
present in the process of individuation that each of us can travel if we
are willing to respond to the call.

APPENDIX
The Cycle of Individuation

✦ ✦ ──

JOSEPH CAMPBELL in *The Hero with a Thousand Faces* identifies the unfolding of the heroic journey with its rites of passage and phases of transformation. The diagram on the next page is derived from his work and carries many of his ideas into the territory I am exploring within this book. The basis of this diagram evolved from conversations with two colleagues, Nigel Wellings and Philippa Vick, with whom I taught at the Centre for Transpersonal Psychology in London. While Campbell considers this cycle within the context of a single life, I have intentionally wished to include the Buddhist notion of reincarnation to complete the cycle. The implication of this is that we do not come into this life from nothing, so to speak, as a blank slate. The Buddha spoke of an endless cycle of existence, and reincarnation is a central premise of Eastern thought. Some Western Buddhist practitioners may dispute the validity or usefulness of this idea; however, I suggest that this is often a result of the fear of its implications rather than any particular logic. There is no doubt that we do come into this life with certain susceptibilities and predispositions which could be seen to originate in previous lives.

The Tibetans speak of beginningless mind and the constant re-circling within the cycle of existence. If we consider this a possibility, then the diagram above offers some thoughts on the nature of our individual evolution through that cycle. Campbell recognized a process unfolding that begins with a call to awaken. This may arise through

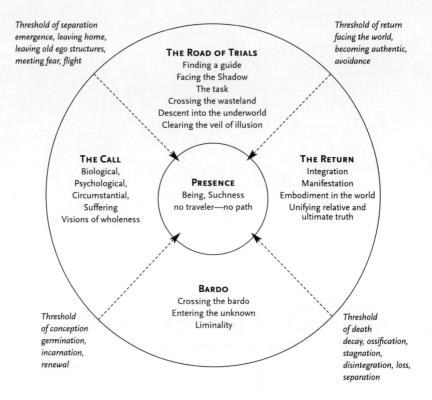

Threshold of separation
emergence, leaving home,
leaving old ego structures,
meeting fear, flight

THE ROAD OF TRIALS
Finding a guide
Facing the Shadow
The task
Crossing the wasteland
Descent into the underworld
Clearing the veil of illusion

Threshold of return
facing the world,
becoming authentic,
avoidance

THE CALL
Biological,
Psychological,
Circumstantial,
Suffering
Visions of wholeness

PRESENCE
Being, Suchness
no traveler—no path

THE RETURN
Integration
Manifestation
Embodiment in the world
Unifying relative and
ultimate truth

Threshold
of conception
germination,
incarnation,
renewal

BARDO
Crossing the bardo
Entering the unknown
Liminality

Threshold
of death
decay, ossification,
stagnation,
disintegration, loss,
separation

THE INDIVIDUATION PROCESS: THE HERO'S JOURNEY

both inner and outer conditions, and whether we respond to it deter-
mines the next phase, which is the entry into the path of trials. Between
each phase on this diagram is a threshold which marks a rite of passage.
These thresholds are often experienced as a kind of death and rebirth
as an old way of being passes away and a new one begins. Each phase
has its own characteristic challenges to be addressed and learned from.
Each phase, in this respect, will bring to the forefront its own potential pathology that needs to be uncovered and resolved. In its resolution comes the capacity to eventually move across the threshold into
the next phase.

In this book I have found it necessary to limit some of the themes
within the path of trials. One domain of exploration I am conscious I
have excluded is that of the masculine and feminine and the nature of

sexuality and its inclusion within spiritual life. This is in part because I have explored this in some detail in *The Psychology of Buddhist Tantra* (published in the UK under the title *The Alchemical Buddha*).

One phase, which Campbell does not include in his own version of this map, is that of the *bardo*, or intermediate state. Since this is an aspect of Tibetan Buddhist teachings that offers useful insights as to the threshold of conception, it feels important to include. The bardo between death and rebirth can be seen either literally or psychologically. If we consider the possibility that we may cycle around this map more than once in a lifetime, then the bardo is a significant phase of liminality that has its own particular dynamic. In a literal sense as the period between incarnations, we may only speculate on the process that unfolds. The Tibetans have their teachings on the "Books of the Dead" that offer some clues, but even among Tibetans there is some debate as to their validity.

Finally, central to this diagram is what has been called Presence. This is not so much the presence of something, rather the quality of being utterly present. What we see in this map therefore is the recognition that while the process may unfold as a relatively linear albeit circular movement, the experience of awakening comes as a shift of awareness into the immediacy of the present moment. In Buddhism this is a central paradox. We may practice a path towards awakening and yet what we discover is that the enlightenment experience comes as an opening to the nature of the present moment. We see that the unfolding of relative experience is an illusion in time and empty of substantiality.

We could therefore at any point in our journey shift perspectives, or shift awareness from relative forms and processes to the intrinsic formless spaciousness of the present moment. This shift is fundamentally liberating and unlocks the solidity with which we can hold the process of our path. Our map becomes a mere appearance, a concept, and an illusion. Ultimately there is no unfolding, because there is nothing to unfold; all is empty. As it says in the *Heart Sutra*: in emptiness there is no suffering, no cause of suffering, no cessation of suffering, and no path.

◆ ◆ ————————————————————————————

Absolute Truth	The false creation of a truth that holds relative forms to be ultimate truths.
Alchemy	The process of transformation of gross substances into a refined material—a metaphorical system for personal transformation studied by Jung.
Archetype	A primordial patterning for psychological life that emerges through the psyche of an individual in symbolic form.
Archetypal image	A metaphorical or symbolic form that represents an individual's experience of an archetype.
Archetypal intent	The nature and dynamic of intention set up by the presence of a deep archetypal pattern.
Arhat (Skt.)	Literally "foe destroyer." One who has gone beyond the cycle of existence and ceases to manifest in form.
Awakening mind (Skt. *bodhichitta*)	The intention to awaken to Buddhahood for the welfare of all sentient beings.
Buddha nature	Our intrinsic potential for Buddhahood—the natural pristine quality of our nature.
Bare awareness	The natural awareness of phenomena free of conceptualization.

Bodhichitta (Skt.)	Literally "the awakening mind/heart." A bodhisattva's intention to attain Buddhahood for the sake of all beings.
Bodhisattva (Skt.)	One who aspires to attain Buddhahood for the sake of sentient beings.
Chenrezig (Tib.; Skt. Avalokiteshvara)	The Buddha (sometimes called Bodhisattva) of compassion.
Chöd (Tib.)	Literally "to cut." Meditation practice performed in cremation grounds.
Collective unconscious	Jungian term for the level of the unconscious that lies deeper than personal unconscious and is considered to contain the archetypes shared by us all.
Dharmakaya (Skt.)	The wisdom truth body of a Buddha—purified mind.
Dionysian	From Dionysus; relating to a natural, instinctual disposition that values intoxication, passion, and sensuality in spiritual life.
Disidentify/ disidentification	The capacity to begin to create an objective relationship between our sense of identity and emotional states. Being able to witness emotional states rather than be them.
Dualistic	Creating duality and division, splitting reality into relative oppositions.
Dukkha (Skt.)	Suffering, unsatisfactoriness.
Emergence	Literal translation of Tibetan *nge jung*, renunciation. Emergence implies the willingness to wake up and face ourselves in the unfolding journey.
Emptiness (Skt. *shunyata*)	Without inherent existence or inherent substantiality; the nature of reality.

Four immeasurable thoughts (Skt. *brahmavihara*)	Meditation on immeasurable compassion, love, joy, and equanimity.
Four noble truths	The first teaching of the Buddha. The truths of suffering, the cause of suffering, the cessation of suffering, and the path leading to the cessation of suffering.
Gelugpa	One of the four main schools of Tibetan Buddhism.
Ground of being	A term for *Dharmakaya* implying the basis of reality.
Individuation	The process of unfolding of the individual towards his or her innate potential for wholeness.
Lama (Tib.; Skt. *guru*)	A spiritual teacher.
Lung (Tib.)	Energy-wind.
Madhyamaka (Skt.)	Literally "middle way"; a Buddhist philosophical school.
Mahamudra (Skt.)	Literally "great seal"; the meditation practice focusing on the nature of mind.
Mahasiddha (Skt.)	A tantric adept in India; the eighty-four mahasiddhas.
Mahayana (Skt.)	Literally "greater vehicle"; the school of Buddhism associated with the bodhisattva's path.
Mandala (Skt.)	Circle—a symbolic design expressing totality.
Manjushri (Skt.)	The Buddha of wisdom.
Mara	A mythical entity like the devil; hindrances to the practice of Dharma.
Mindfulness	A capacity of the mind to maintain an awareness that witnesses the arising and passing of experiences.

Ngöndro (Tib.)	Preliminary practices.
Nigredo	The first stage of the alchemical process in which the shadow and dark elements come to the surface.
Nirmanakaya (Skt.; Tib. *tulku*)	The emanation body of a Buddha.
Nirvana (Skt.)	A state of being where all causes for suffering within the cycle of existence have been extinguished. This is not the same as Buddhahood.
Nonduality	A quality of awareness in which subject and object are no longer split into two.
Numenosity	Being imbued with a quality of inspiration, charge, and attraction.
Pathology	The study of the roots of emotional, psychological, or physical disease or dysfunction.
Penetrative insight (Skt. *vipash-yana;* Tib. *lhak tong*)	A quality of awareness that sees into the nature of reality.
Paramita (Skt.)	Literally "perfection." The six practices of a Bodhisattva—morality, generosity, patience, perseverance, meditation, and wisdom.
Prasangika (Skt.)	Literally "consequentialist." One of the Madhyamaka schools of philosophy.
Puella	Female form of Puer.
Puer Aeternus	Eternal youth; an archetypal psychological disposition.
Relative Truth	The level of reality in which objects are defined in terms of their relationship to other objects and to the subjective mind; the way objects appear to exist as opposed to their actual mode of existence. The phenomenal world.

Refuge
(Tib. *kyab su chi wo*)
To take refuge in the three jewels of Buddha, Dharma, and Sangha.

Renunciation
Common translation of Tibetan *nge jung*. To abandon attachment to worldly concerns.

Samadhi (Skt.)
The perfected experience of tranquil abiding.

Sambhogakaya
(Skt.)
The complete enjoyment body of a Buddha—purified energy-wind body.

Samsara (Skt.)
The cycle of rebirth and death.

Sangha (Skt.)
The community of practitioners.

Self
Jungian term referring to the archetype of wholeness and meaning—the center of an individual's totality.

Self-existent
The view that objects exist inherently with a substantial nature independent of conditions or of the mind that sees them.

Senex
The archetypal old masculine principle.

Shadow
Jungian term for the aspects of our nature repressed and held in the unconscious.

Siddha (Skt.)
One who has developed certain psychic powers, *siddhi*, through meditation practice.

Tantra
(Skt.; Tib. *gyu*)
The esoteric or mystical system of Buddhist practice.

Thangka
A Tibetan painting on cloth depicting meditation deities or venerated teachers.

Theravada
Buddhist school common to Thailand, Burma, and Sri Lanka.

Tranquil abiding
(Skt. *shamata;*
Tib. *shi né*)
Meditation practice aimed at stabilizing the attention on a single object of concentration.

Transference

When unconsciously a person endows another with an attribute that is actually projected from within themselves.

Triple gem

The objects of refuge – Buddha, Dharma, and Sangha.

Tulku (Tib.; Skt. *nirmanakaya*)

Literally "manifestation body." The name given to a lama who has been recognized as an incarnation of a previous lama.

Ultimate truth

The nature of reality lying beneath ordinary appearances and forms. In Buddhism ultimate truth is emptiness, i.e., empty of substantial form and inherent existence.

Vajrapani (Skt.)

The Buddha associated with the embodiment of power.

Vajrayana (Skt.)

Literally "diamond vehicle"; another name for Tantra.

Yidam (Tib.)

Literally "mind bound"; the principal deity practiced by a tantric meditator.

Notes

❖ ❖ ─────────────────────────────────

PART I *The Call to Awaken*

1 *Man and His Symbols*, edited by C.G. Jung (London: Pikador, 1978).

2 Shantideva, *A Guide to the Bodhisattva's Way of Life*, Chapter VIII, verses 10-15. Trans. Stephen Batchelor (Dharamsala: Library of Tibetan Works and Archives, 1979). All quotations from Shantideva cited in this book are from Batchelor's translation.

3 "The truth of cessation" is the third of the four noble truths taught by the Buddha in his first turning of the wheel of Dharma.

4 Arya Maitreya & Asanga, *The Changeless Nature, The Mahayana Uttara Tantra Shastra,* trans. Ken and Katia Holmes (Eskdalemuir, Dumfriesshire, Scotland: Kagyu Samye Ling, 1985), p. 34.

5 John Welwood, *Towards a Psychology of Awakening* (Boston: Shambhala Publications, 2002), p. 11.

6 Shantideva, *A Guide to the Bodhisattva's Way of Life*, Chapter V, verse 13.

7 Stephen Batchelor, *Flight: An Existential Concept of Buddhism* (Delhi: Buddhist Publication Society, 1984).

8 Rob Preece, *The Psychology of Buddhist Tantra* (Ithaca: Snow Lion Publications, 2006); previously published in the UK under the title *The Alchemical Buddha* (Devon, UK: Mudra, 2000).

9 Arya Maitreya & Asanga, *The Changeless Nature*, p. 31.

10 Shantideva, *A Guide to the Bodhisattva's Way of Life*, Chapter I, verse 28.

11 Emma Jung and Marie-Louise von Franz, *The Grail Legend* (Boston: Sigo Press, 1986), p. 40.

12 Herbert V. Guenther, trans. *Kindly Bent to Ease Us* (Emeryville, CA: Dharma Publishing, 1976).

13 Shantideva, *A Guide to the Bodhisattva's Way of Life*, Chapter III, verses 29-32.

14 C. G. Jung, *Symbols of Transformation,* The Collected Works of C. G. Jung, Vol. 5 (Princeton, NJ: Princeton University Press, 1976), pp. 330, 510.

15 C.G. Jung, *Psychology and Alchemy,* The Collected Works of C. G. Jung, Vol. 12 (London: Routledge & Kegan Paul, 1980), pp. 71, 118.

16 Chögyam Trungpa, *Cutting Through Spiritual Materialism* (Berkeley: Shambhala Publications, 1973).

17 Joseph Campbell, *The Hero with a Thousand Faces* (London: Fontana, 1993), p. 73.

18 Herbert V. Guenther, *The Life and Teaching of Naropa* (Oxford: Clarendon Press, 1963), p. 34.

19 Geshe Ngawang Dhargyey, *The Tibetan Tradition of Mental Development* (Dharamsala: Library of Tibetan Works and Archives, 1974), p. 112.

20 Erich Fromm, *The Fear of Freedom* (London: Routledge, 2001).

21 Joseph Campbell, *Myths to Live By* (New York: Viking, 1972), p. 106.

22 C. G. Jung, *The Archetypes and the Collective Unconscious,* The Collected Works of C. G. Jung, Vol. 9, Part 1 (Princeton, NJ: Princeton University Press, 1971), p. 275.

23 C. G. Jung, *Two Essays on Analytical Psychology*, The Collected Works of C. G. Jung, Vol. 7 (London: Routledge & Kegan Paul, 1966), p. 171.

24 C. G. Jung, *The Structure and Dynamics of the Psyche,* The Collected Works of C. G. Jung, Vol. 8 (London: Routledge & Kegan Paul, 1969), p. 226.

25 Ibid.

26 Shantideva, *A Guide to the Bodhisattva's Way of Life,* Chapter VII, verses 49-55.

27 H.H. the Dalai Lama, *Universal Responsibility and the Good Heart* (Dharamsala, India: Library of Tibetan Works and Archives, 1976).

28 C.G. Jung, *Psychology and Religion*, The Collected Works of C. G. Jung, Vol. 11 (London: Routledge & Kegan Paul, 1969), p. 391.

29 Jung, as cited by Anthony Stevens in *Archetype: A Natural History of the Self* (London: Routledge & Kegan Paul, 1990), p. 92.

30 Rob Preece, *The Psychology of Buddhist Tantra*, Chapter 5.

31 Emma Jung and Marie-Louise von Franz, *The Grail Legend*, p. 40.

32 Ibid., p. 50.

33 Erich Neumann, *Amor and Psyche* (Princeton, NJ: Princeton University Press/Bollingen Foundation, 1956).

34 Marie-Louise von Franz, *Puer Aeternus: A Psychological Study of the Struggle with the Paradise of Childhood* (Boston: Sigo Press, 1970), Chapter 1.

35 Fromm, *The Fear of Freedom*.

36 Dakini: a female figure who has achieved a depth of spiritual insight principally with the practice of Tantra. The Dakini can be seen as both literal and symbolic. See Preece, *The Psychology of Buddhist Tantra*, Chapter 16.

37 Herbert V. Guenther, *The Life and Teaching of Naropa* (Oxford: Clarendon Press, 1963), p. 24.

38 Preece, *The Psychology of Buddhist Tantra*, Chapter 6.

39 Jung, *Psychology and Alchemy*, pp. 36, 41.

40 James Hillman, et al., *Puer Papers* (Dallas: Spring Publications, 1979), p. 23.

41 Von Franz, *Puer Aeternus*, p. 5.

PART II *Encountering the Shadow*

1 Campbell, *The Hero with a Thousand Faces*, p. 97.
2 Ibid., p. 59.
3 Jung, *The Archetypes and the Collective Unconscious,* pp. 284, 513.
4 Garma C.C. Chang, *The Hundred Thousand Songs of Milarepa* (New York: Harper Colophon, 1970), p. 5.
5 Preece, *The Psychology of Buddhist Tantra*, Chapter 14.
6 Walter F. Otto, *Dionysus: Myth and Cult* (Dallas: Spring Publications, 1965).
7 Preece, *The Psychology of Buddhist Tantra*, Chapter 15.
8 Ibid., Chapter 6.
9 Keith Dowman, *Masters of Enchantment: The Lives and Legends of the Mahasiddhas* (Rochester, VT: Inner Traditions International, 1988).
10 John Welwood, *Towards a Psychology of Awakening* (Boston: Shambhala Publications, 2002), p. 11.
11 Shantideva, *A Guide to the Bodhisattva's Way of Life,* Chapter V, verse 14.
12 Anthony Storr, *The Art of Psychotherapy* (Oxford: Butterworth-Heinemann, 1994), pp. 138-139.
13 Peter A. Levine, *Waking the Tiger: Healing Trauma: The Innate Capacity to Transform Overwhelming Experiences* (Berkeley: North Atlantic Books, 1997), p. 111.
14 This is taken from a verse within the Heruka Sadhana of Pabongka Rinpoche, in an unpublished translation.
15 See, for example, *The Great Treatise on the Stages of the Path to Enlightenment* by Tsong-kha-pa, trans. Lamrim Chenmo Translation Committee, ed. Cutler and Newland (Ithaca, NY: Snow Lion Publications, 2000-2002), vol. 1, chapter 4.
16 Jung, *The Archetypes and the Collective Unconscious,* p. 121.
17 Ibid., p. 398.
18 Hillman et al., *Puer Papers,* p. 20.

PART III *The Path of Individuation*

1 Jung, *Psychology and Religion*, p. 144.
2 Trungpa, *Cutting Through Spiritual Materialism.*
3 C. G. Jung, *Alchemical Studies,* The Collected Works of C. G. Jung, Vol. 13 (London: Routledge & Kegan Paul, 1983).
4 Jung, *Psychology and Alchemy,* p. 375.
5 Emma Jung and Marie-Louise von Franz, *The Grail Legend*, pp. 10-11.
6 Ibid., pp. 67-73.
7 *Twelve Russian Fairytales,* translated by Thomas P. Whitney (London: Evans Bros., 1974), Chapter 7.
8 Hillman et al., *Puer Papers,* Chapter 5.
9 Shantideva, *A Guide to the Bodhisattva's Way of Life,* Chapter VII, verses 54, 55, 66.

10 Robert Bly, *Iron John: A Book About Men* (Reading, MA: Addison-Wesley, 1990), p. 5.

11 For example, the "Six-session Guru Yoga" by Kyabje Pabongka Rinpoche (unpublished translation by Alex Berzin) says:
> From this moment on until I am Buddha
> May I never give up though my life be at stake,
> The attitude wishing to gain full enlightenment
> In order to free from the fears of samsara
> And nirvana's complacency all sentient beings.

12 Shantideva, *A Guide to the Bodhisattva's Way of Life,* Chapter I, verse 19.

13 Ibid., Chapter III, verses 29-32.

14 Ibid., Chapter I, verse 10.

15 *Thirty-seven Practices of all Buddhas' Sons* by Togme Zangpo, trans. Alex Berzin, verses 2, 5.

16 Shantideva, A *Guide to the Bodhisattva's Way of Life,* chapter VIII, verses 25-27.

17 Murray Stein, *In Midlife: A Jungian Perspective* (Dallas: Spring Publications, 1983), p. 24.

18 Shantideva, *A Guide to the Bodhisattva's Way of Life,* Chapter VII, verses 47-49.

19 Ibid., Chapter III, verses 8, 11, 18, 21.

20 Alice Miller, *The Drama of the Gifted Child: The Search for the True Self* (London: Virago, 1991), p. 23.

21 Dowman, *Masters of Enchantment.*

22 Edwin Bernbaum, *The Way to Shambhala* (Garden City, NY: Anchor Press, 1980), p. 201.

23 Levine, *Waking the Tiger,* p. 5.

24 Elizabeth Wilde McCormick, *Surviving Breakdown* (London: Vermilion, 1997).

25 Jung, *Psychology and Alchemy,* pp. 36, 41.

26 Stein, *In Midlife: A Jungian Perspective,* p. 24.

27 Jung, *Symbols of Transformation,* pp. 330, 510.

28 Jung, *Psychology and Religion,* p. 258.

29 Sylvia Brinton Perera, *Descent to the Goddess: A Way of Initiation for Women* (Toronto: Inner City Books, 1981), p. 70.

30 Bernbaum, *The Way to Shambhala,* p. 199.

31 Energy-wind body: Tib. *lung ku.* See Preece, *The Psychology of Buddhist Tantra,* Chapter 8.

32 Campbell, *The Hero with a Thousand Faces,* p. 82.

33 Stephen Batchelor, *Buddhism Without Beliefs: A Contemporary Guide to Awakening* (London: Bloomsbury, 1998).

34 Garma C. C. Chang, *The Six Yogas of Naropa* (Ithaca, NY: Snow Lion Publications, 1986), pp. 25-30.

35 *Heart Sutra,* unpublished translation by Alex Berzin.

36 Trungpa, *Cutting Through Spiritual Materialism.*

37 Herbert V. Guenther, *The Royal Song of Saraha: A Study in the History of Buddhist Thought* (Boston: Shambhala Publications, 1973), pp. 135-136.

38 See, for example, D. T. Suzuki's *Manual of Zen Buddhism* (New York: Grove Press, 1960), Part IV, section 8.

39 Jung, *Psychology and Alchemy,* p. 335.

40 Primordial mind: Tib. *nyug sem.* Commentary on the "Song of the Spring Queen" by Geshe Jhampa Tekchok, unpublished typescript.

41 Geshe Kelsang Gyatso, *Clear Light of Bliss* (London: Wisdom Publications, 1982), p. 139.

42 Oral commentary by Gen Jhampa Wangdu and others on Pabongka Rinpoche's Heruka Body Mandala teachings.

43 Alaya: a term used in particular schools of Buddhist philosophy, principally the Yogachara, or Chittamatra ("mind only"), school, to denote a consciousness that acts as the basis of all relative appearances, i.e., a universal consciousness. This view is refuted by the Prasangika Madhyamaka school, which holds no such universal consciousness to exist.

44 Campbell, *The Hero with a Thousand Faces,* Chapter II.4.

45 Jung, *Symbols of Transformation,* Chapter 5.

46 Preece, *The Psychology of Buddhist Tantra,* Chapter 18.

47 Zopa Rinpoche, *The Wish-fulfilling Golden Sun* (Kathmandu, Nepal: Kopan Monastery, 1973).

48 Geshe Kelsang Gyatso, *Clear Light of Bliss,* p. 211.

Bibliography

◆◆ ───

A.Kya Yong.Dzin. *Compendium of Ways of Knowing*. Trans. Sherpa Tulku and Alex Berzin. Dharamsala, India: Library of Tibetan Works and Archives, 1976.

Arya Maitreya & Asanga. *The Changeless Nature, The Mahayana Uttara Tantra Shastra*. Trans. Ken and Katia Holmes. Eskdalemuir, Dumfriesshire, Scotland: Kagyu Samye Ling, 1985.

Batchelor, Stephen. *The Awakening of the West: The Encounter of Buddhism and Western Culture*. London: The Aquarian Press, 1994.

Batchelor, Stephen. *Buddhism Without Beliefs: A Contemporary Guide to Awakening*. London: Bloomsbury, 1998.

Batchelor, Stephen. *The Faith to Doubt: Glimpses of Buddhist Uncertainty*. Berkeley: Parallax Press, 1990.

Batchelor, Stephen. *Flight: An Existential Concept of Buddhism*. Delhi: Buddhist Publication Society, 1984.

Bernbaum, Edwin. *The Way to Shambhala*. Garden City, NY: Anchor Press, 1980.

Bly, Robert. *Iron John: A Book About Men*. Reading, MA: Addison-Wesley, 1990.

Bolen, Jean Shinoda. *Ring of Power: the Abandoned Child, the Authoritarian Father, and the Disempowered Feminine: A Jungian Understanding of Wagner's Ring Cycle*. San Francisco: HarperSanFrancisco, 1992.

Campbell, Joseph. *The Hero with a Thousand Faces*. London: Fontana, 1993.

Campbell, Joseph. *Myths to Live By*. New York: Viking, 1972.

Chang, Garma C.C. *The Hundred Thousand Songs of Milarepa*. New York: Harper Colophon, 1970.

Chang, Garma C.C. *Six Yogas of Naropa*. Ithaca: Snow Lion Publications, 1986.

Cooper, J. C. *Fairy Tales: Allegories of the Inner Life*. Wellingborough, UK: The Aquarian Press, 1983.

Dalai Lama. *Stages of Meditation*. Ithaca, NY: Snow Lion Publications, 2001.

Dalai Lama. *Universal Responsibility and the Good Heart*. Dharamsala, India: Library of Tibetan Works and Archives, 1976.

Dhargyey, Geshe Ngawang. *The Tibetan Tradition of Mental Development*. Dharamsala, India: Library of Tibetan Works and Archives, 1974.

Dharmaraksita. *The Wheel of Sharp Weapons: A Mahayana Training of the Mind.* Trans. Geshe Ngawang Dhargyey et al. Dharamsala, India: Library of Tibetan Works and Archives, 1981.

Dowman, Keith. *Masters of Enchantment: The Lives and Legends of the Mahasiddhas.* Rochester, VT: Inner Traditions International, 1988.

Dzogchen Ponlop Rinpoche. *Wild Awakening: The Heart of Mahamudra and Dzogchen.* Boston: Shambhala Publications, 2003.

Edinger, Edward F. *Ego and Archetype.* Boston: Shambhala Publications, 1992.

Epstein, Mark. *Going to Pieces Without Falling Apart.* London: Thorsons, 1998.

Epstein, Mark. *Thoughts Without a Thinker.* London: Duckworth, 1996.

Fromm, Erich. *The Fear of Freedom.* London: Routledge, 2001.

Fromm, Erich, D. T. Suzuki and Richard De Martino. *Zen Buddhism and Psychoanalysis.* London: Souvenir Press, 1974.

Greene, Liz and Howard Sasportas. *The Development of the Personality.* London: Routledge & Kegan Paul, 1987.

Guenther, Herbert V. *The Life and Teaching of Naropa.* Oxford: Clarendon Press, 1963.

Guenther, Herbert V. *The Royal Song of Saraha: A Study in the History of Buddhist Thought.* Boston: Shambhala Publications, 1973.

Guenther, Herbert V. *Treasures on the Tibetan Middle Way: A Newly Revised Edition of Tibetan Buddhism Without Mystification.* Boston: Shambhala Publications, 1976.

Guenther, Herbert V. trans. *Kindly Bent to Ease Us.* Emeryville, CA: Dharma Publishing, 1976.

Guggenbuhl-Craig, Adolf. *Power in the Helping Professions.* Dallas: Spring Publications, 1971.

Gyatso, Kelsang. *Clear Light of Bliss: The Practice of Mahamudra in Vajrayana Buddhism.* London: Wisdom Publications, 1982.

Herrigel, Eugen. *Zen in the Art of Archery.* London: Arkana, 1953.

Hillman, James. *The Dream and the Underworld.* New York: Harper & Row, 1979.

Hillman, James. *Healing Fiction.* Barrytown, NY: Station Hill Press, 1983.

Hillman, James, et al. *Puer Papers.* Dallas: Spring Publications, 1979.

Jung, C. G. *Alchemical Studies.* The Collected Works of C. G. Jung. Vol. 13. London: Routledge & Kegan Paul, 1983.

Jung, C. G. *Answer to Job.* London: Ark, 1984.

Jung, C. G. *The Archetypes and the Collective Unconscious.* The Collected Works of C. G. Jung. Vol. 9, Part 1. Bollingen Series. Princeton, NJ: Princeton University Press, 1971.

Jung, C. G. *Psychology and Alchemy.* The Collected Works of C. G. Jung. Vol. 12. London: Routledge & Kegan Paul, 1980.

Jung, C. G. *Psychology and Religion.* The Collected Works of C. G. Jung. Vol. 11. London: Routledge & Kegan Paul, 1969.

Jung, C. G. *The Structure and Dynamics of the Psyche.* The Collected Works of C. G. Jung. Vol. 8. London: Routledge & Kegan Paul, 1969.

Jung, C. G. *Symbols of Transformation.* The Collected Works of C. G. Jung. Vol. 5. Bollingen Series. Princeton, NJ: Princeton University Press, 1976.

Jung, C. G. *Two Essays on Analytical Psychology.* The Collected Works of C. G. Jung. Vol. 7. London: Routledge & Kegan Paul, 1966.

Jung, C.G., ed. *Man and His Symbols.* London: Pikador, 1978.

Jung, Emma and Marie-Louise von Franz. *The Grail Legend.* Boston: Sigo Press, 1986.

Levine, Peter A., with Ann Frederick. *Waking the Tiger: Healing Trauma: The Innate Capacity to Transform Overwhelming Experiences.* Berkeley: North Atlantic Books, 1997.

Longchenpa. *The Four-Themed Precious Garland: An Introduction to Dzog Chen, the Great Completeness.* Dharamsala, India: Library of Tibetan Works and Archives, 1979.

McCormick, Elizabeth Wilde. *Surviving Breakdown.* London: Vermilion, 1997.

Miller, Alice. *The Drama of the Gifted Child: The Search for the True Self.* London: Virago, 1991.

Miller, Alice. *Thou Shalt Not Be Aware: Society's Betrayal of the Child.* London: Pluto Press, 1984.

Monick, Eugene. *Phallos: Sacred Image of the Masculine.* Toronto: Inner City Books, 1987.

Neumann, Erich. *Amor and Psyche.* Princeton, NJ: Princeton University Press/Bollingen Foundation, 1956.

Norberg-Hodge, Helena. *Ancient Futures: Learning From Ladakh.* London: Rider, 1991.

Otto, Walter F. *Dionysus: Myth and Cult.* Dallas: Spring Publications, 1965.

Pearson, Carol. S. *The Hero Within: Six Archetypes We Live By.* San Francisco: HarperSanFrancisco, 1986.

Perera, Sylvia Brinton. *Descent to the Goddess: A Way of Initiation for Women.* Toronto: Inner City Books, 1981.

Preece, Rob. *The Psychology of Buddhist Tantra.* Ithaca: Snow Lion Publications, 2006. Previously published under the title *The Alchemical Buddha.* Devon, UK: Mudra, 2000.

Rabten, Geshe and Geshe Dhargyey. *Advice from a Spiritual Friend.* Delhi: Publications for Wisdom Culture, 1977.

Rabten, Geshe. *The Essential Nectar: Meditations on the Buddhist Path.* Boston: Wisdom Publications, 1984.

Rabten, Geshe. *The Preliminary Practices of Tibetan Buddhism.* Dharamsala, India: Library of Tibetan Works and Archives, 1974.

Rycroft, Charles. *Anxiety and Neurosis.* Baltimore: Penguin Books, 1968.

Shantideva. *A Guide to the Bodhisattva's Way of Life.* Trans. Stephen Batchelor. Dharamsala, India: Library of Tibetan Works and Archives, 1979.

Sonam Rinchen, Geshe. *The Three Principal Aspects of the Path.* Trans. and ed. Ruth Sonam. Ithaca, NY: Snow Lion Publications, 1999.

Sopa, Geshe Lhundup and Jeffrey Hopkins. *Practice and Theory of Tibetan Buddhism.* London: Rider, 1976.

Stein, Murray. *In Midlife: A Jungian Perspective.* Dallas: Spring Publications, 1983.

Stevens, Anthony. *Archetype: A Natural History of the Self.* London: Routledge & Kegan Paul, 1990.

Stevens, Anthony. *On Jung.* London: Penguin, 1991.

Storr, Anthony. *The Art of Psychotherapy.* Oxford: Butterworth-Heinemann, 1994.

Thogme Zangpo. *The Thirty-seven Practices of All Buddhas' Sons.* Trans. Geshe Ngawang Dhargyey et al. Dharamsala, India: Library of Tibetan Works and Archives, 1973.

Trungpa, Chögyam. *Cutting Through Spiritual Materialism.* Berkeley: Shambhala Publications, 1973.

Tsong-kha-pa. *The Great Treatise on the Stages of the Path to Enlightenment.* Trans. Lamrim Chenmo Translation Committee. Ed. Joshua W.C. Cutler and Guy Newland. 3 vols. Ithaca, NY: Snow Lion Publications, 2000-2002.

Von Franz, Marie-Louise. *Individuation in Fairy Tales.* Dallas: Spring Publications, 1977.

Von Franz, Marie-Louise. *Puer Aeternus: A Psychological Study of the Struggle with the Paradise of Childhood.* Boston: Sigo Press, 1970.

Von Franz, Marie-Louise and James Hillman. *Jung's Typology.* Dallas: Spring Publications, 1971.

Whitney, Thomas P., trans. *Twelve Russian Fairytales.* London: Evans Bros., 1974.

Wehr, Gerhard. *Jung: A Biography.* Boston: Shambhala Publications, 1987.

Welwood, John. *Awakening the Heart.* Boston: Shambhala Publications, 1985.

Welwood, John. *Towards a Psychology of Awakening.* Boston: Shambhala Publications, 2002.

Winnicott, D. W. *The Maturational Processes and the Facilitating Environment: Studies in the Theory of Emotional Development.* London: Karnac Books, 1980.

Yeshe, Lama Thubten. *Introduction to Tantra: The Transformation of Desire.* Boston: Wisdom Publications, 1987.

Yeshe, Lama Thubten. *Mahamudra.* Boston: Wisdom Publications, 1981.

Yeshe, Lama Thubten. *The Tantric Path of Purification: The Yoga Method of Heruka Vajrasattva Including Complete Retreat Instructions.* Boston: Wisdom Publications, 1995.

Yeshe, Lama Thubten. *Wisdom Energy 2.* Ulverston, UK: Publications for Wisdom Culture, 1979.

Zopa Rinpoche. *The Wish-fulfilling Golden Sun.* Kathmandu, Nepal: Kopan Monastery, 1973.

Zweig, Connie and Jeremiah Abrams. *Meeting the Shadow.* New York: Putnam Books, 1991.

Readers wishing to learn more about the author's psychotherapy and mentoring work, retreats, and courses may do so by visiting the website www.mudra.co.uk.